Unmanned

Unmanned

Drone Warfare and
Global Security

Ann Rogers and John Hill

PlutoPress
www.plutobooks.com

Between the Lines
TORONTO

First published 2014 by Pluto Press
345 Archway Road, London N6 5AA
www.plutobooks.com

Distributed in the United States of America exclusively by
Palgrave Macmillan, a division of St. Martin's Press LLC,
175 Fifth Avenue, New York, NY 10010

First published in Canada in 2014 by Between the Lines
401 Richmond Street West, Studio 277, Toronto, Ontario M5V 3A8 Canada.
1-800-718-7201
www.btlbooks.com

Library and Archives Canada Cataloguing in Publication
Rogers, Ann, 1964-, author
    Unmanned : drone warfare and global security / Ann
Rogers and John Hill.
Includes bibliographical references and index.
Issued in print and electronic formats.
ISBN 978-1-77113-153-7 (pbk.).—ISBN 978-1-77113-154-4 (epub).—
ISBN 978-1-77113-155-1 (pdf)
    1. Drone aircraft. 2. Military robots. 3. Security, International.
4. Military weapons (International law). 5. War--Moral and ethical
aspects. 6. War and society. I. Hill, John (Journalist), author II. Title.
UG1242.D7R65 2014   623.74'69   C2013-907913-0
                                              C2013-907912-2

Copyright © Ann Rogers and John Hill 2014

The right of Ann Rogers and John Hill to be identified as the authors of this work has
been asserted by them in accordance with the Copyright, Designs and Patents Act 1988.

British Library Cataloguing in Publication Data
A catalogue record for this book is available from the British Library

ISBN   978 0 7453 3335 9   Hardback
ISBN   978 0 7453 3334 2   Pluto Press paperback
ISBN   978 1 77113 153 7   Between the Lines paperback
ISBN   978 1 7837 1147 5   Pluto Press PDF eBook
ISBN   978 1 77113 155 1   Between the Lines PDF
ISBN   978 1 7837 1149 9   Kindle eBook
ISBN   978 1 7837 1148 2   epub eBook
ISBN   978 1 77113 154 4   Between the Lines epub

Library of Congress Cataloging in Publication Data applied for

This book is printed on paper suitable for recycling and made from fully managed and
sustained forest sources. Logging, pulping and manufacturing processes are expected to
conform to the environmental standards of the country of origin.

Between the Lines gratefully acknowledges assistance for its publishing activities from
the Canada Council for the Arts, the Ontario Arts Council, the Government of Ontario
through the Ontario Book Publishers Tax Credit program, and the Government of
Canada through the Canada Book Fund.

10   9   8   7   6   5   4   3   2   1

Typeset from disk by Stanford DTP Services, Northampton, England
Text design by Melanie Patrick
Simultaneously printed digitally by CPI Antony Rowe, Chippenham, UK
and Edwards Bros in the United States of America

In memory of our fathers
Jack D. Rogers, 1929–2007
Rowland C. Hill, 1925–2013

Contents

Abbreviations

ABM	anti-ballistic missile
COIN	counter-insurgency
CT	counter-terrorism
DARO	Defense Airborne Reconnaissance Office
DARPA	Defense Advanced Research Projects Agency
FATA	federally administered tribal areas
GPS	global positioning system
HALE	high altitude long endurance
IADS	integrated air defence system
IAF	Israeli Air Force
IAI	Israeli Aircraft Industries
IDF	Israeli Defense Force
IED	improvised explosive device
ISAF	International Security Assistance Force
ISR	intelligence, surveillance and reconnaissance
JDN	Joint Doctrine Note
LARS	lethal autonomous robotics system
MALE	medium altitude long endurance
NRO	National Reconnaissance Office
NSA	National Security Agency
PGM	precision guided munition
PTSD	post-traumatic stress disorder
RAF	Royal Air Force
RMA	Revolution in Military Affairs
STAG	Special Task Air Group
SAM	surface to air missile
UAS	unmanned aerial system
UAV	unmanned aerial vehicle
UCAV	unmanned combat air vehicle
UNAMA	UN Assistance Mission in Afghanistan
USAAF	US Army Air Force
USAF	United States Air Force

Introduction

What's that buzzzzzzzzzzzzzzzzzzzzzzzzzzzzzzzzzzzing?

Marshall McLuhan and Quentin Fiore[1]

During the early 1970s, running water was installed in the houses of Ibieca, a small village in northeast Spain. With pipes running directly to their homes, Ibiecans no longer had to fetch water from the village fountain. Families gradually purchased washing machines, and women stopped gathering to scrub laundry by hand at the village washbasin.

Arduous tasks were rendered technologically superfluous, but village social life unexpectedly changed. The public fountain and washbasin, once scenes of vigorous social interaction, became nearly deserted. Men began losing their sense of familiarity with the children and donkeys that once helped them haul water. Women stopped congregating at the washbasin to intermix scrubbing with politically empowering gossip about men and village life. In hindsight the installation of running water helped break down the Ibiecans' strong bonds – with one another, with their animals, and with the land – that had knitted them together as a community.

Is this a parable for our time?[2]

As Richard Sclove's narrative demonstrates, a technology can produce consequences that may seem clear enough in hindsight but were not considered or intended at the time of its introduction. This book represents an effort to investigate the unmanned aerial vehicle (UAV) or 'drone' as a human artefact, bringing together its diverse forms and histories, current and projected uses, and the ethical, philosophical and legal challenges it raises, with a view to better understanding its large-scale effects on the human environment.

The arrival of drones on the international stage has been both slow and rapid: slow in as much as experiments with the idea have been going on for over a hundred years without it becoming mainstream, and rapid in that since the technology caught up with the concept at the end of the twentieth century the growth in UAV use has been explosive. The US military's inventory increased 40-fold between 2002 and 2010, and upwards of 70 countries now possess UAVs in one form or another. They have also been controversial, both because of how they have been used – most notoriously as tools for assassination – and because of what may be a fundamental public suspicion towards the idea of robotised warfare. It is with the connection between these aspects that we are most concerned here: does the nature of this technology have an impact on how it is used, and does this usage constitute a step change in how we carry out our global affairs?

The essence of the question lies in the uniquely 'unmanned' nature of this technology. In general, contemporary unmanned aerial systems consist of one or more vehicles linked by satellite to a ground station. On the face of it, they can do what manned aircraft can do, and indeed they carry out the same kinds of missions using the same kinds of surveillance equipment or weapons that manned aircraft carry. But by creating a profound separation between operator and target, drones remove the physical risk to the side using them, and this leads to a change in perception about how they can be deployed. The corollary of removing physical risk is a corresponding diminution of political risk – political fallout is minor compared to what it would be if bodies, not machines, were on the line. Drones solve the 'Gary Powers problem' – Powers was the CIA's U-2 pilot shot down by the Russians in 1960 and sentenced to ten years in prison for espionage (he was eventually traded in a spy swap in 1962).

Less risk, both material and political, allows drone performance to be optimised: they penetrate into spaces and territories where humans cannot or will not go; not bound by physical needs like rest or food, they are an enduring presence over their target area. Although the weapons and sensor suites they carry may be no better than those of manned systems, in combination with these qualities of access and persistence, their intelligence gathering and targeting abilities are greatly enhanced. More curious, however, is that drones are also viewed as less problematic by the states they are in operation *against*. Drones seem to manifest a less obvious trespass than a manned incursion, making a lower imposition on national sovereignty. The fact that they are tacitly tolerated further enhances their ability to access areas that manned aircraft can't or won't go.

This nexus of access–persistence–accuracy is the core of drone warfare: it facilitates what we call here *nano-war*, that is, the ability of states to bring military-scale force to bear on specific individuals in situations where the delivery of such force would otherwise have been difficult or unacceptable. The low imposition and the relative disposability of the

UAV allows force to be used where in the past it would not be used (or only much more rarely). Thus we now regularly see the search for, and pursuit of individuals in territories where otherwise the pursuing state's writ does not run. The relatively tight focus of contemporary precision guided munitions (PGMs) then allows the use of this technology for the killing of such individuals. It is not that states have not done this sort of thing before – it is that UAVs are normalising it. This is a change. Military action is now substituting for normal security/policing operations, or being taken where previously there would have been no action because there was no 'opportunity' for it. Thus, for example, we are seeing extrajudicial killings rather than the due process of law or the conventional military operation. The arrival of the UAV has dangerously lowered the threshold for the application of military-scale violence, both in terms of crossing borders and in terms of scale of target.

A New Kind of War

This kind of nano-war against individuals is not something the international system has seen on any kind of large scale before. War, as Rousseau reminds us, is between things – states, political communities – and the individuals fighting them are there as combatants, that is, representatives of the cause being fought over. Terrorism is a method, not a cause, and the individuals engaged in it have traditionally been dealt with through law enforcement and juridical apparatuses – only occasionally have governments deployed their national militaries to deal with policing problems. However, following 9/11 the US invoked its right to use military force in self-defence to pursue Bin Laden's Al Qaeda in Afghanistan, claiming that its actions were authorised by the UN. Legal experts have argued that the UN resolutions did not in fact authorise the use of armed force and that the mechanisms provided by criminal justice were sufficient because Al Qaeda had committed criminal acts of terrorism rather than acts of war.[3]

Thus from the very outset the war on Afghanistan was problematic from a legal perspective, but even so since 9/11, the US has continued to assert itself militarily in situations that are not war, meeting minimal resistance, if not tacit acceptance. Along with the UAVs, special forces units and private military companies have been part of this expansion, and, like the drones, a large part of their appeal is their deniability. Small interventions arouse only small controversies, and these are all ways of extending coercive military power without provoking costly political (or military) fallout.

As the infamous 'Blackhawk Down' incident in Mogadishu in 1993 illustrated, when manned operations go wrong they cannot be easily swept under the carpet. That special forces attempt to capture two Somali militant leaders led to a battle that caused hundreds of casualties, drove the US from Somalia and deterred Washington from intervening in the Rwandan genocide the following year. While post-9/11 debacles have not been repeated on such a scale, they have nevertheless caused political headaches. When contractors working for private military company Blackwater opened fire in Baghdad in 2007, killing 17 people, the ensuing outcry led to changes in how private military companies were licensed and deployed and included legal changes to make contractors prosecutable under US law (as of October 2013, four of the men involved were still on trial). Another contractor, Raymond Davis, became a latter-day Gary Powers: part of the CIA's top secret spying mission in Pakistan, he killed two people in Pakistan in 2011 and languished in a prison in Lahore while the Pakistani and US governments wrangled over whether his diplomatic passport should protect him from prosecution. A special forces incursion into Libya in October 2013 to snatch an Al Qaeda suspect was immediately denounced by the Libyan president, while a simultaneous raid on Somalia was botched. And of course relations that were damaged by the US special forces raid on Bin Laden's compound in Pakistan in May 2011 have still not been repaired.

Unmanned vehicles simply do not create these sorts of political nightmares. Throughout all these ups and downs, US drones have continued to kill civilians and militants regularly in Pakistan, Somalia, Yemen and of course Afghanistan, patrol in international airspace and penetrate enemy skies while escaping wider scrutiny and discussion. It wasn't until P.W. Singer's *Wired for War* was published in 2009 that the effects of the roboticisation of battle began to be considered in a wider geopolitical context, even as President Obama amped up the drone programme he inherited from his predecessor. Even so, drones fired on and/or brought down in Iran and Somalia scarcely raise an eyebrow, and in spite of the ongoing furore over US drone policy in Pakistan, no one was really surprised to find that Islamabad had secretly approved the strikes while publicly denouncing them.[4] Pilotless drones are perceived differently – as less provocative – by both the side using them and by the countries in which they are used.

'The Medium is the Message'

These observations around how UAVs are perceived and used has prompted us to think about them in the way suggested by Canadian media theorist Marshall McLuhan, who advises against a focus on the ostensible purpose or content of a technology or medium (he uses the terms interchangeably); we do not care, as he puts it, whether a factory produces 'Cornflakes or Cadillacs'.[5] Instead we should try to work out the unlooked for, real social consequences that flow from the introduction of 'each extension of ourselves, or by any new technology' by considering

> the psychic and social consequences of the designs or patterns as they amplify or accelerate existing processes. For the 'message' of any medium or technology is the change of scale or pace or pattern that it introduces into human affairs.[6]

For Sclove then, the significant message of the pipes was not the delivery of water, but rather a new kind of social separation. For McLuhan, the message of the Gutenberg press was not simply its content – that is, the reading materials it produced and the messages they contained – but something much larger: the tools for enquiry and rational discussion were taken from the hands of those in power, particularly the church, and placed in the hands, ultimately, of everyone who could read. Reading became ubiquitous, and reformation, revolution and enlightenment followed. By spreading the products of the two worlds represented in existing books, the ancient (Greco-Roman) and the medieval, McLuhan claims that, 'the printed book created a third world, the modern world'.[7] Thus the message of the printing press is not the book, but modernity. It's a big claim, but reflects a larger modern intellectual tradition. Marxism can be similarly technologically determinist: for example, as Marx saw it, 'the wind-mill gives you society with the feudal lord; the steam-mill, society with the industrial capitalist'.[8] We are neither so absolute in our technological determinism nor as bold in our findings, but rather see in this a way to start uncovering the potentially large-scale changes introduced by drones by documenting what is specifically new or different about this particular medium.

There are ground-based and sea-based unmanned systems as well, and it is likely that the biggest innovations and effects will ultimately occur in the civilian sector, although at the moment civilian airspace regulations severely limit the use of drone technologies, be they driverless cars or pizza-delivery quadcopters. We have limited our investigation to air-based systems carrying out military-derived tasks in an effort to get at the details that can reveal their effects on global security. The literature on UAVs is vast, varied and scattered across disciplines, running the gamut from philosophical ruminations on robo-ethics, to the scientific intricacies of human–machine interfaces, to the exegesis of legal regimes that enable the US president to decide who to kill each week. To capture this diversity, we modelled McLuhan's 'probe' approach designed to open up discussion and debate, in contrast to presenting a 'package' of exhaustive findings on a specific aspect of drone warfare.

The UAV, on anything like its current scale and efficacy, is a new phenomenon, and even within these limits it is a challenge to assess its intended effects for the militaries and states operating them, let alone the wider unintended spinoffs. One difficulty is to delineate what changes are introduced by drone technologies specifically, as opposed to changes that are attributable to the evolving nature of global violence. It is impossible to decisively separate the technology from its use, to imagine what the history of a Predator might have been had 9/11 not taken place, and had grossly asymmetric battles not been joined by western militaries against 'global terrorism'. For the purposes of analysis we have attempted to sketch some of the various realms where the specific attributes of drones produce unique effects, which in turn impact the ways in which wars are being fought, by looking at the history of drones, current military doctrine, and how ethics, legal regimes and military culture are adapting to fit around this new weapon.

The Path of Drone Development

The history of the UAV's development is instructive with regard to how users see them and the range of distinctive uses they offer, and the first three chapters of this book trace their military development and the impact of digital technologies on war-making, both in terms of weapons and doctrine.

Originally, drones began as attempts by both the US and the British to remove the pilot from the aircraft in the carnage of World War I, turning the plane itself into a kind of flying bomb that risks no one's life in the course of its delivery. At this stage the effectiveness of controlling the aircraft, whether at a distance by radio or via internal gyroscope-based autopilots, is really inadequate, and the experiments do not progress to the field. What they are adequate for is training anti-aircraft gunners, and most of the drones used up until after World War II are used for this mission, one that requires the 'unmanned' quality of the UAV, to produce a *disposability* essential for this dangerous activity.

Although some minor but successful uses of UAVs in combat occurred during World War II, including of course the technology seen in the flying bombs of the German 'V' programme, these experiments were largely put on the back burner under the distinctive conditions of the Cold War. At this time surveillance, or perhaps more accurately spying, becomes key. The attempts to produce high-flying long-range drones for this mission were highly expensive and of limited success, operating under black budgets controlled by intelligence services rather than the military. The major advantage of the drone over the manned aircraft seems to have lain both in its pilotless disposability, and in a special kind of deniability. In various Cold War situations, neither side felt that there was as much at stake in this kind of purely technological intrusion, whether over the Soviet Union or China. The drone was somehow less 'there' than a manned aircraft, and already its usefulness as a 'low imposition' technology was apparent.

As the technology for data processing and networking matured under the conditions of the technological revolution in military affairs (RMA), the ability to navigate accurately and acquire and transmit useful amounts of data enhanced the drone's versatility. As a result UAV usage began to proliferate. An early adopter was Israel, which remains a leader in the field. UAVs helped address particular challenges in Israel's local security environment – for example, their disposability meant they could be used to suppress enemy air defences in conventional wars with neighbouring states. But it is in Israel's role as the dominant power in the region that UAVs proliferated. In the not-quite-sovereign territory of the West Bank and the Gaza Strip, UAVs are used for surveillance, targeting and killing those individuals and groups identified as Israel's enemies.

Exhibiting the same sort of hegemonic behaviour on a global scale, the US has also come to depend on the UAV. Following Israel's lead, both technologically speaking and in terms of mission, the current embrace of this risk-free, low-imposition technology is based on its success in hugely asymmetric conflicts: initially in Kosovo, latterly in Iraq and Afghanistan, and significantly in countries involved in some way in the US 'War on Terror', especially in similarly ambiguous territories such as Pakistan's tribal lands.

Types of UAV have proliferated. The controversial strike drones, Predator and Reaper, that have generated most of the public discussion are but the tip of the iceberg. The vast majority of UAVs are used purely for intelligence, surveillance and reconnaissance (ISR) missions. In current military usage they range from the Global Hawk, with a wingspan greater than a Boeing 737 airliner, to nano-helicopters that weigh a few grams, and all points in between. Many soldiers now have access to some kind of dedicated aerial reconnaissance even at the level of the smallest patrol, and these small drones grant access for surveillance/reconnaissance to areas previously unavailable for such activities, such as the deep 'urban canyon', and even indoors. UAVs promise effective coverage at sea – even the smallest warships can easily carry a highly effective UAV, such as the Scan-Eagle, giving commanders their own persistent aerial reconnaissance. Increased stealth, speed and autonomy promise higher levels of combat ability and ever lower levels of imposition.

As part of the wider RMA, and with their own particular qualities of availability, through numbers, persistence and scale, UAVs have added hugely to the information available to military decision-makers at all levels. This of course is the intended effect. There is some indication in the latest thinking from the US military that the *unintended* effect is to dangle the promise of an (ever elusive) end to the need to make decisions in Clausewitz's fog of war. This may be producing an unrealistic expectation of situational clarity, leading to reduced risk-acceptance in military decision-makers faced with continuing real world complexity. The rush towards introducing systems with greater autonomy that could substantially reduce reliance on human performance is similarly problematic in terms of expectations and possible consequences.

The Human Factor

An acolyte of McLuhan's, Neil Postman, said that 'technological change is not additive; it is ecological. A new technology does not merely add something; it changes everything'.[9] Extending far beyond narrow considerations of how wars are fought, drones affect how we think about war itself: what makes someone a soldier, a warrior, a combatant? In a networked, decentralised assemblage of people and machines, who is accountable for any given civilian death or war crime or human rights violation? Chapters 4–8 of this book consider some of the cultural, legal and ethical implications of drone warfare on individuals, and on existing laws and norms governing the use of force in the international system.

While the vehicle itself is of course unmanned, at a ground station somewhere sits a crew flying the machine and watching the mission – whether ISR or kinetic – unspool before it on computer screens. Physically they are far removed from the dangers of war, but mentally the effects of being a drone warrior are not well understood. Accounts of operators psychologically damaged by the daily grind of killing people by remote control are beginning to dot the mass media. Clinical diagnoses of post-traumatic stress disorder (PTSD), which have usually been based on the effects of exposure to mortal fear, are being realigned to consider the 'moral injury' that is inflicted on drone pilots who are required as a matter of routine to launch missiles at groups and individuals thousands of miles away, watch them die, and then go home at the end of their shifts each day to their otherwise ordinary lives and families.[10]

This is but one of many issues to which the military culture within the United States Air Force (USAF) is struggling to adapt in the face of new conditions created by drone warfare. Operators are lauded and even decorated for their kills; but they are also overworked, underpromoted and mocked as the 'Chair Force'. There are other areas that need to be resolved regarding responsibility and accountability in the decision-making chain; whether the distance between a soldier and his or her target, or the fact that the relationship is a virtual one, makes any kind of qualitative difference between mounting manned and unmanned missions; and indeed, at the other end of the equation, whether it matters if one is killed by a Hellfire missile fired by a drone or by a manned aircraft (the USAF thinks not).

The whole point of unmanned missions is that they reduce risk to pilots, and this supposedly allows for them to make better decisions. If burnout, PTSD and a general difficulty around recruiting UAV operators begin to affect military performance adversely, then such human frailties will become one more plank in the argument to remove not only the bodies of soldiers, but their minds as well, from the sordid business of killing people. There is a strong push to introduce greater autonomy into weapons systems so that mere soldiers will no longer even be required to fight wars. The replacement of soldiers with so-called killer robots, designed to decide who to kill based on programming specifications implanted in the machines themselves, is a near-term prospect, with ethical and legal considerations lagging far behind the research and development programmes underway that are making such weapons possible.

At the other end of the drone's kill chain lie the populations being targeted. While drones are celebrated for their counter-terrorism capabilities – their ability to track and kill single militants from among the civilians below their gaze – they do this by placing entire populations under surveillance, and this omnipresent threat is leading to changes in how lives are lived under drones. The scale of civilian deaths in the non-war zones of Pakistan, Yemen and Somalia is concerning, but the Obama administration maintains that only militants or terrorists are killed, and this oft-repeated fiction seems to largely satisfy US public opinion. In countries under attack, however, there are indications that the drone strikes are undermining security as well as social structures, and creating far more problems than they purport to solve. Former US deputy chief of mission in Yemen from 2004 to 2007, Nabeel Khoury, recently suggested that 'the U.S. generates roughly forty to sixty new enemies for every AQAP [Al Qaeda in the Arabian Peninsula] operative killed by drones'.[11]

Meanwhile, waves of increasingly damning reports claim that the US is trampling international laws and committing war crimes in this ostensibly low-risk way of war. If world opposition does not coalesce around placing curbs on its practice, then it is likely that new international norms will emerge in which other states also feel free to engage in nano-wars against populations they find it inconvenient to deal with. As UN human rights expert Christof Heyns said in his major UN report:

> The expansive use of armed drones by the first States to acquire them, if not challenged, can do structural damage to the cornerstones of international security and set precedents that undermine the protection of life across the globe in the longer term.[12]

McLuhan noted, 'Control over change would seem to consist in moving not with it but ahead of it. Anticipation gives the power to deflect and control force'.[13] In attempting to anticipate the effects of UAVs, the directions for future policy, use and regulation may become clearer. Thus far the message of drones is deeply worrisome: the reasons that make this technology attractive to militaries and politicians are the very reasons that raise concern. Their technical qualities permit access in a wide range of scenarios, enabling the delivery of a massively expanded source of ISR data at every level of a military operation. Their strike/combat capacity, although still limited in a military sense, has clearly been very useful for political purposes, and it is here that the unlooked for larger-scale effects are manifest. When used to target individuals in acts of nano-war, drones increase instability in the international system. This increased propensity to resort to force risks a proliferation spiral as other states rush to possess such systems, while the commission of war crimes and human rights violations, and the erosion of international regimes and legal standards, threaten what fragile security the world has managed to achieve.

1

From Balloons to Big Safari: UAV Development

The US intelligence community is the single greatest contributor to US operational UAV development.

Thomas Erhard, Special Assistant to the Chief of Staff, USAF

Air power, as USAF Major Carl Baner puts it, enables 'observation ... the collection of data and information. The elevation and extent of air and space provides the airman with a perspective of the theater that is not afforded to the soldier or sailor'.[1] As he notes, it also provides the means to *act* on that information. Particularly since 2001, UAVs have evolved to the point at which they provide commanders with effective tools to address both aspects of air power. The road has not always been smooth, however, with manned aircraft and satellites competing over key missions, and expensive failed programmes littering the way. UAVs seem to have finally found their niche as the technological capacity and the appropriate operational environment have come together in the asymmetric conflicts of the twenty-first century. However, this niche is highly controversial, associated with the extension of an imperialist surveillance and militarised violence into situations previously unavailable for such action.

Balloon Warfare

Although UAVs have only come to prominence in the public eye in the last couple of decades, they have been a part of the military inventory for much longer than that. The history of unmanned flight is of course longer than the history of manned flight, and the usage of unmanned flight in war also predates the use of manned aircraft; in fact, its development was tied up with military applications from the very beginning. The Montgolfier brothers, credited with the development of the hot-air balloon, were inspired by the potential they saw for the usage of such a craft in war.[2] This potential was borne out in as much as unmanned balloons undertook the first verified aerial bombing raid in history, when in 1849, during the Austrian siege of Venice, an attempt was made by the Austrians to drift balloons carrying 30 lb bombs over the Venetian defences. The bombs were released either by timer or, according to a contemporary account in *The Scientific American*, by an electric switch connected via a long trailing copper wire. Unguided as well as unmanned, the attempt was a failure, as a change in the wind drove most of the balloons off target, even bringing some of them back over Austrian lines.

The balloon had a long manned history as a military observation tool, but even as late as World War II both the Allied and Axis powers used unmanned balloons to attack each other. Curtis Peebles describes how the British Operation Outward sent almost 100,000 small balloons towards Germany, carrying either a small (6 lb) incendiary device or trailing wires with the intent of causing short circuits in power-lines – a task at which they had some success, resulting, for example, in the destruction of a power plant in 1942. A by-product of the programme was seen in the attempts by German fighters to intercept the balloons – much more costly to the Luftwaffe than the very basic balloons were to the British: an early example of how cheap UAVs might swamp air defences. The Japanese attempted a similar thing, but with a more sophisticated device operating over an intercontinental distance, when late in the war they released over 9,000 balloons carrying small bombs – either incendiary or anti-personnel weapons – which then crossed the Pacific riding on the jet stream. Three hundred are known to have reached North America although they caused little damage, the most serious event being the killing of six curious picnickers in Oregon. The only control these devices had was an estimation of the jet stream speed and direction, and a timing device.

Radio-Control Versus Autopilot

However, the real path towards the effective delivery of air power by UAVs lay with heavier-than-air craft, lightweight engines and wireless technology. A radio-control system was first patented by Nikola Tesla in 1898, a system he demonstrated on a radio-controlled boat to amazed onlookers at Madison Square Gardens. Experiments applying radio-control to aircraft came hard on the heels of the Wright Brothers' first manned flight, with war once again driving the technology. Archibald Low, an eccentric British engineer and inventor known as 'the father of unmanned guidance systems',[3] worked on developing radio-control for aircraft during World War I, conducting the first demonstration of wirelessly controlled unmanned flight in 1917 for the British military, under the code name Aerial Target – in reality the aircraft was intended to be used as a flying bomb, a kind of early cruise missile. The project was not taken up.

This development was paralleled with a different technology in the US, where the Hewitt-Sperry automatic plane underwent a number of trial flights in 1917 and 1918, again with the intention of functioning as a flying bomb, particularly with the aim of attacking enemy shipping. The US Army commissioned a similar aircraft, the Kettering Bug, to function as an aerial torpedo over a range of around 40 miles. Ultimately, 45 of the 12-foot-long biplanes were built but were not used in action. Neither of these aircraft were remotely guided, but rather they flew a programmed course using an autopilot system consisting of the new Sperry-developed gyroscope, a barometer and a timer, to manage height, direction/attitude and distance. As Thomas Mueller notes, this made the Kettering Bug 'the first airplane capable of stabilizing and navigating itself without a pilot on board'.[4]

This approach labels the Hewitt-Sperry and the Kettering bug true 'drones', for although the term is common in describing contemporary unmanned aircraft, the more accurate term for most of this type of aircraft currently is 'remotely piloted', reflecting the fact that decisions are being made about course, height and so on by a human being reacting in real time. A drone is bound to do what it has been programmed to do (we will, however, be following accepted practice and using the terms interchangeably). The advantage of this kind of autopilot guidance at this stage of development is range: the aircraft can fly out of sight of any human controller, whereas radio-control was dependent on the remote controller being able to see the aircraft that he or she was controlling. This means range is limited (or that the controller has to accompany the aircraft in another manned aeroplane). The third category would be 'autonomous', that is, there is no human pilot remote or otherwise, but nor is the aircraft simply following a course by rote: rather, the machine makes choices based on changing conditions, reacting perhaps to terrain changes, or enemy radar signals, or maybe even target recognition. This doesn't come until much later, and indeed is only a partial reality today.

Experiments in radio-control continued between the wars, on land, sea and in the air. The Soviet Union developed tele-tanks, a system in which a manned tank operated a partner unmanned tank via radio-control. These saw use in the Winter War with Finland.[5] The US Navy used radio-control to direct target ships for gunnery practice, such as the obsolete USS Iowa, sunk in 1923. The system of radio-control in this instance was developed by John Hays Hammond Jr, a protégé of Thomas Edison and Alexander Graham Bell.[6] Military experiments with unmanned aircraft also continued between the wars. The British Navy acquired a radio-controlled aerial target aircraft based on parts from a couple of manned aircraft, the de Havilland Tiger Moth and the Moth Major. This task is one eminently suited to basic radio-control as it does not require the plane to travel long distances, but perhaps circle a ship at a distance of no more than a few miles. The aircraft, known as the Queen Bee (some accounts suggest that this name was the original source of the term 'drone'), first flew in 1935 and was quite effective in its role. Over 400 were built, both in land and seaplane versions – the latter launched by steam catapult. Robin Braithwaite reports that the aircraft had an automatic landing system to allow the aircraft to land safely should radio-control be lost, and that 'In its heyday, it was not uncommon to discover an orphaned Queen Bee, devoid of fuel but otherwise serviceable, quietly bobbing about at sea'.[7] The novelist and aircraft engineer Nevil Shute Norway's Airspeed company was commissioned to build a dedicated UAV as a successor to the Queen Bee, the Queen Wasp. This aircraft, also designed both in floatplane and land-based versions, was much less successful, and no more than a few prototypes were built.

Towards Guidance Beyond Visual Range

Many of these early developments have as much to do with the development of guided missiles as with unmanned aircraft, since both Low's radio-controlled Aerial Target and the US Sperry gyroscope-guided aircraft were designed as weapons rather than as aircraft designed to return for reuse. This technology would be advanced in the course of World War II, both in the form of guided weapons and reusable unmanned aircraft. To some extent it was still the province of the talented amateur. Reginald Denny was one such, a Briton who, having served in the Royal Flying Corps in World War I, emigrated to the US to become a film actor (in which he was successful, acting in many well-known movies). He developed a hobbyist's interest in radio-controlled aircraft, started a modeller's shop on Hollywood Boulevard, and promoted his belief that drones had a useful role in gunnery practice to the US military. He made his first sale in 1940, and over the course of the war around 15,000 'Denny Radioplanes' were produced. These aircraft were conventional-looking single-engine monoplanes with a 12-foot wingspan. Few survive, a testament, as one commentator put it, to the trainee gunners' accuracy.[8] The company was later taken over by Northrop, which today, as Northrop Grumman, remains in the UAV business. A number of other radio-controlled target drones based on manned aircraft were used in World War II, from the US Navy's Curtis N2C-2 biplane, which first flew in 1937, to the US Army Air Force's (USAAF) Culver PQ-8/14 based on a light civil monoplane. These were controlled from an accompanying aircraft and were successful in their role, with over 2,000 of the later PQ-14 variant being built. In a footnote to UAV history, Marilyn Monroe was discovered by an army photographer who took pictures of her assembling the Denny Radioplane when she was working at the Denny plant in 1944.

The US military also continued to experiment with radio-controlled 'aerial torpedoes'. But the Navy team that developed the N2C-2 based target drone were to take the concept a fundamental step further. The officer in charge, who retired as Rear Admiral Delmar S. Fahrney, US Navy, writes, 'Back at the Naval Aircraft Factory in April 1939, as officer in charge of "Project Fox," I began planning, design, and development work on a guided missile that could be successfully controlled beyond visual range'.[9] The key to this step was television, and Fahrney records how a contract with RCA led to the provision of a small TV transmitter. By 1941 successful flight tests had been carried out and development went ahead with what they called an 'assault drone'. He describes how in 1942 a TG-2 biplane torpedo bomber, converted into a drone and controlled by an operator looking at a six-inch television screen on an accompanying aircraft, carried out a successful torpedo attack demonstration on a US destroyer. Since the drone was not acting as the missile itself, this can be seen as the first use of an unmanned combat air vehicle (UCAV). In later tests they were also flown directly into the target, acting in a secondary role, in effect, as cruise missiles.[10]

Laurence Newcome, who was heavily involved in the Pentagon's UAV development programme, recounts how almost immediately after its initial success with the TG-2 the Naval Aircraft Factory sought to overcome the limitations of the new TV–equipped drone, namely its inability to deal with night-flying or bad weather. They did this by adding a radar guidance system, and developed two drones able to use both systems, the TDN-1 and the TDR-1. These were fairly basic plywood monoplanes capable of carrying around 2,000 lbs of bombs, but they proved the worth of the UAV concept in the war in the Pacific. Three Special Task Air Groups (STAGs) with 99 control aircraft, 891 drones and over 3,000 personnel were stood up in 1943, and in 1944 STAG-1 was deployed near Guadalcanal and rapidly demonstrated their aircraft's value by flying four drones into a grounded Japanese vessel. This led to further successful attacks on a range of fixed targets, often attacking through heavy anti-aircraft fire, while, as Newcombe writes, 'their [Grumman] Avenger mother ships orbited 6–8 miles away'.[11]

In this kind of attack the drone weapon is deployed as a missile: it is destroyed in the process, as it is directed on to the target as a kind of flying bomb – along the lines of the better-known German V-1, which, however, used a gyroscope and compass along with a range-counter, to fly automatically. But most interestingly, especially given the long post-war emphasis on the drone as a *surveillance* tool, STAG-1 also experimented in action with the use of the drone as a bomber rather than simply a bomb. Newcombe describes how 'armed with a combination of ten 500- and 100-lb bombs, a single TDR-1 dropped the bombs on gun emplacements and then headed for home'. Although it crashed on the way back due to battle damage, this key event 'had proven the operational validity of the unmanned combat air vehicle (UCAV)'. Later attacks used a combination of approaches, with the drones dropping their bombs on targets then being guided into Japanese shipping in what Newcome calls 'a pilotless prelude to the Japanese Kamikaze attacks that began a week later'. He assesses the effects of the drone attacks as follows:

> Of the 50 drones STAG-1 had sent into combat, 15 were lost to mechanical/technical causes, three to enemy fire, and 31 hit or damaged their targets. More importantly, not one STAG-aviator was lost or injured on these missions during some of the bloodiest contests of the war in the Pacific.[12]

The significance of this seems to be twofold: these aircraft proved the worth of the UAV and indeed the UCAV concept in as much as they worked, delivering a weapon accurately on to the target without a human pilot on board. Secondly, the fact that Newcombe draws attention to the lack of US casualties involved in the process indicates one of the fundamental advantages of the UAV: they can carry out dangerous military operations at no risk to the military personnel operating them.

That said, not all UAV operations at this time were risk-free. The US approach to remotely piloted vehicles included the adaptation of large military aircraft at the end of their operational lives, such as the four-engined Liberator and Flying Fortress bombers. USAAF chief General H.H. Arnold, in supporting the effort to bring 'the greatest pressure possible against the enemy', wrote in a 1944 staff memo, 'If you can get mechanical machines to do this, you are saving lives at the outset'.[13] Unfortunately, in this case that was not quite true. These aircraft required a crew of two on board to achieve take-off, who then bailed out. This left the accompanying mothership to control them by radio, the controller having the benefit of a new control technology: a television picture of the view out of the cockpit of the controlled aircraft as well as a view of the control panel to help them in the task of directing the explosive-filled plane on to the target. Despite these aids, this programme was of limited success, creating as much danger for the American crews, accompanying aircraft and towns surrounding the English airfields from which they were launched, as they did for the enemy. Possibly the biggest historical impact of these 'Weary Willies', as they were nick-named, lay in the premature detonation of one such converted B-24 Liberator, which resulted in the death of Joseph Patrick Kennedy, intended by his family for the position of US President. This task then fell to his younger brother, John.

Newcome finds additional, and provocative, significance in the way the drone programme was managed during the war, which he suggests would not be unfamiliar today. Firstly he identifies, in the apparently positive way in which new capacities were rapidly added to the drone (TV, radar, etc.), the phenomenon of 'requirements creep' that delayed availability, complicated production and increased costs. He also saw an institutional resistance to supporting this new and untried technology, as well as a failure to bring operational commanders on board early in the process. This all happened in the context of war, which he characterises as a 'come as you are' affair in which few major technological developments occur, with most major wartime weapons systems in production before the war began.[14]

Cold War Surveillance

As Rebecca Grant points out in the introduction to Thomas Ehrhard's study, 50 years passed between the end of the war and the Predator's appearance in the Bosnian war, a period in which the UAV seemed to have fallen from grace. 'Vanished from sight' might be a more accurate term, as key programmes, if not yet the drones themselves, became stealthy, operating to some extent under the cover of black or secret programmes of shadowy organisations such as the National Reconnaissance Office (NRO) or, later, the Defense Airborne Reconnaissance Office (DARO), and operated by, in some cases, the CIA, rather than the USAF. In fact, as Ehrhard points out, 'the US intelligence community is the single greatest contributor to US operational UAV development'.[15]

Newcome describes how the particular exigencies of the Cold War had some influence on how UAVs developed after World War II. One factor was the perception that the next war would be a nuclear one. Experience with flying manned aircraft over the Bikini Atoll nuclear tests illustrated the dangers of putting aircrew into such a radioactive environment to see what was going on, and so out of this scenario came the pressure to create unmanned reconnaissance aircraft to deal with such 'dirty' missions. The 'cold' nature of the Cold War also meant that such operations as were flown by US forces over hostile territory were reconnaissance flights rather than strike missions. As such, Newcome notes that these surveillance flights were among the hottest missions of the Cold War, posing real risks to the pilots manning the aircraft involved, with 23 aircraft and 179 aircrew lost between 1946 and 1990. There was the additional risk of creating diplomatic incidents if personnel were captured.

For Newcome, these three factors – planning for nuclear war, risks to aircrew and potential for diplomatic embarrassment – 'helped make the reconnaissance mission a logical candidate for delegation to unmanned aircraft'.[16] The early swing towards the UCAV that happened under the exigencies of 'hot' warfare therefore went on to the back burner. Nevertheless, hot wars did of course occur during the Cold War era, and unmanned aircraft saw action in them. The Korean War provided another occasion for the use of outmoded manned aircraft laden with explosive (in this case Grumman Hellcats) adapted to serve as radio-controlled missiles. These were flown off aircraft carriers and then remotely piloted to their heavily defended targets from an accompanying aircraft. Such radio-controlled Hellcats were also used to monitor the mushroom clouds from the tests at Bikini Atoll in 1946.

One of the earliest potential reconnaissance drones failed for one of the reasons Newcome identified above. The high altitude Northrop/ Radioplane B-67 Crossbow started out as a target drone, was adapted for the suppression of enemy air defence mission, and was being considered for the reconnaissance mission when it was cancelled in 1957, as costs escalated and performance deteriorated – the result of 'trying to ask too many missions from a design optimized for one: i.e. the notorious program death by "requirements creep"'.[17]

More successfully, Newcome notes that Radioplane fitted cameras to the successful wartime OQ-19 drone, and sold 1,445 of the resulting SD-1 Observers to the US Army, as well as 32 to the British Army. This aircraft added a key element to the UAV technological mix, in as much as it had a radar beacon on board allowing it to be tracked and sent radio commands by a controller on the ground well beyond visual range. A number of other unmanned surveillance aircraft were developed in the US at this time (SD-2 through 5), but none went into service.

According to USAF Major Christopher Jones, 'The genesis event for the UAV was the downing of Francis Gary Powers' U-2 spy plane over the Soviet Union on 1 May 1960 by an SA-2 missile'.[18] The U-2 had been produced specifically as a response to the Soviet Union's development of nuclear weapons; able to fly at altitudes beyond the reach of Russian interceptors and anti-aircraft missiles, for four years it was able to gather data on Soviet military activities with impunity, and even without official complaint from the Russians since, as Jones puts it, 'To have accused the U.S. of overflights would have been to admit the Soviet military's inability to defend the Soviet Union against U.S. planes'.[19] This all changed with arrival of the Russian SA-2 surface to air missile (SAM) and its successful interception of Gary Powers's CIA intelligence gathering mission. Powers survived the incident and was paraded before the world as a self-admitted spy, in a major embarrassment for the US. Eisenhower stopped overflights of the Soviet Union as a result. UAVs were not immediately seen as the solution as the US had other irons in the fire, notably the CIA's high-speed manned reconnaissance aircraft (later known as the SR-71) and the Corona satellite, Discoverer 14, which as Ehrhard points out flew just three months after the Powers incident. He writes that 'Competition between the three modes of strategic reconnaissance – drones, satellites and manned aircraft – continues to this day', and he adds, 'drones lost all the early battles'.[20]

Nevertheless, at this stage satellites did not provide all the answers as the resolution of the imagery they provided was very low, and their availability to monitor a given target always limited. The SR-71's imagery was higher quality, but its high cost and limited availability also meant that coverage was limited in tactical terms. Then another U-2 was shot down by an SA-2 over Cuba in the 1962 missile crisis; the pilot, Major Rudolf Anderson, USAF, was killed, giving him the unfortunate distinction of being the only person killed by enemy fire during the crisis. Jones suggests that this event gave another push to UAV development, resulting in the most successful surveillance drone of the Cold War period. It was developed from an existing jet-powered target drone, the Ryan Firebee. Known as the Lightning Bug, it became operational in 1962 after a short development period by the US Air Force's 'Big Safari' office, operating under NRO auspices. In tests it immediately showed its advantages over a manned aircraft. Being small, and what Erhard calls 'stealth-enhanced', it was able to avoid radar-lock from opposing fighters in tests against US fighters. Later versions had a quite impressive performance, being able to reach 50,000 feet and fly at over 600 mph. Launched either from the ground or, more typically, from an underwing position on a C-130 transport, it could travel a preprogrammed course of up to 1,300 miles, before being recovered by parachute – either descending to the ground with a thump, or, again more usually, being collected in mid-air by a helicopter. Resistance to the concept from senior air force officers led to a struggle to find anyone to operate it, but eventually the commander of an element of the Strategic Air Command was sold on the idea. As Ehrhard puts it, 'He had just bought into the most significant operational UAV system in history'. Northrop Grumman is still upgrading the aircraft for use as aerial targets by US forces today, five decades later.

The aircraft was first used for reconnaissance missions over China as part of a mission named Blue Springs. Erhard tells of a special unit being sent to Japan to overfly China in pursuit of intelligence regarding China's nascent nuclear weapons programme and its air defences. Success was limited in the early days, with aircraft lost, damaged on recovery, or simply too inaccurate in their navigation to be useful. But changes were made and Blue Springs moved to Vietnam in late 1964, flying missions into China: 'China had minor success shooting down this robot intruder but, unlike the Powers incident, it did not seem to matter politically'.[21] Thus these operations formed something of a proof of concept for the unmanned reconnaissance mission in conditions short of war.

Although developed as a response to the need for unmanned strategic reconnaissance in the context of the Cold War, the Lightning Bug came into its own during the Vietnam War under the programme name 'Buffalo Hunter', flying tactical missions into North Vietnam from 1965 right through to 1975. They operated both as reconnaissance aircraft, mostly at low altitude (the AGM-34L model, 29 feet long with a 13 foot wingspan), and as what Ehrhard calls 'bait', to force enemy anti-aircraft defences to reveal their position as they engaged the drones. But the primary mission was low-level aerial reconnaissance flying at between 500 and 3,750 feet. Air Force Major Paul Elder reports that at 1,500 feet the Fairchild camera provided a useable 120 nautical mile strip of imagery that covered a swath of 3 nautical miles, and resolved objects down to six inches in size.[22]

Lawrence Spinetta notes that over ten years these relatively straightforward UAVs flew 3,450 missions. Some 544 were lost – two-thirds to enemy action, one-third to mechanical failure – which was a much better success rate than expected: 'A drone dubbed Tom Cat set the record with 68 sorties before being lost in September 1974'. He also reveals an unlooked for element of the drone's success: despite being unarmed, several Lightning Bugs managed to earn MiG 'kills', since North Vietnamese fighters sometimes crashed or were hit by errant SAMs while trying to intercept the drones. One drone actually earned ace status, as it contributed to the loss of five enemy fighters'.[23] In another twist to this tale, Elder writes that 'some Air Force officers speculated that North Vietnamese gunners used U.S. drone sorties for target practice and that MIG pilots used them to practice intercepts'.[24] In effect they got a free target drone, which was after all the original Firebee's mission.

That many other UAV programmes failed where the Firebee/Lightning Bug did not may be in part because the programme did not over-reach technically. Nevertheless, the aircraft was not an unmitigated success, failing to achieve its reconnaissance target more than 50 per cent of the time. Part of this was due to the focus on low-altitude operations, to minimise the SA-2 risk and to go under the monsoon weather, as well as to obtain the highest definition imagery. With the margin of error in the drone's onboard guidance in the order of 3 per cent according to Elder, this meant that after 100 nautical miles the drone was up to 3 nautical miles off track, enough to miss its objective, given the 3 nautical mile width of the area of coverage. The course could be corrected by the Microwave Command Guidance System from the C-130 mothership, but it had issues determining its own location to the necessary level of accuracy, and the telemetry from the drone was not always good.

It should also be noted that despite its relative simplicity compared to some other drone projects at this time, the Lightning Bug could not be called cheap. For example, its launching and recovery procedures were demanding both in terms of equipment and manpower. In part because of its success, and the numbers built, it actually stands as what Ehrhard calls 'the most expensive UAV operation of its time'. As many subsequent programmes have demonstrated, removing the pilot from the aircraft does not necessarily save money. In the end however, in a secret report for the Air Force declassified in 2006, Elder was able to conclude that 'Buffalo Hunter is a combat-tested, unmanned system which has functioned effectively in a combat environment', part of its virtue being that they 'never lost a crew-member'. Elder quotes General John Vogt Jr, commander of the US 7th Air Force in Vietnam in 1972: 'I know of no other way we could have obtained the information we needed ... [during] the intensive combat activity of the December period'.[25]

By way of contrast to the Lightning Bug, one of a number of very ambitious secret UAV programmes that Ehrhard describes as starting under NRO auspices in the 1960s was the D-21 Tagboard. Faced with the difficult task of overflying China's nuclear weapons facility at Lop Nor, in Xinjiang, northwest China, a CIA–sponsored programme of surveillance using nominally Nationalist Chinese U-2s saw five aircraft shot down by the dangerous SA-2 SAMs. An unmanned aircraft able to handle the demands of this mission was needed, and Lockheed's famous skunk works came up with a solution. Tagboard was an extreme development: a one-use mach 4 UAV launched at mach 2, in order to fire up its ramjet, off the back of an SR-71. Four missions were flown over China and four drones were lost. This programme bit the dust after one example had a fatal collision with the launching mothership. Other even more expensive programmes followed, with little ultimate success, such as the disastrous $1bn per copy Advanced Airborne Reconnaissance System (AARS). Finally, in 1974, as Ehrhard describes it, the NRO washed its hands of the drone business, becoming purely a satellite-based organisation, reflecting the fact that satellite technology had matured in a number of ways. It transferred its drone operations, as well as its manned reconnaissance aircraft, to the air force – specifically, by 1976, to the Tactical Air Command.

Beyond the US

On the other side of the Cold War divide the Soviet Union also experimented with UAVs. The National Museum of the USAF records that, 'In 1950 the Soviet Air Force began development of a radio-controlled aerial target for training fighter pilots'.[26] Production of the high speed, high altitude Lavochkin La-17 began in 1954. Originally air-launched with basic radio-control, a crude ramjet and strictly limited endurance, the La-17 underwent numerous improvements right up until the last one was built in 1993. These included the addition of an autopilot and a new turbojet, which allowed the development of a ground-launched reconnaissance version (La-17R) in the early 1960s. This carried 'a variety of payloads that included high-resolution cameras, real-time television cameras and radiation monitoring equipment'. The example at the museum was found floating in the Black Sea by the US Navy after it crashed while flying from a Soviet test facility.

The superpowers were not alone in developing UAVs in this period. China's experience with unmanned aircraft benefited from both the Soviet and the US programmes. In the 1950s, when relations between the two communist powers were good, Kimberley Hsu explains that the Soviet Union provided La-17 target drones to the PLA. When this supply was cut off after 1960 as relations soured, the Chinese reverse-engineered the aircraft to create the Chang Kong-1 target drone. The Firebee programme had a role in China's UAV development too. Hsu notes that when 'The PLA recovered a U.S. AQM-34 Firebee UAV in North Vietnam in the 1960s. Chinese reverse engineering yielded another early Chinese unmanned platform, the low-altitude deep-penetration Wu Zhen-5 (WZ-5)'.[27]

Israel has today become one of the global powers in UAV development and production, and the industry has its origins in the events and technology of the 1960s. Firebee, seemingly the ur-drone of the international UAV industry, had a role in the establishment of that capacity. Following Israel's strategic gains in the Six-Day War of 1967, the conflict with Egypt settled into the three years of what is known as the War of Attrition. The Israeli Air Force (IAF) note that with Soviet assistance Egypt deployed SA-2 and SA-3 SAMs, which resulted in losses for the IAF and 'harmed the Air Force's ability to gather intelligence from the frontlines. During the search for a method of intelligence gathering that would not put the lives of air crew at risk, the possibility of acquiring UAVs was explored'.[28] In 1970 a contract was signed with Teledyne Ryan for a UAV based on the Firebee, which started arriving in 1971.

Also in 1971 the IAF acquired the Northrop Chukar (Telem in Israeli usage), developed as a target drone for the US Navy, to carry out another of the central tasks of the UAV: contributing to the suppression of enemy air defence mission. At about 12 feet in length, the Chukar was half the size of the Firebee and straightforwardly launched from a ramp with rocket assistance, to be recovered by parachute. For guidance, it combined an autopilot with radio-control. The IAF write that 'The Chukar's main aim was to draw enemy antiaircraft fire, making it easier for combat planes to locate and destroy the missile batteries'. And in 1973, as they put it, 'The Chukar received its baptism by fire during the Yom Kippur War'. The system was first used to fool the Syrians into believing they were under attack. Overall the IAF say that each group of 2–4 Chukar decoys resulted in the launching of 20–25 enemy missiles.

Other NATO powers were also engaged in the development of UAVs. As the result of a jointly funded Canada/UK/Germany project in the 1960s, Canadair developed a surveillance drone for artillery spotting, the CL-89 (later developed into the CL-289 which was also sold to France). Known as the 'midge', the 12-foot UAV was a rocket – launched off the back of a truck, with a small jet engine taking over once in flight. This was a true drone, following a preprogrammed flight path. The aircraft was recovered by parachute, protecting itself by deploying airbags on landing. Reg Austin writes that 'A major requirement of the UAV was that it be highly survivable in the face of a sophisticated enemy. With its small diameter (0.33m) stub wings of 0.94m span and high speed (740km/hr, it [the Midge] was difficult to detect and destroy'.[29] Simple and reliable, in British service it was to see action in the first Gulf war, as well as with the French and Germans in the Balkan conflicts.

Out of the Cold

The way UAVs were developed and funded in the US during the Cold War period seems to have been a mixed blessing. Ehrhard observes that the covert wealth of the NRO – 'an agency so secret even its name was classified until just after the end of the Cold War' – channelled through the new-born CIA (with its foreign intelligence mission) and the Air Force (a newly independent service), both the product of the 1947 National

Security Act, enabled sophisticated UAV technologies to be developed.[30] However, it also led to a certain distortion in the tasks pursued and the tools developed: 'NRO UAVs cost billions, yet the NRO produced designs ill-suited to the highest priority conventional military challenge of the Cold War', writes Erhard.[31] The costs, even though buried in black budgets, were astronomical enough to raise eyebrows, and the failures multiple.

From the 1970s on, conditions seemed to be coming together to favour unmanned military flight. For one thing, the air defence challenge offered by the Soviet Union was, following the Vietnam experience, understood to be very significant, and the UAV offered a possible solution to managing that threat. Also, science seemed to be on the point of delivering what Erhard describes as a technical revolution in the form of 'micropro-cessor-based automated flight control and high-bandwidth real-time communications'.[32] This is of course part of the wider RMA. In spite of this favourable scenario, Ehrhard suggests that the USAF fared little better as the custodian of the UAV dream than the NRO, with several expensive programmes – such as the ambitious high latitude/long endurance (HALE) Compass Dwell and Compass Cope programmes – collapsing without delivering a useable aircraft. They remain of interest in that they attempted to manage some of the problem (i.e. the high expenditure) areas of UAV usage by using conventional runways under remote pilot control, and Compass Cope experimented with the use of satellites for control, an approach that promised to extend that remote-control globally. Another programme that failed to get anywhere at this time was the BGM-34C multi-mission drone, worthy of note in that one of those missions was weapons delivery – in other words, it was another instance of a plan to develop a UCAV, long before the CIA strapped a Hellfire on to a Predator.

Ehrhard puts the failure of these ambitious programmes down to two factors: one being 'the myth of affordability that haunted UAV programs of the 1970s (and persists today)', the other being that the technology was still not up to the particular demands of the UAV. Thus the USAF was continually confounded by the rising costs of its UAV programmes, and, without the NRO's deep pockets, sought to cut those costs, leading to loss of capacity and failure of the programme. With regard to technology, despite the rise of the microprocessor computing power at this time remained inadequate for automated flight, and communication with the UAV formed a 'kite string' that 'could be clipped quite easily by electronic countermeasures'.[33] Likewise, location was still mostly determined by inadequately accurate inertial systems. Interestingly, too (and this forms an ongoing element in UAV development, especially with regard to autonomy), some proposed UAVs and the way they were intended to be used, fell afoul of European air traffic control regulations. All this meant that the new post-Vietnam focus on the demanding European NATO theatre revealed that the UAV was still not up to the task of dealing either with a sophisticated air defence environment, or a busy civil airspace.

Towards the Working Drone

Despite the teething troubles, the improved communication and control technology available began to deliver real benefits in terms of transmitting digital imagery from the surveillance drone. This allowed analysts and commanders to see what was happening on the ground as it happened, rather than having to wait for the drone to return, be recovered, and have its film processed. A step change in UAV effectiveness was on its way by the 1980s.

A team of Israeli Aircraft Industries (IAI) engineers writes that, 'One of the main lessons of the 1973 war was the lack of good operational intelligence'.[34] The IAF records that it was 'The growing use of Unmanned Aerial Vehicles to gather real time intelligence on the front lines' that led IAI to develop its own UAV capable of broadcasting pictures from a stabilised camera: the IAI Scout. In 1979, 20 of these small (12 foot long) machines were acquired. Initially the Scout required rocket assistance to launch, but a lengthening of the wings enabled conventional take-off controlled by a remote pilot. As an aside, all of these aircraft have the distinctive twin tail-boom formation. The IAI engineers write that 'it could be said that this became the "house configuration,"' explaining their choice in terms of 'Ease of modification – changing engine, modifying tail, modifying wing' and 'Convenience of integrating payloads, including nose space and the use of the booms for antennae and installations'.[35]

The Scout provided effective service to Israeli forces in Lebanon in 1982, and it crossed into US use when it was developed into the Pioneer UAV for the US Navy, who used it in Operation Desert Storm in 1991. One example became famous as the drone that a group of Iraqi troops surrendered to (it is now an exhibit in the Smithsonian). Israeli experience and expertise would be important in the next generation of UAVs in the US and Europe, as the arrival of the satellite-based global positioning system (GPS), and digital flight control systems, led to vastly improved range and effectiveness.

The development of the UAV up until the 1990s reveals certain patterns. From the early days there had been a basic choice between automated aircraft and remotely piloted aircraft, a choice that is now sometimes combined in a single mission. That mission can be driven in part by the capacity of the technology, and in part by the nature of the conflict that states are engaged in: in World War II there was a great need for training anti-aircraft gunners, and so the straightforward target drone was where the emphasis lay. But while experiments were done with UCAVs during the war, these were largely put aside under the differing demands of the Cold War, when high-flying surveillance of an enemy you aren't actually at war with becomes key. What these Cold War events also indicate is the way that the UAV offers a political solution as much as a military one. If a UAV crashes or is brought down while trespassing in sovereign airspace it is a much less significant diplomatic (and domestic political) event than if a pilot is involved. This kind of activity is as much strategic intelligence gathering as military reconnaissance, and was managed in the US from within the intelligence community rather than the military. UAVs became spies, and the black budgets that were available for such projects illuminated one of the fundamental misunderstandings of unmanned aircraft: they are not necessarily cheaper than manned aircraft, and they were as vulnerable as any other kind of device to the mission creep that attaches to so many military projects. Many expensive ventures failed as a result. The fast, jet-powered automatic Lightning Bug previewed the successful tactical UAV, although its accuracy was marginal for the kinds of task it was set. Some form of corrective control during the mission would have helped greatly, and it is the technical capacity for that development that moved the UAV ahead to the next stage.

2

The Drone Takes Off

The next logical step ... weaponising UAVs.

General John P. Jumper, former Chief of Staff, USAF[1]

In the last 15 years or so the UAV has seen action in a range of conflicts. A range of classes of UAVs has also developed in response to the demands of these conflicts. This chapter will seek both to explain how the drone finally made the transition into the mainstream, and to describe how it has been used in the contemporary battlespace. It will also indicate some trends for future UAV design.

Although the unmanned aircraft itself is not a new thing, its prevalence in the military and wider security toolbox is new. In recent years the drone has moved from being an often problematic niche player into the mainstream, taking on a range of tasks effectively, in some cases replacing or augmenting existing manned aircraft, and in others fulfilling new roles, ones not previously undertaken by aircraft. The rise has been rapid: the US Department of Defense increased the number of UAVs in service from 167 in 2002 to almost 7,500 in 2010, forming 41 per cent of all aircraft in the US defence inventory. The fact that the number of countries operating UAVs has grown from 41 in 2004 to 76 in 2012, mostly of the smaller tactical types,[2] and that in addition 50 countries are developing drones of a thousand different types,[3] shows that the US is far from being alone, although it has perhaps gone fastest and furthest down this road.[4] In a report for the Congressional Research Service, Jeremiah Gertler explains this rise in the following terms:

> Advanced navigation and communications technologies were not available just a few years ago, and increases in military communications satellite bandwidth have made remote operation of UAS [unmanned aerial systems] more practical. The nature of the Iraq and Afghanistan wars has also increased the demand for UAS, as identification of and strikes against targets hiding among civilian populations required

persistent surveillance and prompt strike capability, to minimize collateral damage. Further, UAS provide an asymmetrical – and comparatively invulnerable – technical advantage in these conflicts.[5]

Thus there is a new technical capacity, part of the digital revolution that produced the overall RMA, and there is a new security reality: the US War on Terror and the spin-off conflicts that it engendered. This security reality is not the sole cause of the drone's rise, however: to some extent the actions of the states, organisations and individuals concerned led to the embrace of the new technology. For example, Micah Zenko, from the Council on Foreign Relations, told the *National Journal* that 'the responsiveness, the persistence, and without putting your personnel at risk – is what makes [the drone] a different technology'. He added, 'When other states have this technology, if they follow U.S. practice, it will lower the threshold for their uses of lethal force outside their borders. So they will be more likely to conduct targeted killings than they have in the past'.[6] Thus, in his view, the availability of drones changes the behaviour of states, increasing the likelihood of doing the kinds of things that the US has been doing with drones in the kinds of numbers that are fairly unthinkable by any other means (conventional bombing, assassins, special forces raids, etc.) in the military scenarios short of war, such as in Pakistan, Yemen and Somalia, but also perhaps in the insurgencies that the wars in Iraq and Afghanistan rapidly collapsed into.

Along with the US, the other big innovator in UAVs is Israel, and the two countries are closely linked in this field. Gertler notes the influence of Israel's activities in its own 'small wars' on US thinking on drones. He writes:

> For many years, the Israeli Air Force led the world in developing UAS and tactics. U.S. observers noticed Israel's successful use of UAS during operations in Lebanon in 1982, encouraging then-Navy Secretary John Lehman to acquire a UAS capability for the Navy. Interest also grew in other parts of the Pentagon, and the Reagan Administration's FY1987 budget requested notably higher levels of UAS funding. This marked the transition of UAS in the United States from experimental projects to acquisition programs.[7]

If, as we have seen, the early Israeli experience with UAVs had been based on the importation of US equipment like the Firebee and the Chukar, the favour was returned, and not just by way of example: there was a direct technical linkage too. As well as the Navy's Pioneer, the US Army acquired the IAI Hunter tactical reconnaissance UAV in 1996. The practical Israeli approach to UAVs crossed over more directly into the US industry in the person of Abe Karem, a former IAF engineer who had been involved in developing decoy drones in the Yom Kippur War. Styled in the *Economist* as 'the Dronefather', Karem arrived in the US in 1977, where, in the traditions of tinkerers like Low and Denny, he started a UAV company, Leading Systems, in his garage.[8]

At a time when vastly expensive US government funded programmes were stalling, the relatively cheap, reliable, long endurance drone, the Albatross, that came out of that process, caught the attention of the Defense Advanced Research Projects Agency (DARPA), who funded its development into a more sophisticated machine known as Amber. Success was not immediate, however, as this programme, too, fell victim to US agency reorganisation when in 1989 all military UAV programmes were brought under the auspices of the UAV Joint Program Office. The main programme left under the Joint Program Office was a joint Air Force/ Navy project known as the Medium-Range UAV, 'a small, fast jet-powered aircraft that amounted to a more stealthy, data-linked Lightning Bug'.[9] This became one more failure, as competing requirements from the two services drove up costs to the point that the Navy pulled out in 1993, killing the programme and damaging the Joint Program Office.

Normalising the UAV

Meanwhile, Leading Systems had been sold, and sold on, ending up with General Atomics, for whom Karem built a low-cost but effective UAV known as the GNAT 750, six of which were sold to Turkey in 1993. Then came war in Yugoslavia. The US need for covert surveillance led them to purchase the GNAT off the shelf, which gave the CIA a useful source of near real-time video – although the unit's potential 40 hour plus endurance was limited by the need for an accompanying manned aircraft to relay the signal to a ground station. The Federation of American Scientists summed the situation up as follows: 'The GNAT System offers the combination of long endurance, large payload capacity, ease of use and low maintenance while providing a very low cost per flight hour'.[10]

Erhard describes how in 1993 a civil agency, the DARO, operating under the Office of the Secretary of Defense, gained budget and oversight control of all airborne reconnaissance programmes, including UAVs. They inherited an acquisition plan for UAVs defined in terms of three 'tiers'. Tier one, the lowest tier, was fulfilled by the GNAT. The overambitious tier three slot became occupied by what was seen as the 'tier three-minus' Global Hawk. Coming out of the DARPA/DARO era, this Ryan aeronautical designed (taken over by Northrop Grumman) UAV is a large jet-powered HALE UAV with a 40-metre wingspan, intercontinental range and endurance, and a 65,000 foot ceiling, able to scan 'large areas' with its sophisticated sensor suite.

It is also hugely and controversially expensive, at up to US$222m per unit, a price which has seen later versions cancelled or scaled back. The aircraft first flew in 1998, but under the exigencies of the War on Terror it was rushed into service in 2001. It saw service in Afghanistan and later in Iraq, where one particular operation illuminates its capacities. Journalist John Croft describes a moment early in the war when Iraqi troops were still seen as a threat. He writes:

According to Air Force Secretary Roche, JSTARS [joint surveillance target attack radar system] had found a line of troops and equipment moving in, using the sandstorm as cover, to reinforce the much-feared Republican Guard Medina Division. The handoff from the JSTARS to AV-3 [a Global Hawk] allowed analysts connected by satellite and chat links at the Air National Guard's 152nd Intelligence Squadron in Reno, Nevada, to see through the storm and help the air operations experts in Qatar guide fighter and bomber aircraft with GPS-guided bombs to the scene; the Medina Division was essentially neutralized.

He also claims that this single particular aircraft

alone identified 55 percent of the time-sensitive targets and led to significant destruction of Iraqi air defense equipment. It located 13 complete SAM batteries, more than 50 SAM launchers, 300 SAM canisters, and more than 70 SAM transporters. And it provided the intelligence that led to the destruction of more than 300 tanks – 38 percent of Iraq's known armored force.[11]

It is in service with the USAF, USN and NASA, but NATO's plan to acquire five Global Hawks for its Alliance Ground Surveillance (AGS) programme appears to be in some danger now that Germany has cancelled its plan to acquire a signal intelligence version known as Euro Hawk, with a loss of as much as 1bn euros. This decision was in part due to problems integrating the aircraft into European air traffic control rules, an issue that has killed UAV programmes before.

Tier two in this three-part scheme was seen as a larger, higher-flying, more capable version of the GNAT, and in 1994 that GNAT derivative, known as the Predator, was ordered from General Atomics. Predator added cloud-penetrating Synthetic Aperture Radar (SAR) to the electro-optical turret of the GNAT, and, for the first time, was able to use GPS positioning along with commercial satellite links, pushing both control and data delivery truly beyond line of sight, independent of any other aircraft. By 1995 it was flying operationally in the Balkans under the auspices of a special army intelligence battalion, but seeing Predator's success in that theatre the USAF pushed to take over Predator operations. It succeeded in 1996, partly driven by a lack of airborne surveillance following the development of satellites and the retiring of some key older aircraft; for as Air Force Chief of Staff, Ronald R. Fogleman put it, 'we were slowly denuding ourselves of air-breathing reconnaissance capability'.[12]

In 1998 the USAF Air Combat Command took full control of Predator, while under pressure from Congress the acquisition end of things was transferred to Big Safari, an Air Force agency with a long history in the UAV business. Journalist David Gulgum explains that:

> This shadowy organization has developed small numbers of classified payloads and specialized aircraft for clandestine reconnaissance missions. It operates under special rules that allow it to avoid much of the cumbersome acquisition procedure in exchange for new, quickly fielded technical capabilities.[13]

Richard Whittle describes it as achieving its success by aiming for 'the 80 percent solution' while ignoring 'administrivia'. It should perhaps be pointed out that the missing 20 per cent wasn't always trivial: the early Predator control panel was described as being such a random assemblage of buttons that pilots thought of it as the child's toy, Mr Potato Head, with the button to kill the engine half an inch from the button to launch a Hellfire missile.[14] UAVs remained an unconventional technology, happening on the fringes of the military enterprise.

A number of events hastened the Predator along its path from reconnaissance to combat, and on into the mainstream. For Whittle, one of these was the war in Kosovo and the air war over Serbia that accompanied it. One of the new F-117 stealth fighters was shot down, and although the pilot was rescued this led to increased care in air operations, with a 15,000 foot minimum altitude established. This kept aircraft above the cloud, and Predator was brought in to fly in this vulnerable lower zone. So once again one of the key drivers of the development of the unmanned vehicle was its sheer unmannedness: its reduction of threat to personnel and its obviation of the Gary Powers problem.

However, the imagery Predator produced was unavailable to the manned strike aircraft, so the Predator controllers had to try to direct them verbally, which was ineffective. This led to the rapid development of a system, 'Exploitation Support Data', to enable controllers to direct such aircraft on to their targets using Predator video with much more accuracy. Whittle describes how Air Force General John Jumper, Commander of Air Combat Command at the time, then suggested adding a laser designator, so that the Predator could illuminate targets for PGMs from manned aircraft to follow. Big Safari swiftly applied a designator turret intended for the US Navy's Seahawk helicopters. In around a month's time the system was in action, with a Predator 'lasing' (i.e. designating) a building containing a Serbian military vehicle that it had tracked for a smart bomb delivered by an A-10 aircraft.

There would seem to be a number of issues here worth emphasising: what made the difference between a working military UAV system in the modern sense, and the restrictive functioning of a system like the earlier Firebee family, was the information networking – the new ability to share the data Predator produced in essentially real-time. The other aspect of note is that UAVs don't deliver a different technology to the battlefield: the Predator's surveillance and target designation equipment were off the shelf, the same as that carried on manned aircraft. It is how UAVs are used because of their lack of crew that makes the difference. The story of this first direct involvement of Predator in a strike also illuminates something of the distinctive characteristic UAVs do bring to the battlespace: persistence. The UAV tracked an individual vehicle over time – not impossible for a manned surveillance aircraft perhaps, but it's the bread and butter of UAV warfare, especially in contested airspace and where tolerance of casualties is limited.

This use of the laser designator on the Predator produced a significant and controversial development, what General Jumper described 'the next logical step ... weaponizing UAVs'.[15] This logicality was added to by what Whittle identifies as pressure from the Clinton White House which had been 'pressing ... for months to find a way to capture or kill Al Qaeda leader Osama Bin Laden',[16] as a result of the US embassy bombings in Kenya and Tanzania in 1998. The outcome was that Big Safari took the Hellfire AGM-114 missile from the Seahawk helicopter (already therefore working in conjunction with the designator turret from the same source) and worked on arming the Predator with it.

This key moment in the evolution of the drone from a surveillance system into a combat system is a controversial one. Article 36 of the Geneva Convention requires new types of weapons to be reviewed to see if they comply with international law. The US didn't conduct a review of its weaponised Predator because it claimed both Hellfire and the Predator itself had already been reviewed independently to assess their compliance. But Human Rights Watch point to an International Committee of the Red Cross guide to Article 36 that states 'reviews should cover "an existing weapon that is modified in a way that alters its function, or a weapon that has already passed a legal review but that is subsequently modified."' Human Rights Watch adds that 'this rule is especially important for robots because they are complex systems that often combine a multitude of components that work differently in different combinations'.[17]

Also noteworthy was the fact that even as this work went ahead teams from Big Safari and General Atomics (the Predator's manufacturer) were being positioned in Uzbekistan to launch, land and maintain the aircraft, and in 'another country that was in the beam footprint of a satellite in orbit over Southwest Asia' to fly the mission in a mode of 'split operations'. This established current practice in which, for example, Reapers would be based in say, Kandahar, and maintained and controlled for take-off and landing by a team there, but controlled during the mission by a team in Nevada. The 'Afghan Eyes' mission was to look for Bin Laden in Afghanistan, a country with which the US was not then at war. After Bin Laden was spotted twice, with no option to send cruise missiles on these occasions resulting in the loss of the opportunity, the CIA became interested in weaponising its drone. CIA Director George Tenet told the 9/11 commission that by arming the Predator with Hellfire missiles, 'we would have a capability to accurately and promptly respond to future sightings of high value targets'.[18] From the start the arming of Predator was to do with the hunting and executing of individuals in territories of nations with which the US was not at war, and in which the hunter had no jurisdiction. This has become a key part of Predator and its Reaper successor's activities with a CIA-run drone-strike programme.

In February 2001 the first live firing of a Hellfire from a Predator was achieved, even as debate went on regarding the legality of using such a weapon in these circumstances (there had been a question as to whether it thereby became a cruise missile, subject to Intermediate Nuclear Forces regulation). Then came 9/11, and according to Whittle 'three days later a Big Safari-led team was in Uzbekistan with the three armed Predators, and a few days after that a Big Safari-led crew began flying them over Afghanistan from a GCS [ground control station] in the CIA's parking lot. On Oct. 7 2001, they fired their first missile'.[19] In 2012 the number of annual drone strikes in the Pentagon-run campaign in Afghanistan had reached 506. The CIA's more covert missions in Pakistan, Yemen and Somalia added over 400 strikes over the whole period of the War on Terror thus far.[20] Predator had rapidly become a staple tool in the US armoury. Already, by 2005 Whittle saw the programme becoming 'normalised', and by 2010 the USAF was training more UAV pilots than those for conventional aircraft.

Scaling Beyond Predators

Along with the HALE Global Hawk, and the medium altitude long endurance (MALE) Reaper and Predator, US forces in Afghanistan have had success with a catapult-launched tactical UAV (TUAV) known as Shadow, described variously as the smallest of the large drones and largest of the small drones. It's used 'to gather intelligence about Taliban movements as well as provide an "eye in the sky" overwatch for US and Afghan National Army troops while they're out on patrol'.[21] Shadow was also used in Iraq. In a 2008 article for the US Army's website, Sergeant Jason Dangel of the Combat Aviation Brigade, 4th Infantry Division, writes that 'Since the initial development of the UAV approximately ten years ago, its use in the global war on terror has increased tenfold and provides vigilant reconnaissance for almost all combat operations in MND-B [multi-national division-Baghdad], thus helping to provide troops an added edge against the enemy'.[22] Interestingly, the kinds of operations that he addresses in most detail are concerned with the apprehension of individuals, rather than the support of anything like conventional combat. He quotes Major Jonathan Shaffner, a brigade aviation officer: 'For the most part, we have a UAV on station for the majority of missions that involve the capture of high-value targets or terrorists'.[23] An operation is described in which Shadow contributes to the capture of such individuals:

> Upon entering the residence of the suspect, Soldiers found that the criminal wasn't there. At the same time however, the Shadow was honed in on a suspicious vehicle nearby the scene. With the camera fixed on the vehicle, the TUAV operator reported to the ground commander of the situation at which time two male subjects fled from the vehicle and attempted to hide in a nearby canal. With precise accuracy, the Shadow operator reported the location of the two individuals to the ground Soldiers, who then apprehended the suspects – one of whom was the criminal they were looking for.[24]

This conflation of military power and criminal apprehension, and in other cases killing, is an example of how drones apply military technology to essentially policing-type situations in the ambiguous zones of the War on Terror. Derek Gregory applies this thinking to allied operations during Operation Iraqi Freedom, in a political landscape he terms the 'post colony'.[25] The drone, with its relatively low initial cost and its low operating costs, seems well-suited to such situations; Dangel emphasises how this efficiency allows the drone to do what would be difficult to achieve with a manned aircraft, that is, pay close attention to an individual. Improved situation awareness also reduces risk to ground troops, and all this is achieved without risking a pilot's life. He quotes UAV Platoon Sergeant David Norsworthy: 'Keeping Soldiers safe on the battlefield is number one. This is definitely a technology that will always be part of the fight'.

The larger aircraft tend to be operated by the USAF, but the Army has its own high-end armed drone, the Predator-derived Gray Eagle, which has recently come into service in both Afghanistan and Iraq. The story of this programme suggests the development acquisition problems around UAVs in the US forces have not entirely been solved, with *Defense Industry Daily* reporting that the USAF tried to kill the project.[26] John Young, a former chief of defence acquisition at the US Department of Defense, was reported as saying on his departure that 'Lack of inter-service coordination in unmanned aircraft programs is wasting millions of dollars and slowing down much-needed modernization'. He pointed at the Gray Eagle programme as an example, noting how the army's automatic landing system had resulted in far fewer crashes than the closely related USAF Predators and Reapers, but nothing had been done to share this facility. He revealed that one-third (65) of the Air Force's Predators (costing $4m each) had been lost in crashes, most commonly on landing.[27]

Predator's larger, more powerful successor in US service, the Reaper, is also used in Afghanistan by the British Royal Air Force (RAF), which currently operates five Reaper UCAVs there, and which by November 2012 had deployed 297 Hellfire missiles and 52 laser-guided bombs against Afghan targets. The UK Ministry of Defence stresses that British drones have not been used anywhere other than Afghanistan. The UK has also been operating a MALE surveillance unit, the Hermes 450, acquired from Israel's Elbit, via a 'service provision' contract with European defence contractor Thales. In 2011, with Hermes having flown over 4,000 missions, Colonel Mark Thornhill, commander of the British Army's 1st Artillery Brigade, the operator of the Hermes in Afghanistan, said:

> We have now achieved 50,000 [now 75,000] operational hours of Hermes 450, helping to meet the significant number of intelligence requirements that TFH [Task Force Helmand] generates each day. The capability has been absolutely key to many of the TFH operations.[28]

The Hermes 450 was acquired as part of an urgent operational requirement for use in Afghanistan. A more sophisticated development of the aircraft by a Thales-led team, known as Watchkeeper, with automated take-off and landing and a wide range of sensors, has been ordered for the army, but it is running three years late, is yet to see service, and may yet miss the Afghan mission.

Like the Americans, the British have had their problems with this technology. The *Guardian*, following a freedom of information request, reported that nine of the large, sophisticated and expensive (£1m) Hermes 450-type aircraft had been lost in Afghanistan, halving the fleet.[29] (However, respected aviation journalist Craig Hoyle reported that this figure had been given in error, and that the real figure was just one loss, with the others damaged but repairable from hard landings and so on.[30]) The RAF has also crashed one of its $16m Reapers, although perhaps its perceived usefulness is indicated by the fact that they are currently doubling their fleet to ten, and patriating the control system from Nevada to the UK.

Although only the US and the UK have used combat drones in Afghanistan, all the major powers involved there have been using UAVs, ranging from mini to medium drones for reconnaissance/surveillance. The Germans use aircraft like the IAI Heron, which 'enables the Bundeswehr and its NATO partners to monitor the entire northern half of Afghanistan, whose surface area of more than 300,000m² almost equals the size of the Federal Republic of Germany'.[31] The Canadians operated Sperwer, a mid-size tactical UAV. The French use the Harfang MALE UAV, derived from the Israeli Heron, for day and night missions including 'monitoring of villages, convoy escort, searching for Improvised Explosive Devices, preparing helicopter landing zones, and tactical intelligence for troops involved in combat operations'.[32]

There are also multiple projects bringing the versatility of rotorcraft into the UAV business, from the Northrop Grumman Firescout, in service with the US Navy as a ship-borne reconnaissance/strike aircraft, to the Kaman K-Max, undergoing trials in Afghanistan as a supply aircraft.

The hybrid air vehicle (HAV) – an airship-like craft that combines a lifting body with helium gas to give very economical, versatile flight – represents another technology that has been slated for use as an unmanned vehicle. The US Long Endurance Multi-Intelligence Vehicle, based on this technology, promised high levels of endurance and potentially significant cargo capacity, but after failing to meet planned performance parameters it was cancelled in October 2013 and the US$297m aircraft was sold back to its British manufacturer for US$301,000.[33]

Israel, Hamas and UAV Strikes

Having developed UAV operations in the hot wars of the 1970s, Israel has also used UAVs extensively in its smaller-scale and ongoing conflicts with, or on the territory of, its neighbours. Lieutenant Colonel Ido, Commander of the IAF's UAV training centre, indicated the UAV's centrality to current thinking in an official IDF blog:

A large percentage of the IDF's operational flight hours are performed by UAVs, sometimes even most of them. At any given time, 24 hours a day, seven days a week, there are drones in the air performing activities that IDF forces are engaged in.[34]

In the controversial Operation Cast Lead in 2008, ground operations with the stated aim of suppressing Hamas rocket fire into Israel were accompanied by waves of airstrikes including those by drones. Michelle K. Esposito of the Institute for Palestine Studies describes three types of UAVs used for intelligence, surveillance, target acquisition and reconnaissance (ISTAR) in the operation in Gaza – the Hermes 450, the Heron and the Searcher 2, all capable of persisting in the battlespace for 20–40 hours at between 9,500 and 35,000 feet.[35] They carry systems for intercepting communications and other electronic data, as well as day and night imaging. The IDF also use drones for strike missions in Gaza: like the US and the UK they operate the Reaper UCAV, armed with Hellfire missiles, but Esposito also indicates that they used an armed version of the Elbit Hermes 450 firing Hellfires and 'domestically made' missiles. She notes that Israel is 'believed' to have used an assault version of the larger IAI Heron TP, armed with Spike missiles (typically used in the infantry anti-tank role), and reports that, according to agencies such as Human Rights Watch, missiles fired from drones seem to have been responsible for a high number of Palestinian civilian deaths during Operation Cast Lead.

Other Israeli operations since then have used UAVs both in surveillance and attack modes. It should perhaps be noted that the narrow focus of the precision attack by drone following potentially long periods of careful surveillance does not provide any guarantee of safety to non-combatants, whether in Gaza or in Pakistan. Human Rights Watch has detailed many such instances of civilian deaths. For example, its report on the 2012 Israeli Operation Pillar of Fire says, 'Human Rights Watch field investigations found 14 strikes by aerial drones or other aircraft for which there was no indication of a legitimate military target at the site at the time of the attack'. The report says that seven of these attacks in Gaza were UAV strikes, and that 'Israeli drone strikes on November 19 killed three men in a truck carrying tomatoes in Deir al-Balah, and a science teacher who was sitting in his front yard with his 3-year-old son on his lap, talking to an acquaintance – only the toddler survived, but was seriously wounded'.[36]

Small Drones on the Battlefield

By far the largest numbers of unmanned aircraft in action fall into a class which gets little discussion – the mini, micro and even nano drones that fly at the opposite end of the scale to the Global Hawks, Predators and Reapers that get all the press. These small, lightweight devices are designed to be man-portable, and provide even small units of troops with their own dedicated aerial reconnaissance.

US troops rely on Aeroenvironment's Raven RQ-11 in the mini UAV class, *Defense Industry Daily* reports that 'U.S. armed forces use Ravens extensively for missions such as base security, route reconnaissance, mission planning and force protection'. In a useful summary, it lists the Raven's attributes as follows:

- Useful at the battalion level, but so simple to operate that one of the best pilots in the Iraqi theatre was a cook.
- Ideal for quick peeks to see what's on the other side of obstructed terrain – like a city block in Iraq, or Afghanistan's hills and mountains.
- Switch-in IR cameras that some called better than an AH-64 Apache attack helicopter's [...]
- Small and unobtrusive (wingspan just over 4 feet, weight just over 4 pounds), with low noise signature relative to larger UAVs.
- So small, in fact, that it can easily be carried by Special Forces scouts and squads.
- No letters to write if the aircraft goes down.[37]

Specialist Joshua Phan, a US Army Raven operator, described how his unit used the system:

As we have our SFAATs [security force assistance and advisory teams] with Afghans leading the way, we can scout a little bit ahead of them so they are not in danger. We can use it in conjunction and to benefit them. If you throw up a Raven and you see enemy activity in an area where you weren't expecting it, you can save your whole team or platoon.

Sergeant Skyler Rose, a forward observer Raven operator, added, 'As far as the Regiment goes, by taking the still imagery, I would be providing them with the most up-to-date and accurate imagery they can get at that time.

Satellite imagery, they get it month-to-month or week-to-week, but I can give it to them right then'.[38]

The British have mainly used a different mini-drone, Lockheed Martin's Desert Hawk, a similar type of small man-portable device, used for tasks of patrol overview, round the corner, over the hill reconnaissance. It's a tool that, like the Raven, delivers aerial intelligence as needed to small units of soldiers. The British Army has more recently taken delivery of what they are terming a 'nano-drone' – a helicopter-type device known as the Black Hornet, acquired from a Norwegian company. This tiny aircraft, two of which, along with their controller, fit into a book–sized case, extends the soldier's ability to look around corners, over walls, deep into the complex terrain of the 'urban canyon'. Alleyways and even buildings become accessible to this small and unobtrusive presence, with its steerable electro/optical camera delivering live video. With a 20-minute endurance and a range of up to 1,000 metres the Black Hornet, like its mini-brethren, can be set to fly an autonomous route, or be controlled remotely via the video imagery. British Army Sergeant Carl Boyd told the BBC it was used in Afghanistan for looking into the kind of walled compounds common there. He described it as 'a good bit of kit' and a 'lifesaver'.[39] He also added that it was very susceptible to wind, as might be expected with such a tiny device, but that its automatic return to base function helped to alleviate that problem.

This class of aircraft is prone to accidents it seems. US forces have taken to marking their Ravens with a request to return them to the US forces if found. In total in Afghanistan the British have lost nearly 450 UAVs, 412 of which are Desert Hawks. An MOD spokesperson told the *Guardian* that:

> Lightweight mini or nano UAVs like Desert Hawk 3 and Black Hornet can be more susceptible to harsh operational conditions and if they fail to land outside the confines of a safe area are sometimes not recovered in order to prevent any risk to life in retrieving it. This can result in a higher loss rate than larger tactical or strategic UAVs such as Hermes 450.[40]

Nevertheless, at perhaps $50,000–$100,000 per aircraft, this is not a trivial loss.

The glory days of the mini-drone, that have seen thousands come into service, may already be over. Yasmin Tadjdeh quoted aerospace analyst Phil Finnegan: 'For mini-UAS … it is going to be a difficult military market', he said. 'The U.S. market is going to be depressed because you've got a lot already in inventory and the services have budget crunches'.[41] However, it seems likely that even if numbers drop, this tool is here to stay; its obvious usefulness in improving situational· awareness, with consequent likely reduction of casualties, of certain kinds at least, will see to that. What is much harder to get at with regard to these smaller aircraft is the wider effect on the battlefield, the nature of war and social attitudes to military action. One likely effect, however, is a further emphasis on force protection and reduced tolerance of casualties. The more solders can know about their environment, the more, perhaps, they should know. This may result in a reduced appetite for risk.

These small aircraft are relatively cheap and straightforward to acquire, and many hundreds of different types of varying sophistication are available, including those from your corner electronics store. All military forces, regular and irregular, are going to have access to some kind of device of this type, so it would seem inevitable that an increased emphasis on UAV countermeasures is going to be part of future military operations. The half-ounce Black Hornet is unlikely to represent the culmination of efforts to shrink the UAV. Experiments with insect-sized machines are under way. In a 2008 article, consultant Richard B. Gasparre suggested a new range of 'tiers' to describe the small drones, based on soldiers' ability to recognise the artefact for what it is:

Tier-1: recognisable when in flight
Tier-2: indistinguishable in flight, but recognisable at rest in a relatively small space, such as a living room.
Tier-3: indistinguishable at rest, but recognisable at arm's length, or by touch and inspection.

Science fiction perhaps, currently, but his final category, Tier-4, is described as 'recognisable only through inspection by CSI teams or their equivalents'.[42]

The Next Generation: Stealth and Autonomy

Getting smaller is one way to make drones less obvious. But some of the tasks carried out by the larger UAVs are not amenable to being miniaturised. Nevertheless, current tactical and strategic UAVs are quite vulnerable to attack. A report by the USAF Scientific Advisory Board observes that 'A modern IADS [integrated air defence system] would quickly decimate the current Predator/Reaper fleet and be a serious threat against the high-flying Global Hawk'.[43] But another route towards mitigating the threat posed to the larger tactical and strategic UAV by more sophisticated air defence systems than they have faced in Iraq and Afghanistan is to make the drone faster and/or harder for those defences to detect.

General Atomics have a development of the Predator/Reaper series already in flight testing. The turbo-fan powered Predator C Avenger is described by the company as follows: 'Its unique design, reduced signature, and speed increases its survivability in higher threat environments and provides potential customers with an expanded quick-response armed reconnaissance capability'.[44]

Stealth technology includes a range of measures designed to make an object harder to detect. Radar is the primary tool for detecting aircraft and directing defences to respond to them, and so a lot of effort in making an aircraft stealthy goes towards reducing its radar reflection. Small size is one aspect of this, but the aircraft's apparent size can be reduced by careful angling and curving of surfaces to help the structure diffuse radar waves rather than reflect them back to the source. This is further reduced by the use of radar-absorbing coatings, the latest of which actively interfere with the radar signal. Colour is also important in making the aircraft harder to see.

Such stealth technology has been successful in manned aircraft. The technology is not infallible however, as the incident with the F-117 in Kosovo demonstrated. But techniques have improved – the hefty F-22 Raptor fighter aircraft is supposed to have the radar cross section of a bumble bee, and it is claimed that the B2 stealth bomber has never been detected by enemy radar. It was an obvious next step to apply stealthy design to unmanned aircraft. The US already has one such aircraft in service, the Lockheed Martin RQ-170 Sentinel. This reconnaissance aircraft gained notoriety in 2011 when Iran showed an almost undamaged example that they claimed to have hijacked by overriding its controls remotely as it overflew their airspace. The US acknowledged an aircraft had been lost, and asked for it back – a request the Iranians declined. This story points again to the kind of activities UAVs allow, in terms of (relatively) low diplomatic risk interventions in sovereign air space. It also, although there is no confirmation that this is what happened, points to the potential vulnerability of the UAV – the electronic 'kite string' that invites cutting. The Iranian incident with the RQ-170 may point to the continued vulnerability of the UAV's control system. Certainly, according to the *Washington Post*, Al Qaeda are seeking to exploit this chink in the UAV's armour.[45] This insight comes from a document acquired from Edward Snowden, the former National Security Agency (NSA) contractor now in political asylum in Russia. Entitled 'Threats to Unmanned Aerial Vehicles', this report represents a summary of a range of US intelligence assessments. According to *Post* journalists Craig Whitlock and Barton Gellman, who have seen this report (and chosen to keep some details of particular drone vulnerabilities to themselves), 'Al-Qaeda's leadership has assigned cells of engineers to find ways to shoot down, jam or remotely hijack U.S. drones, hoping to exploit the technological vulnerabilities of a weapons system that has inflicted huge losses upon the terrorist network'.[46]

The US also has a combat aircraft of this stealth-configured flying wing type under development for the Navy in the form of the Northrop Grumman X-47B. In another key trend for the UAV, this aircraft is also being used to develop much higher levels of autonomy than the current generation of aircraft, that is, the ability to respond to its environment without the intervention of a human pilot, however remote. In July 2013 the X-47B demonstrated its ability to take-off and land autonomously on the deck of an aircraft carrier, an ability that would free US drone operations from the need for local basing. The Department of Defense's *Unmanned Systems Integrated Roadmap FY2011–2036* suggests that this shift to autonomous systems represents not just a development of the existing information technology-driven RMA, but could perhaps form the basis of the next RMA:

> Dramatic progress in supporting technologies suggests that unprecedented levels of autonomy can be introduced into current and future unmanned systems. This advancement could presage dramatic changes in military capability and force composition comparable to the introduction of 'net-centricity.'[47]

The roadmap reports that the USAF considers this trend towards increased autonomy the 'single greatest theme' in its technological development.

The US has its competitors in this advanced arena of UAV technology. The Dassault-led nEUROn programme and BAE Systems' Taranis are both stealthy UAV demonstrators, aimed at fulfilling a joint UK/French demand for a combat capable stealthy UAV. Both Taranis and nEUROn are also aiming for high levels of autonomy. BAE is similarly experimenting with autonomous systems in areas such as sense-and-avoid, weather-avoid and emergency landing functions, drawing on its already flying (albeit non-stealthy) Mantis demonstrator.[48] The UK/French agreement also covers an aircraft in the MALE class, under the name Telemos, that will likely draw heavily on the Mantis programme.

Outside NATO both China and Russia are also experimenting with stealth drones. In April 2013, China revealed a stealth-configured UCAV in a tail-less flying wing form, similar to the X-47/Taranis/nEUROn type of aircraft. Commenting on the aircraft, named LiJian (Sharp Sword), Douglas Barrie of the International Institute for Strategic Studies commented, 'If any more evidence were needed of the strides China continues to take in defence-aerospace, then the taxi-tests of what appeared a tail-less "stealthy" unmanned combat air vehicle (UCAV) design last month certainly provided it'.[49]

The Russian MiG company signed a contract in May 2013 with the Russian government to develop an UCAV based on its stealthy flying wing 'Skat' prototype, as reported by RIA Novosti, who described the aircraft as also able to operate in 'autonomous modes' and which is 'designed to carry out strike missions on stationary targets, especially air defense systems in high-threat areas, as well as mobile land and sea targets'.[50] The US technological lead in this field is clearly not a long one.

The War on Terror and the large-scale conflicts it generated in Afghanistan and Iraq, as well as Israel's persistent conflicts both within and outside its borders, provided an ideal environment for UAV operations, in that Israel and the US (with its broader coalition allied forces) exercised total air dominance. The weakness of Predator and its turbo-prop brethren, designed for long efficient loitering over a surveillance target, lies in their vulnerability to enemy air defences, whether in the form of ground-based missiles or combat aircraft. In these highly asymmetric conflicts that threat did not obtain, whereas the needle in a haystack scenario that counter-terrorist operations entail requires good intelligence in order to succeed. With very limited human intelligence sources from among these hostile and highly 'othered' populations, aerial surveillance became a vital resource in prosecuting the conflict in any fashion. The security arena that the War on Terror provided seemed to come together with developments in technology in terms of command and control to favour the use of the UAV. The availability of the UAV has in its turn had effects on how that war has been carried out, extending the user's military reach into ambiguous airspace in pursuit of individuals in an almost uneventful way, and in situations where manned aircraft or special forces would only be used in exceptional circumstances.

3

The UAV and Military Doctrine

As a counterinsurgency weapon, therefore, hunter-killer drones appear to be losers. They are creating more militants than they kill, and their escalating use is alienating or 'losing the hearts and minds' of the civilian populations in Afghanistan and Pakistan.

Jeffrey Sluka, political anthropologist[1]

One way to address the fundamental question of what drones do – what changes they bring to the battlespace and to the way militaries and governments act; to the way, potentially, that we all *think* about conflict, territory and related concepts – is to consider what the users of this new equipment are saying about this issue. The fact that defence ministries around the world are finding it necessary to issue reports examining and describing their use of drones is indicative of the novelty of this technology, of the fact that it is in some sense making a difference that has to be discussed. Part of this may be genuine inquiry into the phenomenon by those concerned; part of it may be as a more or less reluctant response to the wider public perception that drones do indeed form a new and perhaps worrying addition to the tools of war, a perception that needs to be managed. That a change is on the way is indicated by Colonel John D. Jogerst who writes, 'At some point, we must reduce our reliance on horse cavalry (the A10/F35?) and embrace the mechanized brainpower of a UAS force'.[2]

The UK Ministry of Defence issued a report in the form of a 'Joint Doctrine Note' (JDN) in March 2011 entitled *The UK Approach to Unmanned Air Systems*. The opening statement on the context for such a report has the following to say:

Unmanned aircraft now hold a central role in modern warfare and there is a real possibility that, after many false starts and broken promises, a technological tipping point is approaching that may well deliver a genuine revolution in military affairs.[3]

So the UK armed forces, as one of the more experienced users of a range of unmanned systems, in the context of actual combat at least, see the possibility of such systems becoming some kind of a game changer at the military level.

That military experience has caused some conceptual problems for the UK. Until the much-delayed Watchkeeper appears in service some time in the future, the procurement of all the current systems has come about as a response to urgent operational requirements arising from military needs in the Iraq and Afghanistan conflicts, rather than as a carefully reasoned doctrinal response to a new technology and what it means for UK capabilities. Nevertheless, the document describes the widely held perception in defence, academic and industrial circles that UAVs 'will become more prevalent, eventually taking over most *or all* of the tasks currently undertaken by manned systems' (emphasis added).[4] The report acknowledges that there is a conceptual gap regarding drones, even in their current state, let alone what might be coming down the road, but references the UK government's 2010 Strategic Defence and Security Review which stressed that even in an environment of reduced spending investment, unmanned systems will see an increase in spending.

A number of questions are raised in the JDN that point to the thinking of the UK military establishment, and their concerns over the changes introduced by this new technology. The authors identify a number of emerging issues they consider key:

As unmanned aircraft become more capable and automated, complex issues emerge. What governance and supervisory systems will be required to authorise and control weapon release or, in peacetime, to ensure privacy? How will such systems be integrated with manned air operations and civilian air traffic structures? How will the data generated by different sensors, and analysed by specialists in different locations around the world, be fused into a final product. Is a common ground control station, interoperable with any national or allied unmanned aircraft, feasible?[5]

While these questions are indeed important, and usefully dealt with in the JDN, we focus here on what it says drones *do*, or can do – what they bring to the table in terms of new capacity.

The reasons given for this wholehearted embrace of the UAV are revealing of where the advantages lies, in British thinking at least: 'The over-riding motivation for moving to unmanned systems is a desire to deliver new or enhanced capability by embracing new technology while reducing costs and the threat to personnel'. The clear hope too is that this shift offers the chance to 'reduce force structure size due to decreasing buy-to-deploy ratios'.[6] One factor is that training for this virtual flying activity can be wholly virtual, requiring no airframes dedicated to this purpose. But this comes with the caveat that as a new technology the UK's experience remains statistically limited, and it is hard to infer reliable conclusions from what they acknowledge as limited data. So they believe that UAVs are cheap, and protect your own people – although we don't really know much about just how cheap they are.

Another positive factor for the JDN is what the document calls a 'reduced manpower footprint in theatre'.[7] This gets to what may be the heart of the UAV advantage – and an obvious one at that. Fewer or no personnel are needed on the ground in the territory involved. This offers the possibility of action where politics or security issues would otherwise prevent it.

Dull, Dirty, Dangerous and Deep

In terms of the planned role of UAVs, as opposed to these unlooked for spinoffs in changed behaviour, UAVs particularly suit tasks that the JDN characterises as 'dull', 'dirty', 'dangerous' and/or 'deep'.

'Dull' tasks include low intensity, time-consuming activities such as persistent surveillance. In an inquiry into the difference that UAVs make, it is worth going into this list of tasks in some detail –the report's full complement of 'dull' tasks is as follows:

- Pattern of life surveillance tasks over fixed locations or in support of littoral maneuver.
- Maintenance of standing anti-submarine warfare or anti-surface warfare radar barriers, including counter-piracy tasks.
- Monitoring of arrays of sonobuoys or other sensors.
- A range of electronic warfare tasks, acting as a communications relay.
- Air-to-air refueling.[8]

It should be pointed out that not all of these tasks are currently undertaken by unmanned aircraft – rather, the potential is there. The new phenomenon here is 'pattern of life surveillance'. The relative lack of expense, of some types anyway, and high capacity for persistence of the UAV, allows this kind of activity. It is very much a product of the particular concerns of the War on Terror, where the cheap delivery of high-resolution output enables the routine targeting of individuals, an activity that blurs the division between policing/security and military roles.

'Dirty' tasks are those needing to be undertaken in environments hostile to human health, which would include chemical, biological, radiological and nuclear (CBRN) type missions (or smoky buildings at the other end of the spectrum). UAVs can be thoroughly decontaminated, or even abandoned if it is too dangerous to do so. Thus both size and disposability, itself an aspect of price, feature in the UAV's distinctiveness in managing the dirty mission.

The third category, 'dangerous', describes what would seem to be one of the most obvious military advantages of the UAV: carrying out missions where the relationship between importance and risk to personnel doesn't justify putting human operators in danger. The document identifies two philosophies with regard to the use of UAVs for dangerous missions: either they must be 'cheap, simple and expendable' or they will be 'complex, and therefore probably expensive, but with high survivability'. The latter implies stealth characteristics and some capacity for self-defence. Such aircraft are already flying: the Lockheed Martin RQ-170 Sentinel and the European (Dassault-led) nEUROn demonstrator for example.

Often the UAV's dangerous mission would be defined by the need to deal with a sophisticated ground-to-air defence system. The JDN identifies tactics that the UAV offers in the suppression of such a system:

- Multiple, cheap unmanned aircraft can be used sacrificially to swamp enemy detection and command and control system or to force an enemy to expend large numbers of missiles.
- Penetrate enemy missile engagement zones to gather electronic guidance and fusing data, observe enemy engagement tactics and transmit data back to intelligence collators before they are destroyed.[9]

This use of numbers of relatively cheap, simple, small UAVs in 'swarms' is one of the innovative capacities the UAV promises. Quoting Stalin, the authors note that 'quantity has a quality all of its own'. Rather than using sophisticated, versatile large aircraft that are mostly underusing their abilities on any given mission, cheap, focused, single-role UAVs may be an efficient way to increase capacity in 'novel ways'. They do caution that such swarming ability is still being worked out. However, as we have seen with Israeli tactics, the UAV has already been used to force defenders to reveal their defences, and even to waste missiles on attacking drones.

Other possible future tasks noted for the UAV in high-threat environments include the following:

- Tactical resupply to troops in contact.
- Combat recovery of personnel or casualties.
- Convoying tactical supplies.
- Sweeping for improvised explosive devices (IEDs).[10]

The US Marine Corps is experimenting with an unmanned helicopter in this tactical supply mode in Afghanistan. The K-MAX is an unmanned version of an existing Kaman helicopter, adapted to fly a preprogrammed flight plan using GPS, needing human intervention only to get it started. The aircraft is used to deliver supplies to forward bases, and by May 2013 had flown over 1,000 missions. Lockheed Vice President Dan Schultz told Reuters that K-MAX was 'saving lives by reducing Marines' exposure to improvised explosive devices on cargo convoys'.[11] Obviously a manned version could do much the same thing, but this would require a pilot to be paid, to be kept safe, whose weight would detract somewhat from the cargo capacity, and which, apparently, would require an additional two hours of maintenance per flight.

'Deep' missions are those carried out a long way inside enemy territory. The JDN suggests that 'when operating in uncontested airspace, deep targets could be ideally suited to observation or attack by unmanned aircraft'. The advantages lie in removing the risk to aircrew and preventing their exploitation if they are captured. UAVs, it points out, simply leave wreckage – which can be denied. For some 'static, well-understood' deep targets, existing technology (like cruise missiles) works perfectly effectively; and manned aircraft remain useful in the case of more mobile, time-sensitive targets requiring a high degree of discretion, with stealthy aircraft like the F-35 particularly suited. But looking ahead to higher levels of autonomy, the JDN suggests that by 2030 'unmanned aircraft will eventually have the ability to independently locate and attack mobile targets, with appropriate proportionality and discrimination'.[12]

Cost

Lower cost is one factor driving the British towards UAVs, even though to some extent the implications of UAV acquisition for force structure remain obscure. The evidence shows that UAVs are much more expensive to develop and deploy than anyone expected. The report is clear that the cost advantages of current unmanned systems can easily be eroded by platform-centric rather than capability-centric thinking, leading to the typically spiralling costs of defence acquisitions, with some UAVs already rivalling manned systems in price. The British document points somewhat presciently to the expense of the Global Hawk as an example of this – less than a year after this document was published the USAF cancelled the Block 30 version of the aircraft, only months after it was first declared operational. US Air Force Chief of Staff General Norton Schwartz, speaking at a Department of Defense press briefing on 27 January 2012, commented on this decision:

> The reality is that the Global Hawk system has proven not to be less expensive to operate than the U-2. And in many respects, the Global Hawk Block 30 system is not as capable from a sensor point of view, as is the U-2.[13]

Even so, the perception remains that UAVs offer the opportunity to lower costs overall; as Research and Markets' United States Defence and Security Report Q4 2011 notes, a 'likely scenario as a result of the multi-year spending cuts is a shift in procurement towards unmanned systems'.[14]

The writers of the British JDN also note that along with the escalation of platform prices, there are other less obvious costs associated with UAVs. For example, the lack of a pilot does not necessarily imply lower numbers of personnel, as they acknowledge the possibility that UAVs can end up demanding higher commitments of manpower than manned systems, especially if the capacity of the aircraft to endure for long periods in the air is fully exploited: a 24-hour flight cannot be managed by a single crew. The doubling of the Reaper fleet to ten aircraft that is under way will require 40 crews. A team of 90 currently runs the RAF's operations at Creech Air

Force Base in Nevada. The team in Afghanistan that handles the physical aircraft is in addition to this. Nevertheless, the MOD's bottom-line perception is still that UAVs *can* offer good value, since, as this document puts it, 'relatively cheap and simple unmanned aircraft are already capable of providing situational awareness at a tactical level that simply could not be afforded by manned means'.[15]

One technological trend that has implications for cost reduction in terms of manpower is increased autonomy. In 2009 the USAF released what it called a 'flight plan' for its UASs, and one of its foci is autonomy, which will lead to what the USAF terms 'multi-aircraft control'. In order to maintain 50 combat air patrols with the MQ-9 Reaper, it currently requires 500 pilots plus 70 for transiting the aircraft. This will reduce in the near term with multi-aircraft control going down to 250, and halve again to 125 at some future date. With these systems, one pilot will be able to supervise several aircraft in their missions – and they won't require pilots for transit.[16]

Change in this technology is rapid, and managing it has cost implications. The JDN points out that the RAF only operated Predator for five years before moving on to the MQ-9 Reaper, and that a significant economic effect arises from this change in procurement practice. Aircraft are being bought in much smaller 'blocks' than is typical for manned aircraft – sufficient, in the US case, only to equip troops as needed for training and deployment. The next generation of aircraft will then be ready by the next deployment, so the cost of obsolescence is controlled and new technology is rapidly brought to the front line.

Size and Difference

An interesting aspect of the JDN's analysis, and one particularly relevant to this discussion, lies in its approach to UAV size and its relationship to the change that the device introduces. There is a tendency to focus on the innovations in terms of capacity and policy brought by the largest, most complex aircraft, notably the Predator/Reaper, particularly with regard to US operations in countries that they are not at war with – such as in Pakistan or Yemen. However, the JDN suggests that this may be the least interesting end of the UAV spectrum. It points out that class II and III drones such as Watchkeeper/Predator 'share the attributes and capabilities of manned aircraft. These are usually so clearly similar to manned aircraft that it is obvious as to how they would be employed and on what tasks'.[17] The choice of whether to use a UAV or a manned system would largely be cost/politics driven. This perhaps explains the Global Hawk phenomenon. In the end it didn't do anything differently from the U-2, and was in fact more expensive than the U-2, so the U-2 becomes the obvious choice – the Gary Powers question apparently notwithstanding. Its technological distinctiveness is ultimately limited.

The potential for change, coupled with the undeveloped state of current doctrine, is seen in the explanation of the other two groups – minis and micros. For the minis (2–20 kg in weight), the view is that while they may have some of the same capabilities as manned aircraft they 'could also provide very different capabilities or be able to operate in a very different way',[18] while the most radical capacity is seen in the smallest sub-2 kg micro UAVs, where 'comparisons with manned aircraft break down'. The other compelling aspect of these smaller devices is the ease of entry into this market – they are relatively cheap to develop and produce, which means changes in attitude as costs approach 'use and throw away' levels. By extension, although not addressed by the JDN, there are proliferation issues around these smaller tools.

Testimony by Sharon Pickup and Michael Sullivan of the US Government Accountability Office (GAO) to a 2006 House subcommittee gives some insight into the usefulness of the smaller types:

> Small UAVs such as the Pointer and Raven have been instrumental in enabling troops to find, locate, and destroy numerous targets … Moreover, the use of small UAVs has enabled ground forces to accomplish their missions at greater distances from enemy positions, in effect expanding the standoff distance and thereby reducing the risk to U.S. service members on the ground.[19]

This kind of small UAV appears to extend the soldiers' situational awareness without them having to put themselves in harm's way to develop that awareness. The information from the UAV regarding enemy disposition both allows more efficient targeting, and protects the unit that has UAV support from the risk of becoming a target itself. In that sense the UAV provides an increase in efficiency, thereby operating as a force multiplier.

Raven and mini UAVs such as Desert Hawk are backpackable – they are the size of a model plane, with a wingspan of 55 inches and weighing around 4 lbs. They are very widely used, with several thousand in service with US forces. As such vehicles get smaller they become potentially even more interesting. At the next level of miniaturisation the JDN authors believe that

> biological mimicry will be a key factor for developing Nano Air Vehicles (NAV). These vehicles, which may weigh less than 25g, will be highly specialised and in addition to having miniaturised sensors for ISR tasks, may be weaponised to act as anti-personnel devices. Low cost for such devices will be critical as they are, effectively, disposable. Detecting and countering such systems will be difficult, particularly if they are deployed in large numbers.[20]

The UK military is already in the nano UAV game. A November 2011 Ministry of Defence call for research proposals specified the following: 'UK Armed Forces need the capability to carry out Intelligence, Surveillance and Reconnaissance (ISR) missions within highly complex environments such as inside buildings and deep within urban canyons'.[21] According to the manufacturer the Black Hornet pocketable nano-copter weighs 15 grams including camera. With its base station, the whole system is book-sized and weighs less than a kilogram and went quite rapidly into service. According to an MOD story in February 2013, Sergeant Christopher Petherbridge, of the UK Brigade Reconnaissance Force in Afghanistan, said:

> Black Hornet is definitely adding value, especially considering the light weight nature of it. We used it to look for insurgent firing points and check out exposed areas of the ground before crossing, which is a real asset. It is very easy to operate and offers amazing capability to the guys on the ground.[22]

There are 324 Black Hornets in service with the British Army.[23]

It may be that there is an inverse proportion between the size of the UAV and novelty of the capacity that it offers. Our eyes are taken by the familiar outline, scale and activities of the Predator-type aircraft, but the real action may be happening below the radar, literally and metaphorically. However, it should be pointed out that the JDN elsewhere discusses the special impact of the much larger Predator on military action (although it should be noted that the Predator attacks in Pakistan are carried out by the CIA rather than the military), observing that

The recent extensive use of unmanned aircraft over Pakistan and Yemen may already herald a new era. That these activities are exclusively carried out by unmanned aircraft, even though very capable manned aircraft are available, and that the use of ground troops in harm's way has been avoided, suggests that the use of force is totally a function of the existence of an unmanned capability – it is unlikely a similar scale of force would be used if this capability were not available.[24]

Thus even large UAVs do much more than simply emulate manned aircraft – they enable different behaviours, reducing risk to your own personnel, making war less terrible and therefore risking making war 'more likely' as the JDN authors put it. This is a key observation. Military thinkers themselves are seeing UAVs as effecting a McLuhanite change in human behaviour, and that change is lowering the threshold to the military-type application of violence.

Persistence

Also of note are the UAV's special performance characteristics and the related capacity for endurance. Taking the pilot out of the aircraft frees up designers in a number of ways – the weight of the pilot/crew, and the physical space they need, is removed, allowing more capacity for other purposes such as fuel, equipment and so on, although, as the JDN points out, at the upper end of the UAV classification this may be a modest proportionate gain as other elements (engine fuel, sensors, etc.) may dominate the payload. But taking the pilot out of the cockpit has benefits in terms of design for innovative or more aerodynamic forms. Ultimately, the g-force limitations imposed by the human on board may allow increased manoeuvrability. Pilot fatigue is also more controllable, allowing aircraft to operate with maximum efficiency throughout the mission.

The key factor here, however, is that all of this allows the UAV much greater *persistence* – what the JDN calls the drone's unique selling point. The RAF's Reapers already exceed 18 hours in the air, and the British company QinetiQ's Zephyr demonstrator can stay aloft for several weeks. Supporting this kind of capacity of course leads to the increased manpower costs per aircraft alluded to earlier. But as the JDN puts it, 'it is this ability of unmanned aircraft to persist over the battlespace that has proved to be so effective in Iraq and Afghanistan'.[25]

In time they believe that this will transform the delivery of air power effects, with commanders able to select services (strike, surveillance, etc.) from an in-place air 'cloud', a physical analogy to the current off-site, somewhere-out-there but always available, computer cloud. This idea itself seems to break down some of the binaries of military action. Air forces would potentially in some sense always be operational, available to planners and decision makers. Persistence becomes permanence. The date for this? Sometime after 2030.

Even now the degree of surveillance coverage in time and space that the UAV allows is having important effects, producing what a Ministry of Defence source in 2012 called improved 'past event analysis' that allows, for example, analysts to review the scene of an IED explosion before it happened, with any luck capturing images of the bombers planting their device. There is a cost to this vast outpouring of data, and that lies in the analysis of those terabytes of imagery. But automation of the process is increasing: the Ministry of Defence source reported that software specialising in 'change detection' has come on 'leaps and bounds'.[26]

Clearly this notion of persistence is central to the UAV concept, and features heavily too in US military analyses of UAV operations. The term is connected to the UAV phenomenon in more than one way. In 2010 The US Army produced a substantial document they call a 'Roadmap' for 'how the U.S. Army will develop, organize, and employ UAS from 2010 to 2035 across full spectrum operations'. Subtitled 'Eyes of the army', it opens with a quotation from Major General James O. Barclay, III, Commanding General of the United States Army Aviation Center of Excellence (USAACE) and Fort Rucker, AL:

> We can send a UAS to look down alleys, around buildings, in backyards, or on a roof to see what's up there, dramatically increasing Soldier protection and preserving the force – a vital force multiplier in this era of persistent conflict.[27]

The UAV's useful characteristic is its persistence as a surveillance tool, but this persistence is, a little oddly, useful because of the persistent nature of today's conflicts: in the time of endless conflict, the UAV's patience makes it particularly and peculiarly valuable. The data the unmanned air systems generate, however, produce the need for 'unmanned' analysis too. One level of automation seems to entail another.

Access

As well as its persistence over time, the larger aircraft's range, reduced costs (ideally) and relative political imperviousness make its availability across geographic space a key value. But the smaller aircraft, deployed at platoon level and below, offer something new to soldiers in the field – the ability to deploy 'literally a pair of flying binoculars'. The JDN says, 'The advantages to a platoon commander of having the ability to produce imagery from over a wall or just around the corner, on demand, should not be underestimated'.[28] It is also pointed out that this advantage comes with a price – the additional burden of carrying and operating the system. Clearly, however, the smaller and more sophisticated they become, the less onerous this burden.

These smaller aircraft also have the advantage of *access* to certain kinds of spaces. The JDN points out that this is particularly important in the urban canyon, the dangerous confined spaces of the city environment, where such devices can unobtrusively 'perch and stare', eventually, perhaps, for long periods of time, recharging from the sun. They could also gain access to buildings, and perhaps in the future deploy precision weapons. Very small 'nano' devices bring a new set of poorly understood capabilities associated with their small size – not least the great difficulty of detecting them, exacerbated by the current move to biological mimicry.

The inherent capacity for access and persistence that the drone offers is being enhanced, for the US at least, by an expansion of drone bases overseas. The relatively low infrastructure requirement of drone operations has enabled a vast proliferation of such bases. Reporter Nick Turse claims there are now 60 military and CIA drone bases worldwide, many in locations where the US military has not previously had bases, such as the Seychelles, although official confirmation is not forthcoming regarding this sensitive information. Turse suggests that this 'tell[s] us much about America's war-making future. From command and control and piloting to maintenance and arming, these facilities perform key functions that allow drone campaigns to continue expanding, as they have for more than a decade'.[29]

So drones, by virtue of some of their inherent characteristics in terms of size, avoidance of risk to pilots, and how they are perceived, allow access to spaces that manned aircraft cannot access. The extension of the drone's stare across time allowed by their persistence is thus added to by this extension of access in terms of space.

The Problem of Information Volume

One problem in discussing UAV activities and the difference that they make lies in separating the qualities that lie in their 'umannedness' from the qualities that inhere in the technology they deploy and which could be deployed via a manned device: the U-2 versus Global Hawk problem. Each might carry the same sensors and generate the same kind of information product that gets processed through the same system. Developments in those sensors and in that processing system may be where the difference lies as much as in the 'U' of the 'AV' – it just happens that UAVs are now usually the most efficient way to deliver a capability that would have been delivered even in the absence of the drone.

However, in that word 'efficiency' lies a real difference. The availability of drones at every level of military operations reflects an innovation: platoons, companies, battalions, brigades and even divisions did not have their own dedicated aerial reconnaissance. They are beginning to acquire such capacity as a matter of course. This capacity would not have been delivered or deliverable without the UAV, as scale and cost means that this capacity would have stayed well up the organisational tree and remained restricted in number. Thus *number* is one more change that the UAV brings.

Coupled with the digital information technology that allows such machines to collect a wide range of data goes the need to do something with all that information so that it doesn't go to waste. What this volume of information, coupled with the need and growing ability to integrate it, is doing to the military's perception of their area of operations may ultimately produce some kind of step change in what the military does and how it does it.

British efforts in this direction include the DataMan system deployed in Afghanistan, which fuses information from a wide range of sources (UAVs, manned surveillance assets such as Sentinel, human intelligence) in up to 350 'layers' from which the user can select the kinds of information they are interested in, in the form of a digital map interface called Geo Viewer.

Such efforts help users access useful data, but inevitably information gets buried in volume. Sifting such large amounts of data with human analysts would be prohibitively expensive, so the solution lies in processing these data automatically: the automation or 'unmannedness' needs to extend down the line from collection to analysis, and this is where efforts are now being made. The most advanced instance of this sort of approach lies in systems such as Gorgon Stare and the more advanced BAE Systems Argus (autonomous real-time ground ubiquitous surveillance) imaging system, which combines the input from large numbers of sensors enabling multiple individual targets to be tracked across city-scale areas. According to a BAE press release, 'The airborne processing system can simultaneously and continuously detect and track the presence and motion of thousands of small or large targets over an area covering tens of square miles'.[30] The system is housed in a 15-foot pod that can be carried by an A160 Hummingbird unmanned helicopter, a vehicle with the capacity to fly at 20,000–30,000 feet and loiter for up to 20 hours. The system's 368 five megapixel video chips allow both wide coverage and high resolution, which means multiple individuals can be tracked across a city. To reduce bandwidth consumption, the system only transmits data regarding places and objects of interest. This system allows users to select areas and times of interest from the simultaneous broad sweep of the system.

The stress on the ability to focus on individuals is perhaps characteristic of the time of the drones, but this capacity is not unique to UAVs – the pod could be flown on a manned aircraft. Nevertheless, the persistence and relative cheapness of providing this capacity through a UAV makes it much more readily available, and it is this availability, manifest in a variety of ways, that forms the UAV difference.

Numbers: The Problem of Availability

The fact that UAVs provide (in many cases) a relatively inexpensive military air asset, available in rapidly increasing numbers, is producing, or reproducing, an old air warfare problem: who controls the aircraft? Soldiers on the ground understandably like to have their own dedicated air support, whether it is for ISR or combat purposes. However, military experience from World War II onwards is that this is an inefficient way to marshal such resources, and that a centralised air command allows the provision of air support in the most effective way. Nevertheless the US Army, faced with the kinds of scenarios that combat units hate – in which, for example, air support that has been promised for a long-planned operation is suddenly retasked by that central authority to deal with an emergency elsewhere – has started to acquire its own sophisticated UAVs that it operates 'organically', raising issues of air space coordination among others. USAF officer, Major Travis Burdine, writes:

The army solution to this airspace-coordination issue calls for creating a restricted operating zone [ROZ] around the UAS [...] The disadvantage of this model is that it uses airspace inefficiently, preventing airspace controllers from maintaining situational awareness within the ROZ and making it difficult for other air assets to navigate through the joint airspace. According to joint doctrine, 'efforts should be made to integrate UAVs with manned flight operations to enable a more flexible and adaptable airspace structure.'[31]

This, as Burdine puts it, 'represents a step backwards towards independent and deconflicted operations, which lack the synergy that properly integrated airpower should bring to the joint fight'. Part of his solution is to stress that 'We must treat theater-capable army UAS the same as other similarly capable fixed-wing manned aircraft'.[32] Thus it seems part of the content of the UAV medium is a regression towards a less centralised air power environment, as a result of the proliferation of these systems within and among the US armed services. Burdine sees the solution in the elimination of the difference between UAVs and manned aircraft – they have to be treated the same. Interestingly, the reason Burdine gives for his concern is this: 'The day the enemy starts flying remotely operated flying IEDs will mark the first time in over 50 years that the army will need to worry about enemy threats from the air'.[33] In other words, the internal proliferation that is creating this more confused air environment is a problem because of the inevitable external proliferation, for the same reasons of cheapness and effectiveness that has seen them expand so rapidly within the US inventory, that is going to put UAVs in the hands of US enemies.

Drones and Counter-Insurgency Doctrine

David Kilcullen defines insurgency as 'a struggle to control a contested political space, between a state (or group of states or occupying powers), and one or more popularly based, non-state challengers'.[34] Clearly both the wars in Afghanistan and in Iraq, having started out as state-to-state conflicts, degenerated into insurgencies as multiple more or less popular groups arose in resistance against the new occupying power.

The use of drones in both these American-led small wars functions along the seam of two doctrines regarding these conflicts, or two modes in which they are fought: counter-terrorism (CT), and counter-insurgency (COIN). CT is focused on the on the western nations fighting the war, in the sense that its goal is targeting the performers and supporters of terrorist acts in and against the west; COIN is focused more on the nation and the population from among whom those 'terrorists' arise, with the intention of building up a strong western-friendly state in which the insurgents will not be welcome, and will therefore be unable to function there.

The trouble with these two modes is that they are to some extent antithetical. CT emphasises the pursuit of individual fighters, and in places like Iraq and Afghanistan that usually means employing military-scale force to kill them rather than to capture them, given the difficulties of police-type operations in these environments (especially with the problems that the US has had dealing with captives from these conflicts). Such operations, carried out away from any kind of conventional battlefield, outside of any conventionally declared war, often in the midst of residential areas, look like assassination. Such actions, however efficient compared to past lower-tech military actions, still risk errors in targeting, or killing bystanders as well as the target, which aggravates the resentments on which insurgency and the terrorist acts that accompany it feed. Hence COIN looks at the bigger picture, seeing the insurgency as fundamentally social and political, and seeks to address those socio-political problems while using military tools to the minimum extent necessary. The US Army/Marine Corps *Counterinsurgency Field Manual* observes that 'sometimes the more force is used, the less effective it is'.[35]

UAVs enter this picture in both modes in which they operate, ISR and strike, and potentially as a tool for both doctrinal approaches. David Kilcullen has described the new model of Iraq-style insurgency that differs from the classical Malayan Emergency model (that the British used against communist guerrillas in the 1950s) in a number of ways, and so requires an adjusted approach to COIN operations. One of these differences lies in the transnational nature of the insurgency today, Kilcullen pointing out that 'border security, money transfers, ungoverned areas, ethnic minorities, refugees and media in neighbouring states may all play key operational roles for the insurgent – hence the counter-insurgent must be able to influence them'.[36] Kilcullen also suggests that 'Legal and political considerations will probably prevent military activity outside a single-country "area of operations."' However, this does not seem to have been the case, in that military-type operations have commonly occurred outside of those single-country areas of operations, such as over the border from Afghanistan in Pakistan. One key reason for this mistaken prediction is the existence of the UAV. For the US, especially under the Obama administration, the UAV has become the favoured (although not exclusive[37]) tool for targeting individual fighters, whether in the heartland of the conflict or in the constellation of other countries where the targeted groups operate. As such, narrowly interpreted, it is a very useful CT tool, allowing access to the place where US enemies are to be found, wherever they are to be found.

But it may be that it is very counter-productive in COIN terms, in that this low-risk (to the user) application of military-scale force actually creates widespread public anger towards the US, undermining other efforts to engage with that same population to align them with US interests rather than (say) the Taliban's or Al Qaeda's interests. Jeffrey Sluka notes that UAV-caused civilian casualties (700 in 2009 alone) alienate the Afghan population and act as a recruiting tool for the militants.[38] Sluka also argues that the drone's existence in itself creates this approach: it is 'technology' substituting for strategy, as he puts it. Because drones *can* be used for targeting individuals in ambiguous territory under ambiguous legal justification, they *are* so used.

It should be noted, however, that the vast majority of UAVs are not combat aircraft – rather, they operate purely as ISR resources. Effective ISR is a prerequisite for accurate targeting for air forces, including UAVs. However precise the weapon, it is still necessary to know what to aim it at. The persistent and widespread presence of UAV surveillance is therefore useful in generating targets for the precision weapons. In the absence of reliable human intelligence sources, UAVs may be the most important tool the military or intelligence services have for information gathering among physically and culturally inaccessible populations in zones such as Pakistan's tribal lands along the North-West Frontier Province. The United States has used this kind of information to generate targets in two ways, both distinctively effects of the UAV's ability to deliver lots of relatively low-cost imagery in legally ambiguous situations. Firstly, there are 'personality strikes'; that is, the targeted killings of named individuals: essentially the assassination of particular people for particular activities that the intelligence agencies have attached to them. Secondly, and perhaps more interestingly and even more controversial, are 'signature strikes': people are targeted not because of any specific information about ⁻s individuals, but rather because the 'pattern of life' they exhibit them look like members of a notional class called 'terrorists'. That pattern of life would be unavailable without the persistent and relatively low-cost presence of the UAV.

Micah Zenko, a fellow at the Council on Foreign Relations, describes these activities outside of the US main zone of operations in terms of counter-insurgency. He told the *New York Times* 'We don't say that we're the counterinsurgency air force of Pakistan, Yemen and Somalia, but we are'.[39] He is pointing to the way US policy may be being driven by the requirements of insecure foreign governments rather than its own best interests, but the fact is these kinds of killings, with their understandable tendency to antagonise populations subject to them, work against the goals of COIN operations, which fundamentally seek to separate the insurgent from the population at large, or perhaps reduce the insurgent tendency in that population by addressing what Anderson calls the *pre-insurgent*.[40] The UAV's ISR availability would, however, also be useful for that COIN task, since having knowledge of the territory in which the counter-insurgents find themselves, and of the insurgents against whom they find themselves fighting, is fundamental to the success of the COIN mission. But, it seems, this is not what has been happening. A Department of Defense report on this problem comments:

> In real terms, ISR support of COIN is not as high a priority for the Combatant Commands, Military Departments, and Defense Agencies as CT and force protection, thus adversely impacting the effectiveness of COIN operations.[41]

UAV and other ISR operations are being driven by the CT mission, targeted killings and the like, and also by another key attribute of the UAV: the protection of US soldiers. The eye in the sky over a patrol is not there to manage the counter-insurgency, but to manage US or International Security Assistance Force (ISAF) casualties.

The UAV's special characteristics as a military tool include the capacity to deal with monotony, their relative disposability that allows them to operate in dangerous environments, and their relative deniability/lowered political value in the case of illicit operations. There are also a range of performance factors, such as potential for high-g-force manoeuvres, and long endurance. The use of smaller, cheaper UAVs, in much greater numbers than manned aircraft, seems to provide the best chance for innovative tactics and abilities, such as those arising from 'swarming' behaviours. And it is here that the biggest change to human capacity as a result of this new 'extension to man' may arise, as such devices arrive on the scene with us having very limited ideas of the effects or consequences of this innovation.

The current bottom-line difference that the UAV provides lies in its capacity for *persistence*. The JDN authors write that the UAV's 'most obvious contribution has been to revolutionise the delivery of the core air power role of intelligence and situational awareness'. This has largely been achieved through the ability of *numbers* of unmanned aircraft to persist for long periods in the battlespace, generating transformative detail in the military understanding of their area of operations. In the persistent war that extends across time and space, the UAV's persistent presence, the ubiquity that its endurance lends at one end of the spectrum, and which new levels of access and cheapness offer at the other end, means that a military air presence may be becoming available both everywhere and 'everywhen'. This ubiquity has consequences in terms of the volume of data, leading to a further automation of the analysis.

The weaponisation of this technology adds what may currently be a militarily marginal, but socially and politically significant, additional capacity, enabling behaviours that previously required higher stakes, thereby lowering the threshold to military action. The fact that on 24 January 2013 Ben Emmerson, a UN special rapporteur, announced a UN enquiry into the impact of drone strikes on civilians, from Pakistan to Yemen, is a significant indicator that this change has been noticed. According to the BBC, Emmerson told journalists 'that the increasing use of drones "represents a real challenge to the framework of international law."'[42] But the way these aircraft are being used also constitutes a challenge to, or perhaps an exposure of, the confusion in the very doctrine by which the War on Terror is being fought in its various modes and locations.

4

The Consequences of Killing Without Consequences

Holly Martins: Have you ever seen any of your victims?
Harry Lime: Victims? Don't be melodramatic. Look down there. Tell me. Would you really feel any pity if one of those dots stopped moving forever?

Graham Greene, *The Third Man*[1]

We are investigating whether UAVs introduce large-scale change into human interaction. The purpose of this chapter is to begin to uncover the nature of the relationship between individuals – operators and targets – who are joined in the 'deadly embrace' (the phrase is Gregory's) of UAV technology during surveillance and combat. Here we concentrate on the experience of the operators, considering how they fit into existing ideas about soldiers, warriors and combatants, and where their experiences deviate from prevailing cultural expectations. The operative variables are space (that is, the distances that lie between combatants) and time (that is, the patterns of shift work for drone operators who are replaced on their mediated battlefields according to the discipline of the clock, and return to recognisably normal lives at the end of their shifts).

In McLuhan's language of media, drones *extend* the reach of the soldier's senses – and lethality – through space. The most frequently cited distance between combatants is around 7,000–7,500 miles, the distance between the 732d Operations Group, home to the USAF's Predator operators at Creech Air Force Base in Nevada, and the apparently target-rich environment along the Pakistan–Afghanistan border. Drones also extend the soldier's reach through time: the 732d's MQ-1 Predator is a quiet and responsive weapons platform that can loiter over an area for up to 24 hours, sending intelligence back to its crew, who can respond to what they see on their video monitors by firing two laser-guided Hellfire missiles if required. The time lapse between choosing to fire and the missile reaching its target is about 30 seconds.

Whether it matters if the person who pulls the trigger is thousands of miles away or in an aircraft directly overhead is widely debated: is killing people using drones easier or harder, more intimate or more abstract, less or more ethical? These are difficult questions. After centuries of technological innovation, militaries have finally deployed weapons that routinely remove human risk entirely from one side of the equation while expanding it exponentially at the other. In doing so, the relationship that has bound combatants together throughout history is altered. Everyone who falls under the Predator's gaze is a potential target or victim who cannot answer this violence with a similar response. In addition, combatants we once understood in the conventional way as pilots and aircrew moving in space are now grounded, separated from their airframes as well as from their targets, and bodily detached from these extensions of their senses. For the time being, our evidence must derive from what little we know about how US, and to a lesser extent UK, military culture is struggling to negotiate the effects of removing individual soldiers from their airframes, and therefore from the dangers of the traditional battlefield.

On the technological horizon is the wholesale replacement of traditional soldiering with increasingly autonomous weapons systems. This move on the one hand valorises the life of the soldier by removing him to safety, but simultaneously undermines his value and identity as a soldier by making him interchangeable with, and replaceable by, other soldiers or even civilian contractors, and ultimately by more machines. Williams used the example of the need to change aircrews several times during a single UAV mission. The overall function of the system (the military assemblage of crew and machine) only requires certain human abilities – to see, to monitor, to decide and, only occasionally, to fly. She suggests this 'introduces the idea that the bodies of the aircrew are becoming less important. Instead, they perform more like machine components', and so 'The human elements of the UAV assemblage are thus considered increasingly unexceptional further reducing their importance within the assemblage in relations to that of its machine elements'.[2]

Mediated Warfare

[1]'₂ puts it, 'Communications technologies span distances so that do not have to' and many human interactions are increasingly

contingent on their use.³ Militaries that use drones to fight rely on technologies to carry out their will. Killings are carried out on computer screens: the only suggestion of the 7,000 miles that separates the soldier and the target is a 1.7 second delay between the operator's command and the aircraft's response. There is no conceivable threat to the operator's personal security as events are relayed, watched, recorded and stored. On the other side, destruction (at least in the early phase when drones were not widely used) literally comes out of the blue, as in this description from USAF Predator pilot Matt Martin, flying a combat mission somewhere over Afghanistan:

> The two [Taliban] leaders halted, plopped down on the ground, and leaned back on their packs. It was break time. The other two caught up and joined them in a little circle, all totally unaware of doom already released and screaming toward them out of the sky ... Once the smoke and fire dissipated, I saw four mangled and scorched bodies blown back onto the ground, the contents of their packs strewn all over the landscape.⁴

Geographer Derek Gregory notes that drones are the latest step in a long history of technological innovation that has led us to our current globalised condition. He pairs 'the death of distance' – the way technology has compressed time and space – with the more literal 'death from a distance' whereby the old trope of a soldier fires and an enemy falls remains true, but the experience is now divorced from the danger and discomfort of actual combat.⁵ In the case of drones there is an absolute geographic distance, a measurable space that remains a significant, perhaps insurmountable, obstacle between opposing forces. This geographic distance necessarily plays into political and military decision-making.

Wired western culture is increasingly familiar with what mediated war looks like to a US soldier (and also, thanks to a barrage of widely available jihadi videos, how it is represented by the opposing side). Less obvious are the cultural practices that inform and shape this new relationship with conflict. Watching smart bombs during the first Gulf war, Judith Butler noted that 'the aerial view never comes close to seeing the effects of its destruction' because the smart bomb's screen 'conveniently destroys itself'.⁶ Now multiple cameras continuously capture the instant of destruction as well as the halo of actions that precede and follow it. Smoke and debris, poor picture resolution, as well as the brief washing-out of the picture caused by the thrust of releasing a missile disrupt the view briefly, but these are problems that the technology can already largely overcome.[7]

What fighting war from within a mediated operational environment is like, and what the consequences are, is much debated. Like 'real' war, different people experience virtual war in different ways. Some, like the CIA's drone proponent Hank Crumpton, look through the carnage to find opportunities to introduce greater killing efficiency. Of the CIA's early experiments in drone warfare in Afghanistan, Crumpton writes that in analysing the aftermath of Hellfire missile attacks, 'we realized that some were surviving the hit. We could see them, wounded and stumbling away. This was unacceptable. We needed more fragmentation at the point of impact'. Within two weeks, modifications had increased both the fragmentation and the 'kill-zone' radius by 25 per cent: 'We analyzed several strikes ... Nobody walked away'.[8]

But for others, the experience of remote-control war is deeply intense and sometimes disturbing – evidence of stress and possibly post-traumatic stress disorder (PTSD) among USAF operators has emerged, along with speculation that the 'intimacy' of spending hours and days observing targets, as well as studying the aftermath, is taking a psychological toll. Traditional pilots conduct their missions and return to base, whereas drone operators, despite the vast distance that separates them from the actual battle, see it up close and personal on their video feeds. 'There's no detachment', a Creech commander said of his Predator crews:

> Those employing the system are very involved at a personal level in combat. You hear the AK-47 going off, the intensity of the voice on the radio calling for help. You're looking at him, 18 inches away from him, trying everything in your capability to get that person out of trouble.[9]

Even as the UAV introduces physical distance between operator and target, its cameras and sensors simultaneously bring the operator into proximity – and even prolonged intimacy – with the target. By giving operators a closer view of the effects of their actions than is available to aircrews in traditional platforms, Williams found that drone crews in effect become 'unrealistically close to the detonation of the weapons they have fired'.[10]

Gregory quotes Mary Favret, who noted that in mediated situations 'Distant violence becomes at once strange and familiar, intimate and remote, present and yet not really here'.[11] It is not peculiar to drones, but true of the increasingly global and yet nuanced awareness of the other's experience brought about by steady improvements in communications and media technologies. Our disquiet emerges from a deeper place than the semantics of whether a drone pilot differs from a bomber pilot. We tap into a history/mythology of what soldiers are and what they do. We therefore begin by examining how drones influence the location of the soldier, both in the battlespace and in our cultural ideas about war fighting.

Inside the Trailer

Alison Williams suggests that looking at the lived experiences of operators can help us better understand how human–UAV assemblages perform geopolitical control over space. The way missions are flown, by whom and how, vary by country and service and constantly change, but broadly speaking we can make some observations about the operational experiences of Predator pilots simply because that is where most research and scrutiny has focused. In the USAF, a typical Predator crew includes a pilot and one or two sensor operators. Because missions last an average of 18 hours and skilled crew are scarce, shifts are long, with crew changes mid-mission. The Predator's ground control station is located inside a trailer that can be loaded on to a C-130 Hercules for transport. The cockpit, which resembles an aircraft cabin, is comprised essentially of chairs surrounded by screens and control panels. One large screen carries a live feed of what the Predator sees. The resolution is sharp, but not that sharp – general outlines are clear enough to allow you to distinguish gender, but facial features are somewhat obscure. Additional screens carry information about the system (altitude, fuel levels, temperature) and layer upon layer of collated intelligence and data from myriad sources, including maps, positions of other assets in the area, as well as imagery and chat rooms.[12] The controls have not been designed with comfort, ergonomics or intuition in mind and some commands are difficult to execute, requiring dozens of keystrokes. Depending on the system, there may be pedals controlling rudders, joysticks and computer keyboards. The missile trigger is colloquially called 'the pickle'. The operators sit on comfortable Naugahyde 'La-Z-Boy' type chairs, a detail that is relevant insofar as much scorn is heaped on the so-called 'Chair Force' by fellow soldiers who regard war as an experience that demands soldiers face real danger.

The ability to pilot a drone depends in part on the operator's experience. Aircraft pilots are familiar with the controls on some systems, but are used to relying on the sensory cues – crosswinds, turbulence – associated with sitting in an aircraft. With a drone, there is no physical connection to the vehicle – instead, there is significant time lag, spring-loaded controls and a narrow field of vision on screen that is frequently likened to looking through a soda straw. During an early attempt to land a Predator, traditional aircraft pilot Matt Martin rose from his chair to look over the nose of his aircraft to get a better view of the runway, forgetting that the only view he really had was the one on the screen in front of him. And in a programme designed to train retired pilots to fly UAVs, reportedly a 65-year-old broke his hip falling on the floor of his trailer when he attempted to 'eject' from his plummeting Predator.[13]

Research on whether Predator operators need to be experienced pilots at all points in different directions, probably because some systems resemble traditional aircraft more than others.[14] Missy Cummings, an MIT expert on human–unmanned vehicle interaction, found that pilots sometimes have a negative transfer of training problems and crash more often than people with no training.[15] The offhand solution – to recruit gamers on the one hand, and to make flying drones more like playing games on the other – is problematic. It is inevitable that the media, as well as operators themselves, draw parallels between drone warfare and gaming, but the resemblance is superficial beyond the usefulness of having a readily understood analogy to hand. USAF pilot Matt Martin compared his first Predator combat mission to 'the computer game Civilization',[16] in an effort to capture the 'surrealism' of his experience, while in a rather different cultural context, following the Gaza skirmish of November 2012, the Israeli military made much of its 'star' rocket interceptor, a 22-year-old who attributed his prowess manning the Iron Dome anti-rocket system to hours playing *World Of Warcraft*.[17] In the latter case, clearly Israel needed to mobilise mass support for military action in the face of the Hezbollah threat, and pushing the gamer-warrior model serves a useful purpose. On the other hand, the US manages public unease about its 'drone wars' by demonstrating the seriousness with which it undertakes its missions – having pilots and officers rather than gamers on task underwrites that message.

The question of who should fly drones goes far beyond the technical skills needed for the job. Public relations (PR) optics informed the decision to use pilots to fly Predator, and this is not a new story. Far from being 'the right stuff', the candidates originally proposed for US space missions were chimpanzees and circus performers – the decision to use pilots was supposedly instigated by President Dwight Eisenhower for PR reasons. Genuine flying skills were not required on the trip to the moon, and nor are trained pilots needed to fly drones. The alternative, to use zombie-zapping teenagers to kill American enemies is more cost-effective, but is currently unacceptable in PR terms, while research on fully autonomous killer robots has already sparked a significant backlash. The question is whether the 'death from a distance' that UAVs facilitate will be accompanied by more fundamental cultural and/or moral changes around the concepts of soldiering. While the Chair Force is much derided by some, soldiers operating under its watchful eye and kinetic potential find the Predator's presence reassuring.

Bored to Death

While gamers may be more familiar with the mediated war-fighting environment, they are not used to the tedium of flying long missions where nothing happens. Boredom is a serious occupational hazard that not only effects the health and well-being of drone crews and hampers recruitment and retention efforts, but more ominously heightens the risk of error and therefore the risk of civilian casualties. The main task of drones, styled as 'remotely piloted vehicles' (RPVs) in the USAF, is to perform 'dull, dirty and dangerous' missions while minimising risk: 'Dull missions include situation awareness missions, especially those involving persistent surveillance of unmoving targets or identifying the "normal" activities in an area so that unusual activities can be spotted'.[18] There are many accounts of the mind-numbing tedium of conducting prolonged ISR missions, and even action on the ground does not always make for exciting viewing. Martin described a dull two weeks watching from above as the Marines finished mopping up in Fallujah, 'moving from house to house rooting out stray enemy holdouts. Harrowing enough for those on the ground, to be sure, but a real yawner from the air. Some days it was all I could do to stay awake for my shift in the seat'.[19]

Boredom and burnout have been attributed to poor human–machine interfaces and overworked crews. Weaponised drones were rushed into theatres in Afghanistan and Iraq before their controls could be optimised for efficiency and comfort. Trained operators were few and far between, and so huge demands were placed on competent operators like Martin.

Shifts routinely lasted 12 hours, 50–60 hours a week, with 30-day shift changes. High levels of visual and auditory vigilance were required. A 2006 study found UAV crews were chronically fatigued, with nearly 40 per cent of them reporting a moderate-to-high likelihood of falling asleep at the controls of their aircraft.[20]

More personnel, better ergonomics and interfaces and so on, can mitigate some of these issues, but mediated battle has other effects, the implications of which we are a long way away from beginning to understand. After long hours spent watching war in mediated intimacy, the transition from going off shift and returning to an everyday life among civilians is suspected, but not yet proven, to contribute to operator stress. In manned aircraft, crews work in a milieu that is still recognisably culturally warlike. The pilot returns to a militarised base that may also be under threat (and will certainly be secured against threat), where s/he may encounter similar crews who have experienced similar dangers, or even find out that others have been killed. It is hard to quantify whether this makes combat somehow more real, but people who have flown combat missions and drone missions acknowledge that fighting war from an aircraft *feels* different. Cummings, herself a former F/A-18 Hornet pilot for the US Navy, told *Salon* magazine:

> When I was a pilot and you came back from a mission you would come back to the carrier to be with people who were doing the same thing you were doing. You were all together in it. On your own, it's harder to keep it in perspective ... We don't know if PTSD is more common among drone pilots than among aircraft pilots. It's just different.[21]

Drone operators returning to their homes and families are prohibited from talking about their 'day at the office'. Martin described how his wife pointed out that he was 'not laughing so much anymore'. He cannot explain, and so she cannot comprehend, the extent of his psychological engagement with the wars in Iraq and Afghanistan he is fighting from his Las Vegas trailer: 'After all, we weren't getting shot at, wounded or killed. Even if we got shot down, we didn't *really* get shot down'.[22] Other operators tell similar tales, but again it is not at all clear whether this is simply a case of learning how to accommodate the new and specific demands of remote war fighting, or whether some more profound change is lurking here.

Tactical Patience

Officially the USAF suggests that while there are inevitably teething troubles associated with the rushed introduction of UAV technology, there is nothing very new here to worry about. A study completed for the USAF in 2011 found that 'the majority of occupational stress was reported to stem from operational stress and not exposure to combat (i.e., live video feed regarding the destruction or death of enemy combatants and ground forces)'.[23] Working conditions such as long hours, shift work and career uncertainty were cited as the more likely sources.

Specific concerns about how fatigue and burnout might affect operator performance, particularly around the politically fraught issue of collateral damage, have been bundled into more general USAF troubleshooting exercises on this front. A USAF investigation into using drones and other platforms for irregular warfare found that collateral damage was caused by faults in identifying targets, and by a lack of 'tactical patience',[24] an important tool in successful counter-insurgency that involves ensuring sufficient situational awareness to avoid deadly mistakes. The USAF report suggested that tactical patience could be undermined by a lack of available ISR and the amount of urgency surrounding an action (that is, the immediacy of the threat balanced against the effects of not responding to an opportunity to mitigate it).

On paper, drones should extend both intelligence and response times, and therefore enhance tactical patience, but the cases we have available to study suggest it may not be so straightforward. Unhelpfully, the USAF report did not have 'exact' figures on civilian casualties in Afghanistan, and furthermore it could not break out the numbers of civilian casualties caused by drone strikes as opposed to conventional aerial strikes. It claimed that the distinction didn't matter anyway: 'A missile fired (e.g. Hellfire missile) from a RPA is no different from a Hellfire missile fired from other platforms like the AH-64 Apache' it claimed, stressing that concerns about collateral damage are not unique to drones.[25] Yet the distinction is significant, since a big selling point for drones is that they are 'better' for civilians because they introduce high levels of accuracy and intelligence potential into the mix, thereby enhancing situational awareness and addressing the tactical patience issue head-on. This is no empty marketing ploy: in just war theory, it is a moral imperative to avoid civilian casualties, and that may be extended to include deploying systems that reduce the risks of collateral damage.

It remains difficult to get at whether being in a war zone rather than in a trailer in Nevada makes a difference to the quality of the operator's combat abilities. Drone operators have been criticised for not having a better understanding of the operational environment. Mistakes made by a UAV crew were partially blamed for a botched operation in Uruzgan, Afghanistan, that cost at least 23 civilian lives – the crew misidentified a convoy of vehicles as containing insurgents and then 'downplayed or ignored' information that should have led them to correct their error.[26] Defence analysts are quick to point to these sorts of examples as evidence that there is no substitute for the human intelligence that comes from being on the battlefield itself. Certainly Martin looked 'forward to learning more about the Muslim culture and our enemy' when he was forward deployed to Iraq, demonstrating that for individuals, a great deal of importance is attached to the authenticity of serving from inside a war zone.[27]

Back in the trailer in Nevada, however, tactical patience plays out differently owing to the different tempo of drone operations. UAVs can loiter over their targets for hours, but there are still time constraints: fuel capacity will ultimately force the drone back to base, while the nature of shift work means that operators have to decide whether to hand over their mission or launch an attack after hours of emotional and operational investment in a mission. Martin's first Predator kill involved a suspected insurgent in Sadr City, Iraq, who parked his truck in a densely populated area: although Martin received clearance to fire, 'We had to be cautious with a shot in this neighbourhood to avoid killing a bunch of people who didn't necessarily deserve being killed'.[28] Martin and the crew waited for the target to drive to a less populated area, but as night approached and the Predator ran low on fuel, they decided to attack rather than risk losing their target. In the 30 seconds it took the missile to travel to the truck, an elderly man walked into the killing zone. The video feed was washed out by the blast briefly, then reassembled to show the aftermath. The target in his truck has been obliterated, and the old man, 'who must have been the most unfortunate SOB in Sadr City because he happened to be walking by at the wrong time', has been blasted into the middle of the street. Martin didn't linger to see whether the old man survived, but tells us, 'Those who would call this a Nintendo game had never sat in my seat. Those were real people down there. Real people with real lives'.[29]

The kind of personality best suited for the first key task of monitoring dull drone activity for long periods may not be best suited to the second key task of making difficult and fast decisions about who, what and when to kill. The initial USAF decision to use pilots and officers as drone crews speaks to a recognition that decisions over life and death in line with legal and moral precepts are considered to be very much part of the operator's job. Outside US military circles however, the use of private contractors and civilians to fight the CIA's drone wars distort the legal and ethical boundaries that surround such decision making; the legal and moral morass surrounding the Obama administration's targeted killings programme simply adds yet another layer of complexity – and uncertainty – to how drones might be changing the character of war.

Combatants or Something Else?

Even from a distance it is possible for operators to triangulate their place in relation to a legitimate enemy target and the civilians who get entangled in the Predator's crosshairs, and, as Martin suggests, they recognise that this is unique: 'Flying the Predator allowed me the extraordinary perspective of being not only a "combatant," albeit from 7,500 miles away, but also an observer with a broad overview'.[30] Michael Walzer's classic account of the 'naked soldier' demonstrates why time and distance matter deeply to the relationship between combatants. Walzer investigated what lay behind soldiers' decisions to *not* pull the trigger when the enemy appears in circumstances where they are not threatening, but rather painfully human. In Walzer's examples, the enemy sometimes appears through the gun sight naked, or smoking a cigarette, or drinking coffee, or enjoying a sunrise. He quotes Orwell, who said of a fascist enemy he saw holding up his trousers, 'he is visibly a fellow-creature, similar to yourself, and you don't feel like shooting at him'. Such sentiments led Walzer to draw a distinction between the work of the soldier and the being-ness of the human:

> Two soldiers shooting at one another are quite precisely similar; one is doing what the other is doing, and both are engaged in what can be called a peculiarly human activity. But the sense of being a 'fellow creature' depends for obvious reasons upon a different sort of identity, one that is entirely dissociated from anything threatening.[31]

Reciprocity is an important brake on the decision to shoot. The human targets of Hellfire missiles cannot threaten the source of their destruction. This is thought to unseat the traditional equality of soldiers, and so calls into question the combat status of those who operate UAVs. Asparo writes that by 'fighting a war through pressing a button, one does not fully become a combatant because one has not conformed to the norms of war in which both sides agree to risk death in settling the dispute'. The just war tradition demands that both sides are prepared to sacrifice lives, and so in practice a drone engagement 'could be deemed unjust because those doing the killing are not themselves willing to die'.[32]

But as technologies change us our cultural constructs must also change, and it is this painful process that the USAF is attempting to undergo. Serious efforts have been made to erase the idea that drone operators far from the front occupy some different rung on the war-fighting ladder than those who serve closer to the action, but there is serious resistance among the rank and file. In a decision that was met with much wrath within the ranks, in February 2013 outgoing US Defense Secretary Leon Panetta announced a Distinguished Warfare Medal for 'extraordinary achievements that directly impact on combat operations, but do not involve acts of valour or physical risks that combat entails'.[33] The medal, which would outrank the Purple Heart and the Bronze Star, recognised the changed nature of warfare and the contributions of both drone operators and cyber warriors to post-9/11 military operations. The announcement sparked an immediate backlash within the military: the national commander of the two million-strong Veterans of Foreign Wars group countered that medals earned in direct combat would be degraded and troop morale could suffer. The proposed medal was withdrawn. A month earlier, Congress demanded to know why the USAF was not promoting UAV pilots as often as fighter, bomber and cargo pilots. The explanation was that drone operators are caught in a catch-22 where the shortage of pilots means long shifts and so less opportunity for career development, which in turn leaves pilots unwilling to move over to UAV roles, thus exacerbating shortages.[34]

Battle as Process

While UAVs are a valued asset, the US military struggles with how their crews fit into its combat culture. Much debate revolves around the (lack of) exposure to danger drone crews experience, and there are efforts to recast the traditional concept of combat risk to one of combat responsibility. To make this argument, USAF Major David Blair writes in the USAF's professional journal, *Air and Space Power*, that air force culture needs to evolve to encompass the new realities of drone warfare and cyber warfare:

> what is the differential risk between 10,000 feet and 10,000 miles in current conflicts? When a manned aircraft with two spare engines scrapes the top of a combat zone, well outside the range of any realistic threat, why do we consider that scenario 'combat' yet deem a Predator firing a Hellfire in anger 'combat support'?[35]

Blair argues that it is what soldiers do, not the platforms they do them on, that is the essential issue. He suggests that a sortie should qualify as combat if it involves '(1) lives directly on the line (2) against an enemy in wartime'. The operator, he notes, may not risk his own life, but can take another – he has agency, and responsibility for, the enemy's life as well as for friendly troops in theatre, and for civilian life as well. Blair's arguments were strongly resisted – the comments appended to his article, mostly penned by soldiers, were overwhelmingly opposed to this effort to equate drone operation with boots-on-the-ground fighting. Even at 10,000 feet there are risks, runs the counter argument.

Blair proposes that we reframe the way we think about war and suggests that although drone pilots experience battle as a completely mediated experience, they should nevertheless qualify as combatants. In a straightforward battlefield encounter, if a US soldier under attack calls in a drone strike, the operator is fully engaged in saving the lives of his own side. But Blair notes that, 'Interestingly, people may realize they're going to be in combat only partway through the sortie'.[36] Warfare is deterritorialised; as a result, he suggests that now combat is a process, not a place, and argues that a drone operator enters combat when he has agency over another's life. However, 'Because software is driving these complex and integrated systems, identifying the agency and action, and therefore tracing or understanding responsibility for each air target, is almost impossible'.[37] In other words, the nature of the weapon itself has implications for the agency of the operators – and their status as combatants. On the one hand, it means resistance to decorating drone operators for their contributions to fighting. On the other hand, traditionally the responsibility for life and death decisions could be located somewhere within a kill chain: an important reservation about weapons systems that decentre the decision-making process is that apportioning blame and ascribing responsibility for war crimes is no longer possible either.

Bug Splat

The inequality between target and operator models the power asymmetries introduced by previous military technological advances. McLuhan identified the discovery of perspective as an important step in the creation of modern weaponry: the spears and arrows of yore required close contact, whereas the science of perspective opened up the possibility of extending one's reach across ever growing distances. Students of the Panopticon have considered the power relationships that inhere and operate according to points of view, while students of air power have considered the cultural effects of viewing from a height and how they present in the construction of aerial targets. Kaplan suggests that modernity's aerial view posited 'a belief that this personal eye, liberated from the bounded embeddedness on earth, in movement, [that] can see almost limitlessly and, therefore, with extreme clarity'. This view, she says, is implicitly and explicitly (when it is manifest as air power) imperialistic, 'promising to link subjects in a unified gaze for the purpose of viewing and therefore mastering a world that had hitherto been unknown or unobserved'.[38]

Whereas air power originally saw rival air forces matched in contests between states, UAVs reflect the grotesque imbalance that now obtains in a global War on Terror in which the 'super-powerfulness and the powerlessness of the warring parties' must contend.[39] The view of the drone pilot is augmented by the recorded memory and dense detail facilitated by the Predator.

From Nevada, Martin's war switched from scrutinising the urban battle terrain of Iraq's most densely populated neighbourhoods to patrolling the unpeopled and inaccessible expanses of Afghanistan, depending on his daily tasking. His job was largely to babysit the heavily automated Predator for a 12-hour shift, week in, week out. Occasionally, something happened. Feeling immortal in his trailer he considered human frailty:

> I *knew* people down there. Each day through my camera I snooped around and came to recognize the faces and figures of our soldiers and marines, unbeknownst to most of them ... I truly felt a bit like an omnipotent god with a god's seat above it all.[40]

Martin's account reveals how he set about constructing a heroic, almost comic-book narrative to give purpose to the grinding tedium of his days, an imaginative construction more grounded in civilian chatter about the fighting in Afghanistan and Iraq than that informed by military assessments. With the caveat that this is but one person's experience, the emotions and reactions of Martin seem altogether understandable. Perhaps seeking to compensate for his lack of authenticity as a combatant, he finds purpose in responding to a mass media news agenda that demands public enemies with recognisable faces. Acting on some intelligence on the whereabouts of Osama bin Laden, Martin is excited: 'I was actually in pursuit of Osama bin Laden! How much closer than that could one get to the war?'[41] Many of his dramatic (non)encounters namecheck the War on Terror's biggest celebrities – for example, he obsessively 'hunts' for Abu Musab al-Zarqawi in order to exact justice for the murder of Nicholas Berg and others.

Martin is immersed in mediated combat that fuses with the war-as-entertainment experience provided by the mass media. Drone crews are susceptible to the psychological challenges of having to be fully present both at war/at work and at home/off work, and Martin's account is suggestive of how soldiers try to fit themselves into this new mediated-warrior framework. He composes a compelling narrative for himself, enduring his boring surveillance flights by pretending to hunt for kidnap victims or Bin Laden. Those are indeed real people, but he does not have a real relationship with them, with the civilians he is purporting to help, the same-side soldiers he is essentially spying on, or with the enemies he targets.

Kaplan discusses how the 'monster-enemy' is constructed through the aerial gaze, quoting Keen's observation from *The Face of the Enemy* that 'The lower down in the animal phyla the image descends, the greater the sanction is given to the soldier to become the exterminator of pests'.[42] The military slang for a person killed in a drone strike is 'bug splat', which supposedly describes the way a crushed body looks in the relayed computer image.[43] Martin describes the first insurgent he hunts down and kills in Sadr City in similar language – 'like a rat, he slithered', and so on.[44] The civilian life he must respect is not accorded much more nuance, although he recognises that he is supposed to protect it. From 10,000 feet above Sadr City he sees 'Kids, stray dogs, and rats ... piles of garbage ... junk cars'. He notes kids rolling a tire, a woman hanging out laundry, people walking, and compares it all to 'a summer day in Garden City, Kansas', but adds: 'Leave it to me to spoil their day'.[45]

The Trials of Separation

It is not easy to confront the mortality of the enemy, and every combatant must make his own peace with his decision to kill or not. If there is debate over whether flying a UAV is more like *Call of Duty* than flying an F-16, it is because we grasp at these knowns as a way to explain the complex cultural/ethical negotiation that is occurring as a new kind of soldier struggles to reconcile the complex flows of the twenty-first century's heavily mediated culture. Drone warfare adds yet another dimension to the problematics of reconciling the abstraction of the aerial target with the concreteness of its effects:

> as the sleek, machinic and dispassionate presentation of these abstractions is called into doubt here, what emotions, affects, feelings and rationalities not only irrupt in the violent outcomes of processes of air-targeting, but actually compose the target process and add tension and torsion to its unfolding?[46]

Soldiers both fear and crave danger. Martin may appreciate the power he wields over life and death from his trailer in Nevada, but only when he is sent to Iraq for forward operations does he become a warrior in his own eyes: 'I would be taking many of the same risks as other soldiers in combat ... For the first time since the war began I felt a direct kinship with the troops I had been supporting so long from a distance'.[47] In Iraq, he still participated in the war via video link, but now – authentically – under fire from enemy rockets. It is only by becoming a target himself that he fulfils the traditional role of the soldier.

Persistence, precision and distance combine in a Predator in a way that extends the soldier's senses hugely, permanently and safely into remote and inhospitable regions. The traditional reciprocity of soldiers facing each other in battle is, for the moment, grossly unbalanced by this advent of technology, and western militaries are struggling to catch up, attempting to reimagine what the old tropes of danger, courage and heroics will be in this new world. Cultural problems are joined by moral ones, as both legal and ethical guidelines are pulled and stretched to accommodate the new praxis. It does not take much imagination to extrapolate a near future when other militaries and irregular groups can take similar liberties with time, space and political violence. The implications that such an unbounded approach to military action might have when this deeply asymmetric relationship is rebalanced is seldom discussed.

5

Targets: The View From Below

We don't even sit together to chat anymore.
Taliban fighter[1]

The US failure to achieve any great measure of success in the war zones of Afghanistan and Iraq, its destabilisation of Pakistan, and the resilience of Al Qaeda-inspired movements in Yemen and Somalia, all point to deep-seated problems with American policy since 9/11, including its reliance on high-tech weaponry to achieve security. 'Ordinary' people have long confounded military strategists by refusing to be or to act in the ways planners expect, although perhaps to the rest of us their reactions are entirely predictable. People who live under drones behave in ways reminiscent of other populations who have lived under air attack – they are more likely to become angry and resistant rather than cooperative and compliant, and this creates problems not just for the architects of their misery, but for their own governments who fail to protect them. The limitations of drone warfare are already written in the histories of air power more generally.

Drones promise to revolutionise war fighting, but it is not the first time such promises have been made. The early proponents of air power believed that strategic bombing 'might be revolutionary in its effects because it would enable a new type of war fighting that went right over the heads of armies and navies, and directly to the sources of a nation's strength' wrote historian Tami Biddle. 'Bomber aircraft might ... – quickly and single-handedly – collapse the war-fighting infrastructure and the popular will of an enemy state'.[2] In other words, killing civilians became part of war plans. In the summer of 1917 Germany put this theory into practice and bombed London from the air, killing 227 people and injuring 677, including children at an infant school. Rather than cowing Londoners, it inflamed them. British newspapers published pictures of the child-victims, and 'reprisal maps' of German towns. Revenge, and the paucity of London's air defences, became the subject of public meetings.

Government leaders worried about its restive home front: its citizens were frightened, yes, but also angry – and not just with Germany, but with the failure of the British state to protect them. Would morale hold? It did, but it also helped the civilian population forge its own sense of identity as a particular group that had particular interests – and in this case, faced particular threats. As government conduct of the war was criticised by the British public, revolutionary upheavals in Russia provided a dramatic example of what people-power could achieve. Ordinary people had forced their way, unwelcome, into the calculations surrounding conflict.

An ensuing century of meting out 'death from above' has demonstrated firstly that public morale is generally more robust than military planners credit, and secondly that killing civilians, whether deliberately or not, is problematic from a PR point of view. The correct way to calibrate a military mission that intimidates, but does not kill or wholly estrange, a population remains elusive, although many different approaches have been tried. An 'overkill' strategy that saw 3.4 million sorties flown by US and South Vietnamese combat aircraft between 1964 and 1972 failed to win Vietnam for the west.[3] The citizens of Belgrade flocked to the city's bridges, targets on their backs, acting as human shields to defy NATO attackers during the 1999 Kosovo war; the opening 'Shock and Awe' campaign of the 2003 US war against Iraq was 'an explicitly performative display of violence from the air'[4] whose emptiness was made all too evident as a long, bitter and brutal ground-based insurgency set in. Drone strikes in Pakistan exacerbated existing political divisions and created new ones: stopping the US bombardment of its people became a key issue in the 2013 Pakistan elections. When faced with overwhelming technological superiority from the air, people – even unarmed civilians – refuse to be dominated, and this is their strength. By limiting the range of options political and military leaders can employ, they have proven their ability to shape how wars are fought. Looking at the marked lack of success in achieving victory or even security in the global War on Terror, the early evidence of the drone wars suggests that once again, death from above creates more problems than it solves.

Under Western Eyes

I became accustomed to their sound. It was there all the time. During the day it was mostly absorbed into the hum of daily life, but in the calm of the night the buzzing was all you heard.[5]

Although they are usually unnamed and uncounted in the official histories of the War on Terror, the most important humans in the loop are those who fulfil the destiny of the drone by being at the end of a potential kill chain. While a drone can be used to kill a single person, it can only do so through the surveillance of the wider population – and in turn, this implies that assumptions have been made about that population in advance of any deployment. The mere presence of UAVs in a region suggests trouble. There is a feedback loop whereby strikes kill civilians and militants, rhetoric inflames emotions and the consequences cannot be controlled. While the US drone programme may be called counter-terrorist, many of its intentions and effects resemble counter-insurgency. Anderson writes that: 'Always by definition too late, since it responds after an insurgency has emerged, *counter*insurgency acts once a population has acquired a tendency to become either enemy or friend'.[6] In pursuing its enemies across the Afghanistan border into Pakistan, the CIA seemingly brought its assumptions about the wider population's reliability with it. And a population that falls under the gaze of a drone is already a population with a question mark, if not yet crosshairs, on its back.

Drones 'are employed to amass data about risk probabilities and then manage populations or eliminate network nodes considered to exceed acceptable risk thresholds', write Wall and Monahan, retreating into the clinical language of biopolitics to describe the ostensibly counter-terrorist approach that nano-warfare takes.[7] The system's scrutiny and codification of people's behaviour reduces them to performing 'patterns of life', their talk becomes 'atmospherics', their 'environment' judged to be 'permissive' or 'hostile', the drone 'loiters' – a term, Williams notes, that 'refers to the ability to generate a threat purely through presence'.[8] In common with other forms of dataveillance, these people and their lives are flattened and reduced to machine-readable binary forms. While drones therefore promise the machine-benefits of precision and accuracy, as Walls and Monahan argue:

> in practice, these surveillance systems and their agents actively interpret ambiguous information that continuously defies exact matches or clear responses. In the process, UAV systems may force homogenization upon difference, thereby reducing variation to functional categories that correspond to the needs and biases of the operators, not the targets, of surveillance.[9]

A person who becomes the object of the drone stare is too easily viewed as a potential threat or potential collateral damage – or at best a non-entity, an irrelevant body in the ongoing wargames.

There is a world of difference between the wide-angle bombing of cities and populations and the newfound ability to 'put the warhead on the forehead' with a drone, but the morality and legality of killing civilians remain fundamentally unchanged. What has changed is the scale of the destruction: wholesale bombing of populations is not acceptable now, and possibly never was, but in the drone we have a weapon that makes this kind of up close and personal nano-war not just possible, but quotidian. Body counts in single figures in obscure places scarcely register, while the aggressor 7,000 miles away takes no risks, and so there are no headlines to contend with. The CIA and the US military have carried out drone strikes regularly since 2002. In the non-war zones of Pakistan, Yemen and Somalia, the number of civilian deaths confirmed by the Bureau of Investigative Journalism as of January 2014 lies between 440 and 1,038. For the US administrations of Bush and Obama, PR on the home front have not been a problem. Even now US citizens overwhelmingly support the practice: a mid-2013 poll found that 66 per cent of respondents favoured the use of drones to kill terrorists, against only 16 per cent opposing drone strikes.[10]

The problem of course is that not only terrorists are being killed. As the body counts, so painstakingly assembled, have climbed and details have leaked out, resistance and retribution have been more evident on the killing fields that on the home front. For the White House, drones have offered a low-risk, covert and deniable way to carry out small-scale attacks in Pakistan and elsewhere without risking the ire of the American electorate: when the simple insistence that only bad guys get killed fails to appease the questions, tortuous legal justifications are proffered as well.

However, this comfortable PR position may not last. A partial, but increasingly difficult-to-ignore, picture of what it is like to live under the constant threat of a drone attack and/or to carry on living in the aftermath of an attack is beginning to emerge and inform debate. As the negative effects of this apparently low-cost exercise of the use of force become more visible, the ability to wage nano-war could become more difficult. Important work to record and publicise the experiences of populations living under drones is being undertaken by groups that include researchers, academics, lawyers and investigative journalists. This wider counter-narrative is vital to challenging the way drone warfare is presented by the US administration and in the mainstream media. Beyond the headlines it is clear that it is not only the bad guys getting killed by drones, and the wider effects on populations are extensive, uncontrollable, and in terms of delivering any kind of real, lasting, security, counter-productive.

Slaughter at Datta Khel

One of the most notorious recent episodes of misguided drone warfare occurred in March 2011. US drones launched a missiles attack against a gathering of tribal elders in Datta Khel, North Waziristan, Pakistan, killing some 42 people and injuring 14. Because the effects of drone strikes are grossly under-reported in the mainstream media, the *Living Under Drones* account of the attack is worth reproducing at some length:

> Ahmed Jan, who was sitting in one of two circles of roughly 20 men each, told our researchers that he remembered hearing the hissing sound the missiles made just seconds before they slammed into the center of his group. The force of the impact threw Jan's body a significant distance, knocking him unconscious, and killing everyone else sitting in his circle. Several additional missiles were fired ...
>
> One of the survivors from the other circle, Mohammad Nazir Khan, told us that many of the dead appeared to have been killed by flying pieces of shattered rocks. Another witness, Idris Farid, recalled that 'everything was devastated. There were pieces – body pieces – lying around. There was lots of flesh and blood.'[11]

The son of one of the attendees rushed to the scene, where

> Unable to identify the body parts lying on the ground, all Khalil Khan could do was 'collect pieces of flesh and put them in a coffin.' Idris Farid ... explained how funerals for the victims of the March 17 strike were 'odd and different than before.' The community had to collect [the victims'] body pieces and bones and then bury them like that, doing their best to 'identify the pieces and the body parts' so that the relatives at the funeral would be satisfied they had 'the right parts of the body and the right person.'

Unnamed US officials reportedly insisted to local media that those killed were deliberately targeted as enemies: 'These people weren't gathering for a bake sale. They were terrorists', and, 'These guys were terrorists, not the local men's glee club'. In fact, the gathering was a *jirga*, a consensual decision-making meeting convened in this instance to consider a dispute over a local chromite mine. After extensive research, the Living Under Drones project concluded: 'All of the relevant stakeholders and local leaders were in attendance including 35 government-appointed tribal leaders' as well as four local Taliban members; the nearby Pakistani military post had been informed of the *jirga* ten days in advance; and while the attendees knew that drones were operating in the area, they felt secure because of a perception that 'the drones target terrorists or those working against the government', according to the son of one of the victims.[12]

In spite of clear evidence to the contrary, officially the US administration still maintains that everyone at the *jirga* was an insurgent and therefore a US enemy. This blackwashing of legitimate community gatherings is routine. It is made possible because access to credible information is limited, the applicable laws are complicated and the US government refuses to provide the evidence upon which its targeting decisions are based. In this example we have better information than usual, and in many respects the devil is in the details. As the best propagandists know, it is better to build large lies on small truths. There *were* Taliban in attendance, including Sherabat Khan Wazir, a top local commander associated with a powerful North Waziristan Taliban group led by Hafiz Gul Bahadur. The Bahadur group conducted its activities over the border in Afghanistan and was closely allied with the Afghan-based Haqqani network, and so did represent a genuine threat to US forces. This is the kind of evidence Washington will point to in order to justify the strike, hoping that simple guilt by association will accomplish the rest.

Yet within Pakistan, the Bahadur group was considered 'good Taliban' – that is, it was pro-government and had signed a peace deal with Islamabad years before. As local men of influence, its members were considered an important element to include in the *jirga*. Following the strike, the Pakistan government strongly protested to the US, while Bahadur threatened to tear up his peace deal with Pakistan; and it emerged that even the US ambassador had tried to stop the attack, but had been overruled by the CIA.[13] In May 2013 the Peshawar High Court found the US government and the CIA guilty of war crimes and breaches of Pakistani sovereignty in a case brought by the families of the victims of Datta Khel.[14] The CIA may have succeeded in eliminating an enemy or four at Datta Khel, but in the process it created many new ones.

This is by no means an isolated case. In July 2013, another person in another country not at war with the US sought answers about family members killed by US drones. This time the attack was in Yemen, and propelled Faisal bin Ali Jaber to write to both the Yemeni president and to Barack Obama on behalf of his dead family members:

> Why ... did you both send drones to attack my innocent brother-in-law and nephew? Our family are not your enemy. In fact, the people you killed had strongly and publicly opposed al-Qa'ida. Salem was an imam. The Friday before his death, he gave a guest sermon in the Khashamir mosque denouncing al-Qa'ida's hateful ideology. It was not the first of these sermons, but regrettably, it was his last.[15]

Even as Yemen totters towards democracy, it has been sending clear messages to the US about the effects of the US drone campaign that ostensibly targets only Al Qaeda operatives. In August 2013 its National Dialogue Congress, a US-supported precursor body to help restore democracy in Yemen, voted nearly unanimously to criminalise drone strikes and extrajudicial killings. In spite of this clear signal that drones were not welcome, within a week two children were among those killed in a series of strikes apparently launched in response to US-intercepted 'chatter' about a possible Al Qaeda attack – somewhere in the world – that led the US to close 19 embassies in the Middle East and North Africa.

In Somalia US drones held their fire until June 2011, although surveillance drones have provided intelligence since early 2007, when, for example, a Joint Special Operations Command AC-130 gunship attacked a suspected Al Qaeda convoy tracked by a Predator. At least two civilians, possibly children, were killed in that attack.[16]

The civilian carnage continues in spite of international human rights regimes explicitly designed to protect non-combatants from the ravages of war and extremism. Human rights in non-war zones are first and foremost guaranteed by states themselves; the US has been able to pressure weak and, in the case of Somalia, failed governments to 'allow' drone strikes, skating around accusations of sovereignty violations and accusations of war crimes as the lawyers argue. Habermas, apropos of the 2003 US war on Iraq, described a 'radical breach' with international law as the American administration turned instead to a reliance on 'its own ethical values and moral convictions; it has substituted its own normative values for prescribed juristic procedures'.[17] While the Obama administration has brought legal arguments back into play, it has not returned to the traditional understanding of existing legal regimes but instead reconstructed their meanings to fit American ends. Pakistan's emergence as ground zero in the CIA's drone wars demonstrates how governments and states have been artfully subverted in the process.

Pakistan's Borderlands

The US has been conducting drone strikes in non-war zones such as Somalia and Yemen, but the epicentre of its drone war lies in the Federally Administered Tribal Areas (FATA) of Pakistan that border Afghanistan. It is important to look at the problematic of how sovereign territory is constituted here, as the area offers the richest detail in an otherwise sparse information environment surrounding US drone policy. The FATA is a region that lies within the state borders of Pakistan, although the central government has never asserted effective control and Afghanistan has never recognised the colonial-era Durand Line that became the modern border. Access is difficult, travel is restricted, conditions are dangerous, and body counts are unreliable because they are highly politicised. In the absence of official, verifiable figures, local investigators face threats from both the military and the militants: 'We cannot portray drone strikes in a positive light; we don't want to end up dead', said one journalist.[18] In the absence of hard information, many competing scripts of violence about the FATA have been written, but it is not an imaginary place – real people are trying to live their lives there. Understanding how Pakistan is sited so ambiguously in the (ongoing) global War on Terror that it can be both ally and target requires some background.

First, there is Pakistan's own security situation. The main threat to Pakistan has always been India. Pakistan's management of its borders and support of groups beyond its borders, such as the *Mujahideen* fighting the Soviets in Afghanistan, has been with an eye to securing itself against its great rival. If the aphorism 'my enemy's enemy is my friend' ever applied anywhere, it applies to Pakistan, although enemy is probably too strong a word. Pashtun tribes and Islamist politics are part of the political landscape, and it supported the Taliban regime in Afghanistan as a useful bulwark against the possibility of a more pro-India government. It was the 9/11 attacks that necessitated the *volte face* by the military government of Pervez Musharraf. When President George W. Bush famously announced on 20 September 2001, 'Either you are with us, or you are with the terrorists. From this day forward, any nation that continues to harbor or support terrorism will be regarded by the United States as a hostile regime', Pakistan had little choice but to swap sides and to try to manage the domestic fallout as best it could. The alternative was to watch the US ally with India and designate Pakistan a terrorist state. Still, the choice was sufficiently difficult that the US, aware that it would take a significant push to make sure Pakistan chose the correct side, offered billions of dollars of aid in exchange for Islamabad's material support, including access to airspace, military bases, transport roots and intelligence. Neither side was particularly happy with the deal.

In November 2001 the Afghan Taliban government fell, and Pakistan's northwest, that is, the FATA, the North-West Frontier Province and Baluchistan, became destinations for fleeing Al Qaeda and Taliban fighters. These areas later became staging grounds for the Afghan insurgency. Prodded by the US, Pakistan military units reluctantly went into the tribal areas to try to root out militants, but were largely unsuccessful, perhaps lacking conviction that this was an effective way to solve America's terrorist problem, and certainly aware that they were more than likely to exacerbate their own. Predictably, in response to the military crackdown, the scattering of militant groups within Pakistan grew, spread and began to coalesce into a much more potent threat to Pakistan proper. By 2007, the Tehrik-i-Taliban Pakistan (Taliban Movement of Pakistan or TTP) and other groups were mounting counter-attacks, staging terrorist incidents and exerting control over areas to the extent that the federal government was forced to conclude peace treaties with radical groups and cede governance to them.

Pakistan's double game of trying to cooperate with the Americans without enflaming the groups in its difficult border zones unravelled, while US actors – diplomats, the CIA, the US military and even private contractors – pursued conflicting strategies depending on who their Pakistani counterparts were and how they read the depth of their commitment and reliability.[19] The International Crisis Group describes the 'schizophrenic' nature of Pakistan's view of the drone programme, exemplified by this remark by one of its interviewees: 'The truth is that Pakistan's military approved of both safe havens for the Taliban and the American drone strikes against them'.[20] The CIA drone strategy, as it has become intertwined with Pakistan's own relationship with FATA, corrupted the decision-making process of both states.

The human cost of this misbegotten alliance is high: while the numbers vary, between 2,500 and 3,500 people were killed by US drones between 2004 and mid-2013, and perhaps 20 to 30 per cent of them were civilians. Even if the remainder were 'legitimate' kills of militants, the civilian cost, as measured by the Pakistanis themselves, is unacceptably high. In a 2013 Pew Research poll, 74 per cent of Pakistanis believed that too many innocent people had been killed, 68 per cent opposed the US drone programme and only 11 per cent regarded the US favourably – a new low; 98 per cent now considered terrorism a major problem for the country, and rated the threat posed by the Taliban on a par with the threat posed by their traditional enemy, India, for the first time since Pew began polling on the issue.[21] A decade of drone strikes has turned the Pakistani population, its own security deeply undermined, against the US. Like earlier examples of air power, drone warfare has failed in its attempts to produce peace through targeting civilians.

Revisioning War Zones

Pakistan would likely have been left to manage its security issues without American interference if 9/11 had not happened. Instead, the attacks led the US administration to rewrite the rulebook, starting with a significant shift of power into the hands of the president. Just three days after 9/11, a panicked US Congress passed (with only one dissenting vote) the sweeping Authorization for the Use of Military Force that gave the president the open-ended power to 'use all necessary and appropriate force against those nations, organizations, or persons he determines planned, authorized, committed, or aided the terrorist attacks that occurred on September 11, 2001'. In essence, this meant that rather than being at war with a particular country or countries, the US had authorised the president to make war in any country that Al Qaeda was operating in. Born out of specific circumstances and aimed at meeting specific threats, this piece of legislation continues to underpin Obama's drone campaign against enemies and threats that scarcely resemble those that existed – and that in many cases did not even exist – when the law was passed. In July 2013, a Congressional attempt to sunset the Authorization for the Use of Military Force and finally end this 'endless war' at the end of 2014, by which time all US combat troops should be home from Afghanistan, was defeated.

War envisioned this way is not containable by traditional principles, as is demonstrated by the term 'Af-Pak', a consciously ambiguous name used by the Obama administration to suggest this is an ungovernable swath of territory that will not be bundled into the conventional international relations lexicon of states, borders and sovereignty. Richard Holbrooke, the US Special Envoy to Afghanistan and Pakistan (such a job title suggests how the two countries elided in American thinking) said:

> First of all, we often call the problem AfPak, as in Afghanistan Pakistan. This is not just an effort to save eight syllables. It is an attempt to indicate and imprint in our DNA the fact that there is one theater of war, straddling an ill-defined border, the Durand Line, and that on the western side of that border, NATO and other forces are able to operate. On the eastern side, it's the sovereign territory of Pakistan. But it is on the eastern side of this ill-defined border that the international terrorist movement is located.[22]

This portrayal is more political than territorial, an example of what Duffield labels the global borderlands, 'a metaphor for an imagined geographical space where, in the eyes of many metropolitan actors and agencies, the characteristics of brutality, excess and breakdown predominate'.[23] The logic runs that if an area cannot be captured by the rules, then the rules do not apply, and a space opens up to rewrite them. The US linguistically established this as a discrete area that falls outside conventional understandings of international borders; it then used its own interpretation of self-defence to start carving out a new kind of war zone that was not based on territory, but on people. Extending this logic still further, combat drones have allowed the US to carry out nano-wars on a global scale, relying on the fact that killing individuals (even American citizens, such as Anwar al-Awlaki in Yemen) will not arouse much opposition, or even interest. As long as it is perceived that American lives are saved and terrorists are being killed, US public opinion is quiescent, perhaps reassured by its administration's torturous interpretations of international law that it uses to justify the carnage.

In this new world order, as defined by American power, where is the war? Traditionally, in non-war situations, international human rights laws apply. However, the Obama administration says that international human rights law is not applicable when a state is acting under the self-defence principle enshrined in the UN Charter, as the US claims to be doing.[24] In other words, from an American perspective there are no non-war zones, just places that either contain threats or don't contain threats. The US interpretation of the laws of war offer little help in narrowing this field: in April 2012, CIA director John Brennan offered the US's view: 'there is nothing in international law ... that prohibits us from using lethal force against our enemies *outside an active battlefield*, at least when the country involved consents or is unable or unwilling to take action against the threat'.[25] With this triple-pronged interpretation, the US maintains that its use of drones outside of conventional war zones is legal. The fact that it is the Obama administration that articulated this position 11 years after 9/11 is suggestive of how the War on Terror has leaked across time as well as space, buttressed by legislation passed in the wake of the original terrorist attacks.

Pinpointing the legal basis for identifying US violations of international law in its drone wars is additionally hampered by US praxis, which makes determining where responsibility lies for any given decision or action hard to ascertain. Pilots flying drones operated under CIA auspices are regarded as civilians because officially the CIA is a civilian organisation, but the lines between CIA and military activities have become increasingly tangled; the programs themselves, the evidence on which decisions are made, who is involved and what permissions have been granted and by whom, suffer from a lack of transparency. Sometimes the operators are contractors from private military companies, and so even less accountable. It isn't even clear that a state can legally consent to allow another state to kill its citizens on its territory.[26] Targets are not members of a traditional state military so they are not combatants in the usual understanding of the term: the Obama administration maintains that Al Qaeda has no non-military wing, so all members, whether bomb makers, propagandists or drivers are fair game, and the list of targets grows ever longer, covering threats so far down the command chain that they are likely not threats at all. It is difficult to escape this legal wilderness of mirrors, but it is increasingly clear that these radical interpretations of existing international law threaten to push the global security order in a direction that favours US, and inevitably other, imperial powers.

Afghanistan: Lies and Statistics

In contrast to Pakistan, Afghanistan is clearly a war zone, falling under international humanitarian law as a non-international armed conflict.

While there has not been the same level of controversy surrounding how the US drone war is conducted there, this is largely due to an informational black hole. The ISAF is not forthcoming with casualty figures of any type, civilians included, and when it comes to death from the skies the type of weapons platform used – whether manned or unmanned – is often not possible to ascertain. But even from this sketchy basis, it is clear that civilians are being killed by drones, and in increasing numbers, even as the US combat presence there ostensibly winds down.

The UN Assistance Mission in Afghanistan (UNAMA) reported that between January and June 2013, drones had killed 15 civilians and injured seven in seven separate incidents, noting that there were no civilian casualties in the same period in 2012. While drone casualties make up less than 1 per cent of the mid-year total, overall there was an uptick in casualties from the previous year, suggesting rising insecurity. The report cited a specific example: in June 2013, a humanitarian worker was clearing mines in Panjawi district, Kandahar, when he was killed in an ISAF drone strike. ISAF told UNAMA the victim was not a humanitarian worker, but a mid-level planter of IEDs and the decision was made to kill him rather than risk losing him in an operation to find and detain him. Some 80 other deminers working with him were not injured. [27]

Drones have been eulogised as minimising collateral damage in Afghanistan because they facilitate good intelligence, and by extension good targeting. But there is a dangerous tendency to elide arguments about drones as effective weapons within a responsible military strategy with arguments that are more propagandistic than factual. For example, in 2009 drones were credited with tidily reducing Afghanistan's civilian casualty toll. Examining how such claims work their way into mainstream media and academic discourse is worthwhile. This was a year that in fact saw record levels of civilian casualties, and much was made of a change in tactics when General Stanley McChrystal took command mid-year: 'Under his command, the overall number of air strikes decreased, drone strikes increased, and a UN report cited a corresponding 28 percent reduction in civilian casualties', academics Brunstetter and Braun write, taking this statistic into the academy to suggest how drones could comply with just war doctrine. [28] They drew their observations from an even more gung-ho article by *Wired* writer Spencer Ackerman who, under the headline 'Under McChrystal, Drone Strikes in Afghanistan Quietly Rise as Civilian Casualties *Drop*' (emphasis in original), cited the 28 per cent figure as an 'internationally-validated reduction in U.S./NATO-attributable civilian casualties'. Ackerman wrote this was 'the most important aspect of the increase in drone usage', and suggested that 'the precision capabilities contained within the remotely-piloted drones satisfy McChrystal's guidance for a "a higher degree of certainty, patience and restraint in employing air strikes."' [29]

The actual UNAMA report suggests something quite different. ISAF, supported by Afghan units, killed 828 civilians in 2008, and 'only' 595 civilians in 2009, the 28 per cent drop cited above. But context is everything: the Afghan government of Hamid Karzai had been deeply critical of the high levels of civilian casualties caused by air strikes and night raids, and in response McChrystal implemented a more conservative approach. UNAMA was in fact reporting on a new tactical directive specifically 'designed to reduce civilian casualties' that 'limited the use of force – such as close air support – in residential/populated areas. It also revised the guidelines for operations involving residential compounds, and searches of houses and religious establishments'.[30] In other words, the decrease was due to an overall effort across operations to reduce civilian casualties. The tempo of drone strikes did increase, partly because more lethally equipped drones were arriving in theatre, but how much of any 28 per cent drop is directly attributable to them is impossible to extrapolate from available information.

Furthermore, this drop should be set against the overall rise in casualties, which were in fact up by 14 per cent over the previous year. On the ISAF side, UNAMA reported that airstrikes claimed the most lives (359, or 61 per cent of the total), with the runner-up being search and seizure operations that caused 98 civilian deaths (16 per cent). Collateral damage statistics were far worse for the opposing side (styled in the report as anti-government elements or AGEs), who killed civilians at three times ISAF's rate. Here, suicide and IED attacks accounted for 44 per cent of the overall civilian total. 'Although such attacks have primarily targeted government or international military forces, they are often carried out in areas frequented by civilians', UNAMA reported.[31]

It is very much in the nature of counter-insurgency operations to trap civilians in the crossfire. The practice of locating western forces in civilian areas was criticised for attracting violence into the very communities ISAF was supposedly trying to protect. For their part, anti-government elements found it useful to hide among civilians. The UNAMA report found that traditional codes of hospitality and 'power imbalances' in local communities made it difficult to turn these people away. Militants, of course, are no ardent upholders of international humanitarian law, and as is often the case in asymmetric war the weaker side finds itself pushing boundaries to exploit what few advantages it has, defending such acts as military necessity. This is not news to western military planners, who have done it themselves – as an American major famously said of the 1968 bombing offensive against the city of Běn Tre in Vietnam, 'It became necessary to destroy the town to save it'. However, a disregard for international law on one side does not excuse the other side from observing it. The UNAMA noted that the ISAF bore its own obligation to respect international humanitarian law, rather than compound the problem by committing its own violations.[32]

Life and Death Under Drones

The death and destruction that costs the US so little to mete out is being recorded in the cultures and on the bodies of those who are forced to live under the conditions created by US national security policy since 9/11. The Living Under Drones project spent nine months in northwest Pakistan not just looking for victims, but documenting the experiences of the inhabitants and identifying the kind of harm, beyond death and injury, that is inflicted on ordinary people. What they found suggests the ways in which the social fabric of these communities has been profoundly damaged by the unique characteristics of drone warfare: the 24-hours-a-day threat that loiters unseen, but often heard, over their homes, striking people without warning while they are eating, sleeping, praying, talking – or pulling bodies out of drone strike craters, or attending the funerals of earlier victims. In addition to the 'usual' dislocations and trials of those who experience political violence, the persistence and precision of UAVs bring unique problems that are not just visited on the individual victim and his/her family, but on the community as a whole. Interviewees told researchers that the threat of a drone strike 'anywhere at any time led to constant and severe fear, anxiety, and stress'.[33] To protect themselves, they began to behave differently, to change their patterns of life, to consider this threat when weighing decisions of whether to attend school, go to work or attend a wedding. 'More than two can't sit together outside because they are scared they might be struck by drones', one teenager told the Living Under Drones interviewers.[34] Economic life is affected. In the words of another interviewee:

[Before, e]verybody was involved in their own labor work. We were all busy. But since the drone attacks have started, everybody is very scared and everybody is terrorized ... People are out of business, people are out of schools, because people are being killed by these drone attacks.[35]

It is plain to see that life in these communities is adversely affected, but more ominous still is how those effects are then factored into the targeting matrixes of US war planners. A pattern of life that now includes funerals for so-called militants becomes an exploitative opportunity to find and kill more targets. Perhaps the most indefensible use of drones is the 'double tap', or follow-up strike, a CIA tactic that targets the very human impulses to assist the injured and bury the dead. Between 2009 and 2011 in Pakistan, the Bureau of Investigative Journalism found evidence of 11 double-tap strikes that targeted rescuers who rushed to scenes of earlier attacks to help, and one attack on a mosque. Amid international criticism that killing civilian rescuers is a possible war crime, the double taps more or less stopped, although in 2012 the practice was apparently resumed during the hunt for senior Al Qaeda figures including number two Yahya al-Libi, who was ultimately killed in a drone strike on 4 June 2012.

CIA double taps should be considered war crimes,[36] although when the legal lines are as blurred as they are in the US drone war in Pakistan, mounting a case, or even creating the political will necessary for such an attempt, is difficult. An example will suffice to show the complexity involved, and how the practice is defended as militarily 'justifiable'. On 24 May 2012, drones attacked people gathered for morning prayers at a mosque in a small village known to accommodate foreign fighters near Mir Ali in North Waziristan, Pakistan. In the first attack, four people, probably foreign fighters, were killed. Within 20 minutes, six or seven people, including local men, arrived to help the injured: 'While they were pulling out bodies from the rubble and putting the dead and injured people on *charpais* or beds to take them to the hospital, the drones returned. They fired four more missiles at those involved in the rescue work'.[37] Six were killed on the spot, 12 others were badly injured, of which two later died. Proponents of double taps would argue that the loss of possible civilian life here was proportional to the need to kill foreign fighters, and could even argue that these were not 'innocent civilians' at all, but militants or militant sympathisers. Nevertheless, double taps violate the well-estab-lished rule that injured combatants (and their rescuers) are effectively removed from combat, making further attacks unwarranted. Denying quarter to the enemy is prohibited by military convention, including the 2007 US Manual for Military Commissions, the Hague regulations and the International Criminal Court (Rome) Statute (which the US signed but did not ratify).[38] But any attempts to peg international humanitarian law violations on ostensibly non-military actors (such as the CIA) operating outside of war zones (as is the case in Pakistan) are not likely to get very far.

Yet the CIA does seem to be sensitive to criticisms about its attacks on rescuers, suggesting that resistance emanating from the communities it targets is not entirely futile, and/or that the possibility of being indicted for war crimes does give pause. For example, it engaged in a curious effort to apparently cover up its attacks on rescuers, even though the main target – Yahya al-Libi – was among them. It was widely reported at the time, and has been subsequently confirmed by various sources, that the first drone attack on 4 June 2012 targeted a small house at 4.00 a.m., and killed five. A dozen people ran to the scene and began to recover the bodies when a second strike killed ten more, this time including Yahya al-Libi, who was reportedly 'observing the rescue operation'.[39] Yahya was clearly a high-value target, but the CIA showed Congressional representatives a video in which he appeared to be alone when he was killed in a strike, rather than presenting a wider sequence of strikes that killed up to 16 confirmed militants. The CIA now regularly screens drone attack footage for House and Senate oversight committees as part of an attempt to introduce more accountability and oversight into its drone programme. The oversight process is set up so that the congressional committee can further investigate strikes that it may have qualms about. 'I don't know that we've ever seen anything that we thought was inappropriate', a senior staffer told the *Los Angeles Times*.[40] Perhaps even 'militants', killed as they are pulling charred bodies out of a decimated house, would raise questions of whether denying quarter and deliberately killing people engaged in the work of helping others is something the US Congress would not want to sign off on.

Whatever the military necessity of targeting possible militants and then targeting their rescuers, who may or may not be militants, the wider effect is to damage the impulse of everyone to help the injured. Living Under Drones reported that not only have those who were in the vicinity of strikes been deterred from assisting at attack sites; this reluctance has found its way into the policies of emergency workers. In North Waziristan, for example, it was reported that one humanitarian organisation instituted a mandatory six-hour delay before reporting to the scene of a drone strike:

'Only the locals, the poor ... will pick up the bodies of loved ones' said the source.[41]

In theory, drones could improve intelligence and minimise collateral damage; in practice, they seem to make it easier to take precipitate action that leads to civilian deaths. But the effects of drone warfare cannot only be measured by body counts. The 'othering' afforded by dispersed decision making and mediated assessments based on partial understandings of complex cultures counters the potential positives that drones look like they could bring to military practice. In the changing rules of the game, this is not war – there are no definable frontlines, military objectives or enemies – and the old verities and logics governing war and peace have been reconstituted. And while we debate the finer legal points, the killings continue, and the situation grows graver still: 2012 casualty figures for the FATA surged dramatically, to 4,052 people including 1,463 militants, double the 2011 figure of 1,957 casualties.[42] Although drone casualties fell in Pakistan in 2013, they continued to grow in Yemen and Afghanistan.

6

Unlegal:
Justifying a Drone War

To say a military tactic is legal, or even effective, is not to say it is wise or moral in every instance. For the same human progress that gives us the technology to strike half a world away also demands the discipline to constrain that power – or risk abusing it.

Barack Obama[1]

How was this 'self-defense'? My family worried that militants would target Salem for his sermons. We never anticipated his death would come from above, at the hands of the United States ... How was this 'in last resort'? Our town was no battlefield. We had no warning – our local police were never asked to make any arrest ... How was this 'proportionate'? The strike devastated our community.

Letter from Faisal bin Ali Jaber to President Obama[2]

War is political, but we often forget that international law is also political. Drone proponents and critics are deeply interested in influencing how rules governing the use of force will ultimately accommodate the introduction of UAVs. The UN Charter enshrines the concept of horse-trading in Article 13(1), where 'encouraging the progressive development of international law and its codification' is duly recognised. Consequently, whether drones are some fundamentally new kind of weapon that need to be considered differently from a legal/ethical perspective, or whether they perform the same roles as existing systems, only better, is a highly divisive topic. The hottest controversy concerns how drones are used by the US military and CIA for carrying out targeted killings. This is an issue that is not exclusive to drones, but is part of a more generalised debate over the meaning of self-defence and is rooted in Israel's use of UAVs for assassinations. A closely related question, however, is whether drones, as a 'risk-free' technology, lower the threshold for using force. Many take the position that although they are exotic, UAVs do not represent something fundamentally different from standoff aerial military systems that are manned rather than remotely piloted. While it is not fair to simply blame the technology, it is clear that drones allow policymakers to use force differently. Would the CIA have been permitted to routinely fly assassination missions using manned aircraft? It seems unlikely.

Laws governing the use of force in the international system protect the sovereignty and integrity of states, which is why states generally uphold them even though it means accepting some constraints on their ability to wage war. The legal regimes include the UN Charter, the laws of war (international humanitarian law) and the Geneva Conventions, and in non-war situations, human rights law and criminal justice. There are also domestic laws, such as the US executive ban on assassination and its prohibition on killing American citizens without judicial process. Since 9/11, when the 'gloves came off', the US has engaged in practices that many have convincingly argued violate international law,[3] although it has offered legal justifications for its actions that reference the universally acknowledged right of a state to self-defence. The myriad ways in which the US has used drones – operated by the civilian CIA, by the military, by a combination of both, or handed off to private contractors; on the conventional battlefields of Afghanistan and Iraq, and in the 'friendly' countries of Pakistan, Yemen and Somalia; against clear enemies and those much more questionable in terms of the threats they pose to the US – involve many legal domains. Added to the mix is the emerging concept of 'lawfare', which seeks to move the practice of monitoring human rights during conflict into a more aggressive mode whereby human rights become a weapon in the arsenal of belligerents, for example by placing legal obstacles on war fighters in order to limit their military options.

The scope and intensity of these various discussions illustrate the importance of what is at stake: the future of norms that structure the use of international violence. Habermas argues that in the current world order international law has been effectively constitutionalised, that is, it is widely accepted that international law takes precedence over the laws of nation-states, and breaches can be punished. He suggests there are 'no more just and unjust wars, only legal or illegal ones, justified or unjustified under international law'.[4] While this may be true, in a realist world order dominated by states pursuing national interests, hegemons such as the US can disproportionately influence the ways in which international law is interpreted. Returning to the foundations of international war law – that is, just war theory – allows us to assess current practice against more traditional normative measures. The serious battering of just war conventions by US drone strikes contributes to a new set of norms that are likely to be regressive to the causes of peace and international stability. The consequences are already apparent: the creation of 'accidental guerrillas' who are mobilised in opposition to the carnage exacted on their communities, asymmetric responses in all the wrong places (such as attempted terrorist attacks in Times Square).

Drones and Just War Theory

In the just war tradition, a war must show both just cause (*jus ad bellum*) and just conduct (*jus in bello*). The purpose of this section is to explore how the key principles of just war theory apply to drone warfare. Our focus is on *policies* that see drones deployed to wield force in the international arena while recognising that their unmanned nature likely affects decision making.

An ostensible cornerstone of the post-1945 world order is that while war is sometimes necessary, it should always be a last resort. The only just causes recognised in the UN Charter are that of self-defence against aggression (Article 51); or to aid victims of aggression when explicitly permitted by the UN Security Council (Article 2(4)). An important test is that force must be proportionate to the problem it seeks to address: 'Only if the universal good predicted to result outweighs the universal ill projected, is the military action justifiable'.[5] As Walzer puts it, 'From a moral standpoint, perhaps this is a war that should be fought – because of the character of the enemy, whose success is a prospect more fearful than war itself'.[6]

Just conduct governs the way force is applied, and finds its legal expression through international humanitarian law, particularly in the Geneva Conventions, as well as associated laws, conventions and treaties. Just conduct seeks to limit the *means* of warfare, for example by restricting certain technologies through treaties (such as those regarding chemical weapons, nuclear weapons and landmines), and so speaks to the specific nature of what drones are permitted to do in the military theatre. In addition, international humanitarian law outlines acceptable *methods* of warfare, which are defined and constrained by the Geneva Conventions' protections for combatants and non-combatants, provisions for limiting civilian deaths, and the designation of some acts as war crimes. In assessing just conduct with regard to UAVs, there are three considerations: the proportionality of the response vis-à-vis the potential or actual threat, the distinctions made between civilians and combatants, and the military necessity of the action taken.

Where the unique unmanned nature of drones comes into play is in calculating the costs of using force. An important curb on going to war has traditionally been the prospect that violence will be reciprocated and all warring parties will face losses. This is recognised in the rules of just conduct that accord significant value to the lives of the opponent. The enemy is not expendable, but possesses clearly codified rights and protections. While there is no assumption that warring sides must be equal in strength, there is recognition that some weapons and methods of fighting cross a moral line. Just conduct demands that commanders seek to minimise losses on *both* sides and balance the expedience of slaughter against the morality of a more qualified defeat. Thus actions must be proportionate to their objectives and minimum force must be applied. Because unmanned operations are risk-free, they remove an important moral brake on war fighting: by reducing the risk taken by the attacker, they lower the threshold for action.

However, commanders must also limit or prevent own-side loss of life. Philosopher Peter Asaro points out that innovations in military technology seek to give one's own side the advantage, and there is no convention that suggests stronger, better-equipped armies must down weapons in order to level the playing field.[7] In fact, commanders who do not seek to limit loss of their soldiers' lives through using available technology – or, states that do not equip their militaries adequately – have some moral culpability. The ethicality of using a superior technology to overcome an enemy lurks in many arguments over controversial politico-military decisions: it informs the endless debate over whether the use of atomic bombs against Hiroshima and Nagasaki was militarily justified, and is embedded more generally in nuclear deterrence strategy. Just war theory is not grounded in firm moral positions, but in conventions that are open to widely divergent interpretations that change over time and circumstance. Just war theorising, as Rigstad puts it, is 'the discursive practice of systematic public reflection and argument about how best to distinguish between ethically justifiable and unjustifiable warfare'.[8]

On the face of things, it is apparent that drones, with their ability to enhance intelligence collection and offer highly accurate targeting, should help the US wage just wars. In a legally defined war situation, 'If the killing is legitimate, the fact that it was targeted, or done by a drone ... makes no difference. If anything, targeted killing is better than untargeted killing, which the laws of war call 'indiscriminate' and a war crime', Luban points out.[9] In theory this may be true: in practice, there are significant caveats. We suggest that drones *do* make a difference because the lack of reciprocity seems to make it easier to use force, while, as we will see below, the targeting, intelligence collection and interpretation of international law that also forms the drone assemblage seems to undermine rather than improve just conduct. In making a more general case that drones contribute to just cause, Brunstetter and Braun suggest that:

> Drones arguably provide a government the means to act on just cause more proportionate in responding to ... a (terrorist) threat because they require minimal on the ground logistics, are less expensive and less invasive than ground troops, and can more specifically target the threat itself – that is, individual terrorists.[10]

Logistics, expense and imposition are part of the package of considerations that go into a decision to wage war in the first place, but in the just war tradition the infinitely more important point to be satisfied is that there is no other option available other than using force. As we will argue below, drones seem to facilitate the US desire to 'wage war' against specific individuals, blurring the lines that define and separate the need to go to war from law enforcement as a more appropriate CT strategy. The problems with drones lie in the way they offer an easy option for one side to use force without fear of reprisal, which may distort the more important principle of using force as a last resort, while the combatant/civilian distinction hinges on how targets are chosen – and here the underlying question is: do targets look different when you are watching them from a safe 7,000 miles away? Put simply, the debate is over what is war, and what is murder. We suggest here that drones have facilitated a fusion of the two ideas into one, that is, the waging of nano-war against specific individuals.

Making the Just Cause Argument

> We will apply the right tools in the right way and in the right place, with laser focus.
>
> John Brennan, Chief Counterterrorism Adviser, July 2011[11]

Since 9/11 the US has used Article 51, the right to self-defence allowed in the UN Charter, to justify its use of force in many corners of the world. As Michael Byers demonstrates, this is the continuation of a trend US administrations have been following since the end of the Cold War. Byers noted that the US used Article 51 to justify using force to 'support democracy' (in Grenada in 1983 and Panama in 1989) and to support 'humanitarian' interventions, such as the illegal NATO 'liberation' of Kosovo in 1999 (which received a degree of *post facto* justification via the UN's 2005 adoption of the Responsibility to Protect.)[12] In response to 9/11, the White House argued it was at war not with a state, but with Al Qaeda and its associates, which opened the door to covert actions and targeted killings outside of designated war zones.[13] As Jonathan Masters, pundit for the Council on Foreign Relations explained it:

> the U.S. right to self-defense, as laid out in Article 51 of the UN charter, may include the targeted killing of persons such as high-level al-Qaeda leaders who are planning attacks, both in and out of declared theaters of war. The administration's posture includes the prerogative to unilaterally pursue targets in states without their prior consent if that country is unwilling or unable to deal effectively with the threat.[14]

Washington's decision to pursue militant networks was widely supported in the wake of 9/11, not only because Al Qaeda was clearly a threat, but also because it suited the interests of other regional hegemons. China and Russia readily accepted a gloves-off approach to 'Islamist' militancy, which they could apply against restive Muslim groups in their own regions. The UK, Israel and Australia had earlier approved of such revisionist interpretations of interstate war and terrorism.[15] Other states that fell under US hegemony – such as Canada, with its heavy economic dependence on the US, and Pakistan, fearful of falling too far afoul of US power – acceded to the US course of action.

While there was powerful support for the US's revisionist view of self-defence, over time the US squandered much support, particularly with its decision to go to war in Iraq (although the Bush administration tried hard to suggest links between the Iraqi regime and Al Qaeda.) The more conventional legal view is that small groups like Al Qaeda are guilty of criminal actions rather than of committing violations against the Westphalian system of states. Abele suggests that the danger in following the US path by citing moral grounds for actions disallowed on legal grounds is that it leads to *ad hoc* arguments 'as governments make their decisions to go to war or to take action against international criminal groups, instead of locating such analyses of state actions within the framework of morally and legally legitimate international relations'.[16]

As Masters noted, the US asserted a right to use force to go after targets in states, whether or not those states had given their consent. It is unclear whether the US interpretation of self-defence can trump the normal understanding of territorial sovereignty, or whether states can even give consent for other states to kill their citizens, as this would seem to contravene the right to life protected by Article 6 of the International Covenant on Civil and Political Rights. However, it may be that US praxis, supported by other powerful international actors, will succeed in having these more radical interpretations of the rules adopted.

Lifting the Assassination Ban

Since 9/11 the US has killed somewhere between 2,835 and 4,108 people in drone strikes in Pakistan, Yemen and Somalia, claiming national self-defence as its core justification.[17] Others suggest these are extrajudicial killing, citing Common Article 3 of the Geneva Conventions that prohibits 'The passing of sentences and the carrying out of executions without previous judgment pronounced by a regularly constituted court, affording all the judicial guarantees which are recognized by civilized peoples'. Indeed, some consider them a form of state terrorism.[18] The American Civil Liberties Union has brought numerous lawsuits against the US government, alleging more generally that:

> The CIA and the military are carrying out an illegal 'targeted killing' program in which people far from any battlefield are determined to be enemies of the state and killed without charge or trial. The executive branch has, in effect, claimed the unchecked authority to put the names of citizens and others on 'kill lists' on the basis of a secret determination,

based on secret evidence, that a person meets a secret definition of the enemy.[19]

Carrying out targeted killings outside of designated war zones has been the subject of many debates within the US administration over the decades. Following the Church Committee's exposure of dubious CIA excesses in the 1950s and 1960s, including attempts to assassinate foreign leaders, in 1976 US President Gerald Ford signed Executive Order 11905, a presidential ban on political assassinations. Subsequent administrations extended Ford's ban to make it even more sweeping. While the order had been occasionally violated, citing self-defence, before the advent of the Predator, such actions were rare. Attitudes seem to have shifted in the early years of the War on Terror: perhaps, Mazzetti suggests, as a consequence of the May 2004 Helgerson Report on prisoner detentions and interrogations. With the possibility that CIA officers could face prosecution for violations of the Convention Against Torture, Mazzetti argues that the CIA took the decision that killing people rather than jailing them was a safer option.

Long before the scandal over torture erupted, the CIA had been pushing hard for a licence to kill: it had been seeking approval to train hit squads to carry out assassinations since December 2001. The idea was approved by the White House but never authorised or implemented by then CIA director George Tenet. Private military company Blackwater prepared assassination teams on the CIA's behalf, but in the end they were never used for fear the operations could be traced back to the CIA. There appears to have been a strong reluctance to send people into the field to kill other people. Somehow, the introduction of armed drones to do the job instead eased the uncertainties. 'Killing by remote control was the antithesis of the dirty, intimate work of interrogation', Mazzetti writes. 'It somehow seemed cleaner, less personal'.[20] Now Blackwater employees were hired to load missiles on to drones in Pakistan rather than conduct assassinations directly. Even those within the CIA were somewhat surprised at the sea change in official attitudes: CIA official Henry Crumpton later wondered why it was okay to drone someone in Yemen or Pakistan but not assassinate them in Paris.[21]

Whatever it was that kept the presidential ban on assassinations in place for so many years has been erased since 9/11. Those that assumed there would be a decline in drone killings when Obama succeeded Bush in office were sorely disappointed. Instead, the number increased significantly as the Obama administration widened its kill lists from beyond the high-value targets of Al Qaeda and Taliban leaders to a more blanket approach that targeted militant networks in Pakistan and beyond. By September 2012, CNN identified covert drone strikes as one of Obama's 'key national security policies', noting he had 'authorized 283 strikes in Pakistan, six times more than the number during President George W. Bush's eight years in office'.[22]

Choosing Targets

The just conduct of a war relies on adhering to the principles of distinction, proportionality and military necessity. While the interpretation of normative principles is problematically subjective, these particular conventions are challenged by the fusion of UAV technology with the US's radical new policies regarding the use of force.

Briefly, distinction refers to the cardinal rule of just conduct to discriminate between combatants and non-combatants. 'Combatants are those authorized – legitimately or not – to use lethal force in exchange for which they forfeit immunity from same', writes Jackson. 'Therefore, only combatants are justifiable military targets'.[23] Proportionality speaks to assessing how much force is morally appropriate to the goal sought, while military necessity balances the equation by allowing that collateral damage can be given a moral pass if the objective is legitimate and civilians are not deliberately targeted. We turn back to these just war conventions as a way of moving beyond the problematically thorny discussions of whether the US is in technical violation of specific international laws.

In conventional wars, distinguishing between combatants and civilians is reasonably straightforward, while the body of laws and analyses surrounding more complicated situations, such as when fighting involves irregular troops, or takes place within states, is well developed. However, there is much ambiguity around whom the US is defending itself against. David Chandler wrote that 'it would appear that the much-publicized abuses of the "war on terror" stem from the Western inability to cohere a clear view of who the enemy are or of how they should be treated'.[24] The excessive secrecy surrounding Obama's 'kill lists' does little to dispel such mysteries. Indeed, 'The most agonizing issue in the drone program', Luban says, 'is figuring out who is an enemy combatant, who is not, and how one knows'.[25]

Much of the legal imbroglio lies in understanding the difference between fighting in a designated war zone, such as Afghanistan or Iraq, and fighting non-international armed conflicts (NIACs) in places such as Pakistan, Somalia and Yemen. Critics of US drone strikes cite legal tests of what constitutes a group that is a party to an NIAC: such tests depend on organisational and command structure, as well as intensity of activity. For legal scholars such as Kevin Heller, a shared ideology does not a targetable network make: 'Because of the horizontally fragmented nature of these [copycat or franchise Al Qaeda] groups the United States cannot be considered to be in a global NIAC with "al-Qaeda"'.[26] Others, including UN human rights expert Christof Heyns, have challenged: 'It's difficult to see how any killings carried out in 2012 can be justified as in response to [events] in 2001'.[27] Violations of international humanitarian law are alleged because, in the case of Pakistan for example, 'the individuals who are being targeted are not directly participating in hostilities, and/or because the high civilian death toll from drone attacks means the force used is neither necessary nor proportionate'.[28] The US and Pakistan authorities have attempted to define the legal context to their own advantage, however, and establishing whether or not US drone strikes in Pakistan are legal very much depends on which strike it is, when it occurred, and who you ask: officially Pakistan denies ever giving permission, but it is well established that at least some within the Pakistan government did green-light attacks, and even supply intelligence to facilitate such missions.[29]

Signature Strikes

The principle of distinction is more clearly violated in the US practice of signature strikes that target unnamed/unidentified individuals simply because they exhibit a behaviour the US considers threatening. Signature strikes can be legal if certain evidentiary tests can be met. Such tests involve how manifest the threat posed is – so for example, suspects planning attacks, handling or transporting weapons, or sited in known training camps and compounds offer compelling signatures of bad intent. But mere propinquity to militant camps or terrorist compounds, or to people identified as threats, or to carrying weapons, are not enough, and the principle of distinction is not met. The US turn to assessing 'patterns of life' as a way to distinguish between enemies and non-combatants fails to meet even the most basic tests.

Heller reports that the first reported signature strike occurred in 2002 when a CIA Predator system operating in Afghanistan spotted a tall man dressed in white accompanied by two other men said to be showing him a degree of reverence. They were in an abandoned mujahedeen complex. The tall man, the CIA hoped, was Bin Laden, and a Hellfire missile was launched. All three were killed, and all three were innocent of any affiliations with Al Qaeda or the Taliban. The Pentagon defended the CIA action on the grounds there were 'no initial indications that these were innocent locals' when the decision to fire was made.[30]

Signature strikes soon became a worryingly common tactic. Heller, quoting a Columbia Law School Human Rights Clinic report *The Civilian Impact of Drones*, notes that in 2011 the US killed 'twice as many "wanted terrorists" in signature strikes than it had in the so-called "personality strikes" in which the target is identified as a specific "terrorist" leader'.[31] In both types of strike, the evidence on which the decision to attack is based remains secret. US officials have admitted that in some cases all military-age males in an area of 'known terrorist activity' are considered fair game – they count in the kill lists as dead enemies 'unless there is explicit intelligence posthumously proving them innocent' according to one well-sourced *New York Times* story.[32] Heller concludes that the secrecy surrounding the US extrajudicial killing programme precludes making a definitive decision on whether many of the signature strikes are legal or not, although in numerous cases they certainly appear questionable.

Signature strikes reportedly ceased in Pakistan in July 2013, amid a general decline in drone attacks in response to increasing Pakistani resistance. However, the practice was stepped up in Yemen, where the US is 'at war' with Al Qaeda in the Arab Peninsula. Signature strikes were first approved and used in Yemen in April 2012, with the Yemeni government approving each strike.

Bad Intelligence

The just conduct principle of proportionality has the utilitarian aim of minimising death and destruction, and has been used to justify assassinations on the grounds that killing someone who threatens peace and security legitimately contributes to the greater good. It underlies much of the logic of drone warfare, specifically the drone's alleged ability to find and kill American 'enemies' with singular discretion and with minimal disruption to the wider community. Walzer suggests that arguments focusing on proportionality are nearly impossible to resolve, and instead we should look at responsibility. Responsibility can be adduced, he says, by asking of a state's soldiers if they were diligent in acquiring the intelligence needed to avoid civilian casualties, if they took care to ensure they aimed at a military target, and what risks they accepted in order to minimise civilian casualties.[33] On the first and second points, the surveillance and persistence capacities of drones can improve intelligence collection, but this capability should not be overrated. It is patently clear that in many strikes the intelligence was dirty, whether it was skewed by informants and governments to serve purposes other than eliminating US terrorist threats, or misused and/or misunderstood by those who used it for their targeting. The drone may indeed hit the target, but whether the target should be hit has been questionable in too many cases.

The reliance on signature strikes owes much to poor intelligence: according to Gregory Johnsen, author of *The Last Refuge: Yemen, al-Qaeda, and America's War in Arabia*, 'The US doesn't seem to have good human intelligence. It's essentially bombing and hoping, which is neither sustainable nor wise'.[34] The irony is that drones *should* and *can* improve the quality of intelligence, but, as Brunstetter and Braun suggest, aerial intelligence only tells part of the story: it cannot replace good intelligence from the ground.[35] From Afghanistan to Somalia, the US has frequently relied on untested and untrustworthy players to help draw up its targeting plans. In the FATA, the International Crisis Group reports that it is believed informants provide false information to the US in order to settle local scores with rival groups.[36] In Somalia, investigative journalist Jeremy Scahill described the situation as a proxy war, with the US relying on warlords and militias to help hunt down US enemies, training and funding African Union troops, and carrying out targeted killings under cover of the Ethiopian invasion.[37] In such cases, scrutinising individual strikes to assess whether they adhere to the just war traditions of self-defence, proportionality and/or discrimination is impossible.

Killing the Peacemakers?

The final piece of the just war tradition is *post ad bellum*, that is, the situation that follows the war. A lot of the activity in the international system – from treaties to war crimes tribunals – aims at re-establishing some sort of mutually acceptable outcome to return the belligerents to peace. There are prohibitions even on assassinating the most heinous of leaders because throughout hostilities, the political process does not end: for violence to cease, the warring parties must be able to parley, and to coexist afterwards.[38] There is a prima facie case to be made for removing military commanders – decapitation of the military leadership can be an important element in winning a war. But in outlining some of the downsides to Israel's targeted killing policy David suggests that, for example,

> when Israel killed Arafat's second in command, Abu Jihad, in 1988 it eliminated not only an individual behind several bloody operations, but also someone on the right wing of the Palestinian Liberation Organization whom many saw as a pragmatist capable of making peaceful compromises.[39]

Over the years we have seen spectacular changes in political fortunes, from convicted 'terrorist' Nelson Mandela's 'long walk to freedom' to the more recent historic handshake between Queen Elizabeth and a former senior IRA figure, Martin McGuiness, in June 2012. In other words, the leaders can lead their soldiers in from the cold when fortunes change, and can make vital contributions to post-conflict stability. Peace works best when it is based on trust. Targeted killing, particularly when it appears indiscriminate, when civilian lives are claimed, when no evidence is presented publicly, has the opposite effect. And when war is seemingly declared against an individual, a commitment to making a wider, lasting peace is not triggered. Who is a target and what the effect of killing him or her will be is in itself an extremely fraught analysis.

Lawfare: Changing the Rules

Daniel Reisner, former head of the IDF's International Law Division, told *Haaretz* in January 2009, 'If you do something long enough, the world will accept it. International law progresses through violations'.[40] What is self-defence, what is a proportional response, who is a combatant, what is a threat? Such questions have long generated controversy, while the unique properties of drones have not made the job of answering them any easier. But the fact that just war doctrine *is* mutable makes how we answer them extremely important. Practices can have large-scale consequences. Policies can be instituted to deliberately stretch and even change international norms. The illegal but somehow 'moral' basis of humanitarian intervention gave impetus to a programme of norm entrepreneurship that resulted in the UN adoption of the Responsibility to Protect and its reconfiguration of state sovereignty. There is a similar long-running move to create international acceptance for targeted assassination, a drone specialism.

Law is rightly evolutionary, changing to meet changed circumstances. Since around 2001 the term 'lawfare' has been used, usually pejoratively, as a way of complaining about efforts to constrain military action through an appeal (often legal) to uphold human rights. Eric Prince, founder of Blackwater, complained about the operational constraints that international law places on military commanders and soldiers in the field: 'I mean, you can't drop a bomb from an airplane in Afghanistan without having a lawyer sign off on it'.[41]

Lawfare's arrival into the national security lexicon speaks to the rising awareness that militaries needed to get ahead of defining the new legal game. The IDF has consistently come up with aggressive interpretations of international humanitarian law, including its 'preventative war' justification for bombing Iraq's Osirak nuclear reactor in 1981, and its arguments concerning who is a lawful combatant surrounding its long-term policy of targeted assassinations. This even extended to the bombing of a police graduation ceremony in Gaza on the first day of the 2008–2009 Gaza War, an example of the temporal nature of threat definition. The IDF's legal team reasoned that police cadets were 'civilians' until they graduated, whereupon they instantly became legitimate military targets as part of a potential 'resistance force' controlled by Hamas. Such militant interpretations of international humanitarian law by Israel have served as a basis and 'proof of concept' for subsequent US interpretations.

These efforts to drive international law in specific directions has been tagged 'state lawfare', defined by Lisa Hajjar as: 'the ways in which government officials construct interpretative edifices to project the lawfulness of policies that deviate from international interpretations of international humanitarian law'.[42] The idea of state lawfare begins to capture the way in which the battlespace and the moral high ground converge as militaries strive to create a new legal space for their conduct by carrying out operations that violate conventional readings of laws regarding the use of force. The danger to global security is twofold: new practices create new precedents, and efforts to rebalance the military advantage conferred by drones create new risks.

On the first point, as Reisner himself acknowledged to *Haaretz*, 'an act that is forbidden today becomes permissible if executed by enough countries'.[43] The logic runs that each violation that goes unpunished suggests that it is at least tacitly accepted – and eventually permitted. In 2012 the Chinese defence ministry defended its use of surveillance drones over the Scarborough Shoal, territory disputed by the Philippines and Taiwan, as 'justified and legal', while in February 2013 its Ministry of Public Security's drug bureau revealed it had considered plans to launch drone strikes against drug trafficker Nhaw Kham, operating in Myanmar. Instead, senior political leaders opted to have him captured inside Myanmar by Chinese police. He was later brought to China to face trial, and executed.[44] The decision against carrying out a visibly judicial killing may signal that China is not willing to support the precedent of targeted assassination being set by the US and Israel.

On the second point, while states endeavour to somehow stake out new readings of just war doctrine at the normative level through their operations, there is the potential for blowback as the actors most disadvantaged by the technology look for ways to turn the tables. Walzer has argued that just war conventions tend to favour the stronger side; consequently, 'it is the weaker side that persistently refuses to fix any limits on the vulnerability of enemy soldiers ... pleading military necessity',[45] while Simpson has suggested that 'in a world where robots were a reality, the only realistic option for a protagonist who did not have the resources to field their own robots would be to go asymmetric'.[46] Convicted Times Square bomber Faisal Shahzad demonstrated how a non-state actor fighting drones might interpret military necessity. An ethnic Pashtun from Pakistan, Shahzad told the judge at his sentencing hearing that his action was taken in response to US actions in Iraq and Afghanistan, and specifically drone strikes in Pakistan: 'I am part of the answer to the U.S. killing the Muslim people'. When asked about killing civilians, including children, he said: 'When the drones [in Pakistan] hit, they don't see children'.[47] Shahzad, although a naturalised American, described himself as a Muslim soldier, a combatant who was willing to take risks for his cause that included a willingness to inflict purposeful collateral damage in violation of current just war conventions and international law, thereby turning the tables on the US's flouting of rules.

This is what happens when you start bending norms. The principle of battlespace reciprocity may never sit easily in a twenty-first century dominated by asymmetric warfare carried out by non-traditional actors against militaries that provide no combatants. The practice of a government singling out 'enemies' within another country's population – and killing them in 'self-defence' – runs roughshod over the matrix of human rights, international humanitarian laws and just war conventions designed to protect civilians from the ravages of armed conflict. The US use of force on the international stage, greatly facilitated by the reach of its UAVs, is based on radically revisionist interpretations of international law, and it may be successful in having these views and practices accepted. While Obama's direct involvement in the US drone programme, approving each target and operation, could end with him in the dock as a war criminal, it is more likely that other political leaders will claim the same privileges, using the same rationales.

7

Killer Robots

When robots rule warfare, utterly without empathy or compassion, humans retain less intrinsic worth than a toaster.

Major General (Retired) Robert Latiff and Patrick McCloskey[1]

The 2013 Tom Cruise sci-fi film *Oblivion* captures what Simpson has called our Frankenstein worry: 'the haunting fear that you will be unable to control what you create and that terrible destruction will ensue'.[2] In several scenes in the film we watch an intelligent drone system of the future confronting human protagonists and trying to decide whether to kill them or not. Cruise's character desperately pleads his case. Unable to make a definitive decision based on its information, the drone switches rapidly between its binary kill/don't kill choice, and finally stands down – as it has been programmed to do. Pure science fiction? While the current generation of drones is still manned insofar as a human operator sits somewhere overseeing the machine and its operations, this prospect of increasingly autonomous systems is not far off, with experts predicting that '"killer robots" – fully autonomous weapons that could select and engage targets without human intervention – could be developed within 20 to 30 years', according to Human Rights Watch.[3]

Research and development into lethal autonomous robotics systems (LARS) continues apace, even as opponents struggle to get such systems banned before they are even built. UN human rights expert Christof Heyns warns that 'war without reflection is mechanical slaughter',[4] while Human Rights Watch named its major report on the subject *Losing Humanity*, arguing that autonomous systems cannot fulfil the tenets of international humanitarian law, or even basic morality. On the diplomatic front, in October 2013 France told the UN General Assembly, 'this is a key debate as it raises the fundamental question of the place of Man in the decision to use lethal force', and called on states to discuss regulation of LARS at the Convention on Conventional Weapons meeting in 2014.[5] Meanwhile, Human Rights Watch is coordinating an international 'Campaign to Ban

Killer Robots', already active across 19 countries, and hopes to mirror the campaign to ban landmines that ended in a widely supported international treaty. There is a one significant difference: what is sought is a pre-emptive blanket ban on technologies that do not yet exist.

If the rhetoric is high, then so too is what is at stake as a multi-billion dollar industry, supported by militaries and governments, goes head to head with grassroots campaigns fighting efforts to change the way wars are fought. Getting states to agree to place limits on their ability to win wars has never been easy. While UAVs are still *mainly* used for watching, they are also used for killing, and who is killed and why is a controversial issue, whether drones are used or not. But the more contentious technological issue pivots on devolving decision-making to the drones themselves. There could be dramatic incentives to deploy killer robots in order to gain military advantage, and indeed, deploying weapons that can spare lives – such as so-called smart bombs that limit collateral damage – is a clearly established moral precept in war. There are also powerful gains to be made both economically and in efficiency, making the case for development a strong one. Defensive drone systems are already in place, such as Israel's Iron Dome missile defence system, and South Korea's sentry robots that monitor its demilitarised zone with North Korea.

The public's Frankenstein worries have been measured repeatedly, and while there is opposition to LARS, it is not as robust as campaigners like to pretend. Indicative is a mid-2013 poll showing that while 55 per cent of randomly sampled Americans opposed the development of autonomous weapons, some 26 per cent were in favour, and 18 per cent undecided. Among the strongest opponents were active duty military personnel, at 73 per cent – perhaps reflecting a reluctance to see their artisanal war-making culture downgraded and made obsolete. But for others these attitudes are amenable to change as they become more comfortable with the benefits of the technology. Some of the current unease is generational, with those growing up in highly technologised environments or with less cultural baggage more willing to accept higher levels of autonomy. Driverless cars are a case in point: they are no longer unthinkable as people develop more confidence in systems that promise to improve comfort, safety and efficiency on the roads.

Among the concerns cited by opponents were:

potential malfunctions, the absence of a moral conscience in machines, whether they could distinguish civilians and combatants, the loss of human control over machines with the power to kill, and the possibility that they could be used by dictators to more efficiently violate human rights.[6]

Many of these concerns can be superficially addressed through effective marketing, which is why the pro-drone/pro-robotics charm offensive is already well underway. Proponents insist that existing UAVs are already saving lives, and that future technological developments will only improve the ugly experience of combat: 'I ultimately believe robots can exercise better ethical judgment than human soldiers in the battlefield', said Ronald Arkin, a robotics expert at the Georgia Institute of Technology in a 2007 interview.[7] UAVs are being pushed as potentially powerful witnesses that could monitor human rights in the battlespace, gather evidence and even deter violations by their very presence, while killer robots are touted as the latest and greatest in a long line of weapons purportedly designed to save lives. If these systems are perceived as a means to kill 'enemies' safely and effectively, the tide could turn in their favour. Many people are already broadly supportive of existing drone policy. In the US, 66 per cent of people polled supported drones strikes abroad,[8] while in a similar poll in the UK, 55 per cent of the British public said it would support a government drone attack on a 'known terrorist' abroad, with support dropping off depending on the amount of collateral damage anticipated.[9]

The promotion of autonomous systems as 'more ethical' than we are is part of a PR effort to create wider acceptance for their development and eventual deployment, not to make a meaningful contribution to international peace and security. Groups such as Human Rights Watch may well insist that 'emotions do not always lead to irrational killing',[10] but such caveats face an uphill battle in an American socio-political climate that valorises technological efficiency and innovation, and equally has shown itself willing to accept the abrogation of civil rights and violations of international law in order to combat 'terrorists'. And so defence research money finds its way to experts like Arkin who suggest that while it may be difficult, engineers can create the architecture, algorithms and apps to build ethical robots. Whether this goal can ever be achieved (which is unlikely) is far less important than its rhetorical role in making the case for developing autonomous systems.

We currently still have a choice over whether to pursue the development of killer robots. Serious ethical and legal problems lie behind the easy claims that the industry is creating better, safer systems. To assess this debate we first look at the threat, as well as the promise, of increased autonomy, before moving on to ask, in the mode of Langdon Winner, whether drones have politics – that is, do they structure human associations and power relations in particular ways? We believe they do, and that their inherently authoritarian qualities could contribute to an international order dominated by technologically advanced regional hegemons that will use their extended, low-cost military reach to impose their specific interests, undermining peace and security in the process.

The March to Autonomy

The British military conducts tests of its UAVs alongside manned aircraft in a private airfield, Aberporth in Wales. The owner of the airfield protested the idea that drones are different: 'We are not reinventing flying, we are simply organising a different form of control. The pilot has not gone walkabout, he is on the ground monitoring the situation in the same way as if he was in the air' he told the *Guardian*.[11] In fact, it is exactly that 'different form of control' – specifically, how much involvement people can and should have with their machines – that may make the drone a potentially disruptive technology. Human Rights Watch distinguishes between: 'human *in* the loop' weapons, wherein the robot can only deliver force with a human command; 'human *on* the loop' weapons, where there is human oversight and override; and 'human *out* of the loop' weapons that do not require any human input at all once they are programmed and deployed.[12] We will come back to the ethical issues, but first we need to explore the concept of autonomy.

For proponents, the very epithet 'drone' is an insult, intimating a machine engaged in some mindless, repetitive task. The term *robot*, which first appeared in a 1920 Czech play, has its roots in the Slavic term *robota* – literally 'serf labour', and figuratively 'drudgery'. Much current drone work is indeed drudgery, for both the machine and its human counterpart, making the push for greater autonomy a matter of improved efficiency and convenience. Autonomy essentially describes the extent to which a machine is able to reason its way towards problem solving when confronted with uncertainty. Artificial intelligence expert and drone critic Noel Sharkey explains that when it comes to machines, '"Think" does not mean to imply processing information in the same sophisticated way as humans. Instead "think" refers to processing "if ..., then" commands'.[13] Such capabilities vary in their gradations and capabilities.

Peter Asaro established a useful continuum for describing levels of autonomy in weapons systems and the associated ethical questions that are raised at each level. He notes that in general 'any system with the capability to sense, decide and act without human intervention has a degree of autonomy'.[14] At one end of the spectrum are familiar technologies such as the landmine that 'decides' to explode in specific conditions. A landmine, Asaro points out, does not choose where it is placed, but the morality associated with any damage its causes is determined by whether it detonates in battle, on a playground or along a disputed border. Moral responsibility therefore lies with the human decisions that led to the deployment of the mine, not with the mine itself. Next up is the so-called 'smart' bomb that finds its way to its target using internal navigation and detonation systems. A failure to reach its target may be the fault of the bomb itself; target selection, however, remains a human concern. Then come technologies such as guided weapons systems, automatic anti-aircraft batteries and automatic anti-ballistic missile (ABM) systems. In particular, ABM systems that were used to safeguard countries from nuclear attack were considered to undermine deterrence (that is, the principle of reciprocity that underwrote the doctrine of mutually assured destruction), and so were subject to treaties limiting their deployment.

Still following Asaro, further along the autonomy spectrum lie systems that 'use sophisticated sensor analysis to select appropriate targets on their own and make decisions about the appropriateness of various actions in response to its situation'. Such systems are already online, although currently they keep a human in the loop to oversee decisions to use lethal force. Asaro reminds us that 'this is not a technological necessity' but a sop to human sensibilities, and writes: 'We can identify the choice to use deadly force against a specific target as a critical threshold along the continuum of autonomy, and one which carries a greater moral burden in the design and use of such a technology'.[15]

The end game, already well under way, is to develop fully autonomous lethal systems to fight on what the USAF calls the 'battlefields of tomorrow'. These are the killer robots that will see decisions over life and death outsourced to computers. In July 2013 the US Navy's X-47B, an UCAV demonstrator, piloted entirely by computers, carried out one of aviation's most difficult tasks: it took off – and more importantly, landed – on an aircraft carrier. The X-47B is a human-on-the-loop system, with the operator monitoring the machine but only stepping in if needed. By 2020 the Navy intends to have a UCAV, potentially with significant stealth capability, that will be able to fly missions up to 1,200 miles away completely autonomously, as well as refuel, relying on its preprogrammed onboard computers. It is already being touted as a game changer that 'will give us what the Navy needs the most, which is presence, which is being not just at the right place at the right time, but the right place, all the time', US Navy Secretary Ray Mabus said after watching the X-47B trials. He added, 'It isn't very often you get a glimpse of the future'.[16]

The successful test of the X-47B signalled an important new step in the pursuit of highly autonomous systems, and although it has been developed purportedly for surveillance, it has a 1,000 lb weapons payload capability. China, Russia, Britain, France and Israel are working on similar projects. In fact, while currently only three countries – the US, Israel and the UK – are known to have operated armed drones, as of December 2011 a US Congress report estimated that 76 countries had drones already, a number that had essentially doubled in seven years.[17] Partly autonomous weapon systems are already also used by South Korea, and India is researching into the development of fully autonomous weapons. Where, when and how autonomy and weaponisation will merge in different programmes is hard to predict, but it is likely to occur sooner rather than later as states vie to gain a military edge. Christof Heyns notes, 'experience shows that when technology that provides a perceived advantage over an adversary is available, initial intentions are often cast aside'.[18]

In its 2009 flight plan, the USAF suggested that greater systems autonomy is all but inevitable as it prepares to respond to emerging threats: 'Future UAS able to perceive the situation and act independently with limited or little human input will greatly shorten decision time. This Perceive-Act line is critical to countering growing adversary UAS threats that seek automation capabilities'.[19] Humans making decisions slow things down, and while the USAF intends to keep humans in the loop to monitor UAV operations, the report asks specifically for political direction on how far it should be prepared to go towards autonomy: 'Ethical discussions and policy decisions must take place in the near term in order to guide the development of future UAS capabilities, rather than allowing the development to take its own path apart from this critical guidance'.[20] The report warns that even operations such as nuclear strikes could be technically feasible before we have decided whether it is politically desirable to automate such actions.

The Good Drone

> [E]veryone who benefits or hopes to benefit from unmanned aircraft ... needs to speak up to better tell the stories of how UAS will help cut costs, save lives and improve everyday activities.
>
> *Forbes Magazine*[21]

When it comes to selling weapons, technologies that promise to make war safer is an old trope. Advocates suggest that, unlike physically and mentally flawed and emotional human beings, robots have nothing to cloud their judgement or undermine their performance and so do a better job. Arkin claims that 9/11 need not have happened if robots were protecting America:

> That was completely avoidable with existing technology. You could easily put an anti-collision system onto a commercial airliner that would usurp control from a pilot if it were on a collision course with a building. But we trust people more than we trust robots.[22]

In 2006 the US Department of Defense began to throw money (not much, given what is at stake – it offered $290,000 over three years initially) at Arkin so that he could study the possibility of building moral behaviour into drones with a view to taking unreliable, unpredictable humans out of the loop. 'The net effect of Arkin's research will be to produce robots that can perhaps act more humanely than humans do under highly stressful conditions, as evidenced by acts such as those committed at Abu Ghraib', ran the news release announcing the project.[23]

The following year, Arkin's 'Case for Ethical Autonomy in Unmanned Systems' appeared in the *Journal of Military Ethics*. The premise of this work was to juxtapose human moral failure against the smooth ethical precision of machines. Arkin began by noting what a monumental disappointment the human race is: 'One could argue that man's greatest failing is being on the battlefield in the first place' he wrote, and went on to offer up a litany of battlefield atrocities and wartime abuses to demonstrate 'the shortcomings humanity exhibits during the conduct of war'.[24] His examples focused chiefly on crimes committed by American soldiers in Iraq and Vietnam, along with assorted moral failures in Korea and during World War II. Arkin presented a deeply Hobbesian vision of a permanently flawed, warlike human race, a judgement made more damning still by its emphasis on the conduct of supposedly morally enlightened US soldiers. The conclusion to be drawn is obvious: since we cannot be trusted, replace our fallible presence in the battlespace with humanitarian drones:

> If we can reduce civilian casualties in compliance with applicable protocols of the Geneva Conventions and the ideals enshrined in the Just War tradition, the result will have constituted a significant humanitarian achievement, even while staring directly at the face of war.[25]

At the operational level, Arkin has proposed that 'ethical governors' could regulate the actions of future lethal systems. Machines would be programmed to first, determine whether the action (attack) they are preparing to undertake is allowed under international humanitarian law and rules of engagement; and if so, only proceed if the action is necessary under operational orders.[26] There are practical and philosophical problems with Arkin's proposal. For a start, writing algorithms that are 'ethical' is a misunderstanding of what morality actually is – a social process that involves weighing conflicting values and multiple courses of action, not a simple binary choice.[27] In Arkin's system the human on the loop is left to play the perverse role of overriding the ethical governor function to allow the machine to carry out actions the human deems militarily necessary – actions the machine itself has flagged as somehow unethical or illegal. Matthias shows that Arkin's promises of 'ethicality' actually refer only to compliance to international humanitarian law as interpreted by the side operating the drone, and to the rules of engagement written by the side operating the drone. A robot programmed to resist military overrides on 'ethical' or 'legal' grounds would run directly counter to the tactical interests of its operators who are, after all, there to win a war. Even in Arkin's world, humans are still required to make the ethical decisions.

Human fallibility is similarly at the centre of efforts to justify an increased reliance on UAVs within the military. MIT expert on human–robot interaction, Missy Cummings, used her experience as a former F/A-18 pilot to try to persuade a Washington audience that systems that allow decision making to be decentralised or devolved are superior to humans acting on their own:

> I am here to tell you as a fighter pilot [that] humans make so many more mistakes at the tip of the spear in the cockpit trying to drop bombs.

Conducting warfare from UAVs where you actually have a group of people along with a lawyer sitting next to you or at least on the radio with you trying make these hard decisions is a much better form of warfare than the kind I fought in and so even though we're scared of UAVs in terms of weaponizing them I will tell you that in doing so we have actually saved a lot of lives.[28]

This last statement is impossible to quantify of course. Firstly, there are inadequate data to support her claim. If we are talking about saving American lives, then compared to 'boots-on-the-ground' services like the Army and Marine Corps, the USAF and USN have tiny casualty rates.[29] Researchers have even found that 'in fact, Naval and Air Force personnel in Iraq [had] a much lower death rate than young men in the [US] civilian population'.[30] If we are talking about non-American lives 'saved' then the claim is even more difficult to support. Cagey about body counts anyway, the USAF does not keep (it says) separate body counts for drone and manned missions. If we turn to the CIA use of drones, Alston, after conducting an extensive review of the available statistics for his report on the CIA's targeted killings programme in Pakistan, concluded: 'we simply don't know how many people have been killed in drone strikes and how many of those killed have been civilians', although the evidence showed that civilian deaths occurred frequently enough to be 'legally problematic'.[31] And there is no way to quantify the likelihood that many of the attacks would not have taken place at all if the CIA did not have drones in the first place. A final point is that lethal decisions (and mistakes) don't just occur in the cockpit, but can happen at many points along a kill chain: a US military report blamed 'inaccurate and unprofessional' drone operators who provided faulty intelligence that led to the deaths of up to 23 civilians in Uruzgan province, Afghanistan in 2010 (the attacks themselves were carried out by helicopter-launched Hellfire missiles).[32]

We can concede that computers may make fewer mistakes in carrying out their programmed functions, but the claim that drones save lives is difficult to prove. It is unlikely that any programmer could model the complexities of international violence and write the algorithms sufficiently well that they could imbue drones with anything approaching a moral architecture, although blind adherence to some aspects of international law is perhaps possible. However, given the US tendency to flout international law, there is no reason to believe even this would provide much of a solution.

The Trouble with Robots

Contra Arkin, Ryan Tonken argues that from a moral perspective, the robots we design should be pacifists. Technologies and their uses are constructed by societies, and if we want to prevent war, we should not build killer robots in the first place. He draws a comparison with how we might feel about a robotic torture machine. It may be that a machine could torture humans more 'effectively', for example by being finely calibrated to deliver levels of pain that stop short of permanent injury or death; but the fact that torture is considered immoral is hardly diminished by the fact it is done by machine. While military technology is essentially aimed at killing people, Tonken argues for a value-sensitive design approach that takes things like ethics, conscience and dissent into account: 'if left untouched by a human operator, the hand grenade would not harm and kill humans, although it was created for that purpose. The same cannot be said for the autonomous lethal robotic system' which will be preprogrammed to decide who lives and who dies.[33]

A more practical concern is that such systems will never be able to satisfy the tenets of international law and meet just war considerations such as distinction, proportionality and military necessity. Can such systems distinguish between friend and foe? Do they offer a proportionate response to threat? Is there sufficient accountability when things go wrong? On such questions, technology falls short. While, for example, facial recognition systems can sort people into categories based on available factual knowledge, battle often requires subjective judgements and guessing at intentions is something even humans do with only varying success. The Human Rights Watch report cast doubt on the idea that accountability and meaningful justice are possible where killer robots are employed: 'it is unclear who should be held responsible for any unlawful actions [a robot] commits. Options include the military commander that deployed it, the programmer, the manufacturer, and the robot itself, but all are unsatisfactory'.[34] Ironically, the autonomous lethal system lacks the one thing a moral agent has: autonomy. 'With machines we have a guarantee of perfect obedience, which also means that immoral commands will be executed without any final moral deliberation in the form of a soldier's conscience coming into play', Matthias argues.[35] Because a robot cannot be held responsible for its actions, a moral vacuum opens up. Machines can only be accused of errors, not war crimes.

Do Drones Have Politics?

Michael Toscano, president of the Association of Unmanned Vehicles Systems International, the industry's major lobby group, pushed technological boosterism to a new extreme when he claimed that by using drones in agricultural roles, 'you can almost do away with starvation on the planet'.[36] Such boasts would sound familiar to Langdon Winner, who began his classic treatment of the philosophy of technology by noting 'in controversies about technology and society, there is no idea more provocative than the notion that technical things have political qualities'.[37] We are barraged daily by claims that technology improves lives, and when these claims come from policymakers, military planners and corporate interests we should interrogate them closely for their political implications.

Winner organised the long-running debates over the relationship between technology and society into three broad categories: first, the purpose for which technology is designed; second, how its creation and use are socially, culturally or politically constructed (i.e. its social origins); and third, whether the technology as an artefact has inherent political properties – that is, does it have within itself characteristics that incline it towards a particular structuring of power relationships.

We have covered much of this ground already in relation to drones. In the calls to ban the research and development of LARS, or to demand that robots be pacifists, we recognise the debate over purpose – in other words, that design *is* decision to some extent – and that we should assess whether the embrace of drones is a good thing for society. The second debate, on the social origins of technology plays into this: developers and manufacturers belong to a military-industrial complex that looks to maximise profits by selling technologies to the state, while the state funds and encourages such R&D in its relentless quest to gain military security. To pretend that technologies emerging from this nexus are somehow politically neutral and therefore outside political, ethical and legal concern seems naïve, although such claims are quite common. Winner looked at mechanical tomato harvesters, which were researched in the academies, funded by governments, and purchased by only those businesses large enough to make a substantial investment. In a few decades they transformed the business of growing tomatoes and everything that underpinned it, from economic relationships to the agricultural landscape, to the tomatoes themselves, which were scientifically altered to better conform to the needs of the machines. 'What we have here is an on-going social process in which scientific knowledge, technological invention, and corporate profit reinforce each other in deeply entrenched patterns that bear the unmistakeable stamp of political and economic power', he concluded.[38] This statement seems applicable to UAV development.

But it is the final category – whether artefacts have inherently political qualities that structure power relations in particular ways – that is the most intriguing to open up in relation to drones. Here, Winner used Lewis Mumford's authoritarian/democratic binary to set the stage: authoritarian technologies are 'system-centered, immensely powerful, but inherently unstable', whereas democratic technologies are 'man-centered, relatively weak, but resourceful and durable'.[39] Winner used the sailing ship, an example also used by Plato and Engels, to illustrate an authoritarian technology: 'Because large sailing vessels by their very nature need to be steered with a firm hand, sailors must yield to their captain's commands; no reasonable person believes that ships can be run democratically'.[40] A more democratic technology could be something like solar panels, installed by householders to help them generate electricity independently of the electricity grids that require large-scale organisation to function and can cause widespread misery when they fail. At its most rigid, the argument runs that 'the adoption of a given technical system *requires* the creation and maintenance of a particular set of social conditions as the operating environment of that system',[41] while milder forms suggest more of a practical compatibility with, rather than a requirement for, such social adaptations.

Drones are tools used by individuals to extend their senses, but they also belong to networks, making them system-centred, and given the importance of human–machine interaction here they have cyborg qualities as well. Such a complicated artefact presents some analytical challenges, and it is useful to consider where they sit on the spectrum relative to other weapons. The AK-47 assault rifle, for example, is a democratic technology. Although it was deliberately proliferated by the totalitarian Soviet state to its allies and friends, it was designed for individual use and its qualities – cheap, easy to copy, use and maintain – eventually put it into the hands of even child soldiers in Africa and Asia.[42] Chivers' work suggests that it is not the use of a weapons system per se, but the meaning of that usage as it expands and exists over time, and with the AK-47 we clearly see a democratisation of violence that made guerrilla war easier. Over time, the AK-47 probably contributed more to international anarchy than to the stability of the Soviet empire. Less democratic, because it is more system-dependent, is a manned fighter aircraft like the F-15. The aircraft itself is a highly technologised part of a wider system, while its pilot belongs to a chain of command, so the assemblage is not democratic. But pilots sometimes make decisions that align with their own agency that run counter to their orders. For example, during the Korean War half of the F-86 pilots belonging to the famous 'MiG-Killers' of the 51st Fighter Wing never fired their weapons, explaining that they preferred to stay alive rather than engage their enemy.[43] We can also consider the scores of pilots over the years that have defected with their aircraft, actions that are usually of interest more for their political significance than for the impact on military operations. In any case, pilots defy orders frequently enough to suggest they are masters of their machines and their destinies.

While it depends on the specific system, smaller, simpler UAS, particularly micro drones, are already following the AK-47's trajectory and finding their way into the hands of non-state groups. In 2011, Libyan rebels used backpackable Scout ISR systems made by Canadian company Aeryon for offensive operations, prompting a Canadian police investigation into possible export control violations. Hamas developed a UAV programme of sufficient concern that Israel attacked suspected development centres in Gaza during Operation Pillar of Defense in late 2012. Israel has shot down five drones over the past decade, mainly launched by Hezbollah operating from inside Lebanon.[44] Whether begged, borrowed or stolen, drone technology is already available to the masses. There are parallels to be drawn with the early personal computer industry, as much a product of the Californian hippy counter-culture as the US military's quest for a communications system that could withstand a Soviet nuclear decapitation strike on the political leadership. Like its 'homebrew' computing forebears, the DIY-drone community shares software code and modelling tips freely, and its members can be found on any given Sunday flying their remote-control aircraft, whether home-made or purchased from local electronics retailers. The early personal computer hobbyists started by giving us 'PONG' in 1972 – it didn't look at first blush like a disruptive technology.

It is undeniable that the UAV exhibits some democratic tendencies. The question is how far it is possible – or permitted – to go, and whether more authoritarian system control will become evident or totalising. Apart from their qualities as singular machines, drones are also deeply embedded in networks. Here we see multiple inputs of information and so a diffusion of authority that might be more akin to the 'wisdom of crowds', and might even be 'more democratic' in its dispersal of power. But such systems also reduce transparency. Digitised technologies have political qualities that appear to us as regulatory and voluntary, although they are deeply controlling. The case made by Larry Lessig is that programming code exerts a normative force, and to enter a system means submitting to its invisible rules, for example, by entering a password. 'Controls are imposed for particular policy reasons, but people experience these controls as natural. And that experience ... could weaken democratic resolve'.[45] As Matthias explains, whether autonomous or human-controlled, a killer robot does not resolve ethical problems, it merely codifies a set of responses that may or may not be appropriate to the situation. Whatever responses have been programmed reflect the perceptions of the programmer and his brief, and the thinking that went into the coding is likely to be 'invisible' to us, and therefore beyond democratic scrutiny and control. For example, networked kill chains that include data collected from multiple systems and sources make identifying and assigning ultimate responsibility problematic. Furthermore, the UAVs are embedding within the highly hierarchised, bureaucratic and inflexible structures of militaries: we have noted that the USAF, for one, is struggling to change itself culturally to adapt to UAV systems – a clear case of an organisation changing to accommodate a technology.

Finally there is the cyborg problem of human–machine interaction, where the attempt to fit humans to their machines, rather than vice versa, is apparent in these first iterations of twenty-first century UAVs. Williams quotes Gray's 1997 work on postmodern war: 'the line between the machine, body and object, has never been so vague as it is in contemporary man-machine weapons systems'.[46] Like the tomatoes engineered to meet the needs of the tomato harvester, soldiers will be required to adapt to their machines, which may alter the original goals of both the human and the machine. Such rhizomic structures, in surveillance assemblages at least, have been characterised by Lyon as 'decentralized, polycentric, and only very partially predictable'.[47]

UAVs run the gamut in size, mission and complexity, although once launched, even the largest UAV, the Global Hawk, requires only a two-person crew to operate it – and it can even fly itself to a reasonable extent. However, drone missions can span periods of time that extend beyond the physical capabilities of their operators, so crews must be rotated, making the system personnel-hungry. Writing about the need to constantly 'refresh' UK Reaper crews, Williams argues:

> This interchangeability introduces the idea that the bodies of the aircrew are becoming less important. Instead they perform more like machine components; their eyes and operational skills being privileged within this assemblage whilst the rest of their flying abilities are increasingly replaced by the technologies that enable the airframe to maintain flight and engage with the spaces surrounding it without active control.[48]

Williams develops the idea that the Reaper's visual suite – zoom, night vision, infrared, etc. – gives the machine sight capabilities that are better than those of a human, while the humans we keep in the loop undermine these capabilities. For example, we blink: 'This human inability to remain unblinking upsets the desire within military circles to enable persistent presence through the imposition of the loitering, continually gazing, vision-machine', she writes.[49]

The Message of Drones

'"Very good," Grand Duke Mikhail once remarked of a regiment, after having kept it for one hour presenting arms, "only *they breathe*."'[50] From a machine-biased perspective, it is the human that undermines its performance. As in the past, what the human operator brings to the battlefields of tomorrow falls short of the perfection military commanders seek, a perfection that they now turn to machines to provide. Having been bested by machines when it comes to morality, rationality, trustworthiness, accuracy and flying skills, the human component of the UAV assemblage is threatened with a future where he or she is judged to be worth less than a toaster, which at least can be cannibalised for parts. The machine rejects the human as increasingly superfluous, if not a downright nuisance. In McLuhan's tetrad – his suggested approach to analysing media to uncover their unobvious effects – this is the reversal, the flip, the point where the artefact turns back on its user: in creating ways to save humanity, we create a machine that renders humanity inferior to it.

As for the larger effects on social relations, at the extreme, fully autonomised systems should in theory make no demands beyond what is needed to take care of the systems themselves. (Indeed, this was what the Tom Cruise character was doing in *Oblivion*.) This leaves the system available to authoritarian control. Barack Obama already receives his weekly kill lists, and on his say a small number of CIA operatives enable a drone somewhere to carry out his command. Decision making, evidence, target selection, legality, are tremendously opaque. The programmer and his political leader replaces the soldier; a technocratic society supplants a republic; and the preprogrammed morality is imperialistic insofar as it represents only one side's interpretation of what is ethical, legal or just. Schmitt's motorised partisan is brought to mind:

> all that's left is a transportable, replaceable cog in the wheel of a powerful world-political machine that puts him in the open or invisible war and then depending on how things are developing, switches him off again.[51]

The phrase commonly, although inaccurately, attributed to McLuhan – 'we shape our tools and thereafter they shape us' – crystallises the essentially iterative relationship between technologies and users that we should take into account.[52] Further expanding on this, Neil Postman argued that every technology has

> a philosophy which is given expression in how the technology makes people use their minds, in what it makes us do with our bodies, in how it codifies the world, in which of our senses it amplifies, in which of our emotional and intellectual tendencies it disregards.[53]

While digitised technologies often seem to perform in democratic ways, drones that fight wars are authoritarian technologies. In 1987 the International Committee of the Red Cross flagged its concerns over the automation of the battlefield and warned that: 'all predictions agree that if man does not master technology, but allows it to master him, he will be destroyed by technology'.[54] Complicated decision-making processes will be flattened so they can be codified and outsourced to machines which will amplify our ability to kill without cost, while paying no heed to our emotional and intellectual 'tendencies'. The remaking of the world's militaries to fit UAVs should be attempted with a caution informed by a much fuller awareness of possible large-scale consequences, and killer robots *should* be banned.

8

From Man O' War to Nano-War: Revolutions in Military Affairs

Once, I remember, we came upon a man-of-war anchored off the coast
... there she was, incomprehensible, firing into a continent. Pop, would
go one of the eight-inch guns; a small flame would dart and vanish, a
little white smoke would disappear, a tiny projectile would give a feeble
screech – and nothing happened. Nothing could happen. There was
a touch of insanity in the proceeding, a sense of lugubrious drollery
in the sight; and it was not dissipated by somebody on board assuring
me earnestly there was a camp of natives – hc called them enemies! –
hidden out of sight somewhere.

Joseph Conrad, Heart of Darkness[1]

In the legitimate struggle against terrorism, too many criminal acts
have been re-characterized so as to justify addressing them within
the framework of the law of armed conflict. New technologies, and
especially unmanned combat aerial vehicles or 'drones', have been
added into this mix, by making it easier to kill targets, with fewer risks
to the targeting State.

Philip Alston, UN special rapporteur on extrajudicial,
summary or arbitrary executions[2]

The UAV has clearly effected change across a range of military activities.
It is often seen as forming a *revolutionary* military technology, potentially
transforming the nature of warfare. It may be in the nature of revolutions
that any degree of hindsight seems to reveal them as somehow hollow,
failing to deliver on the radical change that they promised. The new
boss seems much the same as the old boss. With regard to revolutions

in military affairs the same *post facto* tristesse seems to apply. The shiny technology arrives on the battlefield, promising much, but wars, it seems, go on much the same, with substitutions and adjustments rather than transformations. The German blitzkrieg, a classic, even clichéd, instance of a military revolution, was based on rapid manoeuvring of the new(ish) armoured forces, but the latest thinking is that it emulated just what Prussian generals had been doing since Frederick the Great, and while delivering victory after extraordinary victory on the Eastern Front, God remained firmly on the side of the big battalions, and the war was lost.

Nevertheless, the idea of the transformatory event in military affairs has maintained its appeal. According to John F. Guilmartin, Jr, 'It has been over 125 years since Charles Oman referred to the developments that enabled the armies of Habsburg Spain and Austria to halt the westward advance of the Ottoman Turks between 1529 and 1532 as the *military revolution* [my emphasis] of the sixteenth century'.³ Subsequently this term has become a staple of military historical analysis.

The concept of the military revolution is usually tied up with an innovation in military technology, but whether the technological innovations often identified in such discussions as the precipitator of such significant change are genuinely revolutionary in their military impact has often been seen as controversial. The technological component usually arrives as part of a package of social, cultural and doctrinal change, and so addressing simple causes of such complex historical processes can become problematically reductionist.

Lieutenant Colonel W.L. Pickering of the Canadian Armed Forces is one scholar who introduces a note of caution regarding what we can label the RMA: 'Technology has been the key enabler, but has not in itself driven an RMA, although it often spawned the underlying social and economic conditions that fostered an RMA. It was the intelligent application of the technology of the day, rather than the development of new and novel technology, that was most important'.⁴ He cites the efficiency of the Roman Legion, the power of the Mongol cavalry, the success of the Swedish Army in the Thirty Years War and Napoleon's continental dominance as instances of such revolutions, driven less purely by technological innovations, and more by their refinement, combination and use according to an effective military doctrine. He also notes, however, that as technology has grown more sophisticated it has arrived on the battlefield ever sooner after its development. Thus, as the product moves more rapidly from the lab to the battlefield, the consequent change may be becoming more immediate, more visible.

Even so, it is reasonably clear that the introduction of new military technology can have, and has had, large-scale consequences both on and off the battlefield, both expected and unlooked for. Whatever the subtleties of the argument, the technological component of rapid military advancement can be significant. Barry Watts, in a 2011 report for The Center for Strategic and Budgetary Assessments, describes two twentieth-century instances of such change: firstly, 'The advent of motorization, the airplane, and chemical weapons during the First World War', along with the 'maturation' of this technology in World War II in the form of blitzkrieg, strategic bombing, and the replacement of the battleship by the aircraft carrier as the dominant naval weapon. For him, the second instance came with nuclear-armed ballistic missiles. The extension of the military's reach, across continents and into civilian lives far from the battlefield, seems an obvious and significant shift, and one firmly sited at the door of a technological innovation: the aeroplane, and later, the missile.[5]

The most recent occasion for such a revolutionary development in military equipment has become known simply as *The* Revolution in Military Affairs, which began in the 1980s and may still be in process. This particular RMA, the RMA of our times, has arisen from the introduction of digital electronic technology into the battlefield, which has had a huge impact across the range of military activities, from communications and logistics to surveillance and weaponry. In particular, the improvement in accuracy allowed by the new technology has resulted in a vast reduction in the number of weapons needed to destroy a given target: PGMs allow something approaching the one shot, one hit ideal. Watts describes the dramatic Soviet perception of the onset of this revolution as follows:

As Marshal Nikolai Ogarkov, then chief of the Soviet General Staff, observed in 1984, these developments in non-nuclear means of destruction promise to 'make it possible to sharply increase (by at least an order of magnitude) the destructive potential of conventional weapons, bringing them closer, so to speak, to weapons of mass destruction in terms of effectiveness.'[6]

This Soviet understanding of what was going on was brought to a wider US audience in a report originally published in 1992 for the US Office of Net Assessment. Author Andrew F. Krepinovich described this Russian view that the new technologies formed what they termed a 'reconnaissance-strike complex (RSC)':

> This network of networks (command and control, data acquisition, fusion, and dissemination, and weapon systems) can, theoretically, engage a wide array of critical targets at extended ranges with a high degree of accuracy and lethality.[7]

He goes on to describe how Soviet thinkers saw the outcome of this process: 'Entire countries will become the battlefield. The distinction between "front lines" and "rear areas" will be blurred beyond recognition. In future wars, there will only be "targets" and "non-targets."'[8]

The early military effects of this technological development have been seen in the early phases of the wars in Iraq, as the western powers swept aside the Iraqi forces despite their significant numbers, rapidly attaining their immediate military objectives (their broader political objectives proved to be another matter). Iraqi targets were struck wherever they were from the beginning, rather than being taken on in sequence. The wider significance of this change in the order of magnitude of efficiency in the ability to destroy a given target is not immediately obvious. It is nevertheless clear that in military terms it permits smaller numbers of units (aircraft, bombs, etc.) to achieve effects that would have taken a much larger effort in the pre-digital age. Drones are perhaps just the latest iteration of this technology. This military step change is part of what is under analysis here, but the intention is also to move the debate on to a larger board in order to address the question not simply of how technology (in this instance, UAVs) changes military affairs, but also how it impacts more widely on human society. However, the blurring of the lines, the extension of the battlespace to include all potential 'targets', that the Russians foresaw, seems to be coming to pass in the current UAV wars.

McLuhan and Technological Change

If we are to consider the impact of the UAV, we can consider it in two modes. The first is its impact on the battlefield: its transformatory contribution (or otherwise) to the way wars are now fought. The other approach is to consider the UAV's impact on human society on a grander scale. Marshall McLuhan's method in the study of the impact of a given technology instructed that we should focus not on what it is or does, but rather on how the medium 'shapes and controls the scale and form of human association and action'. We should look at, that is, the *medium* as the message.[9]

Interestingly, McLuhan was writing in 1964 at what he thought was the beginning of a new technologically driven social revolution, as he saw that the previous print-made world 'now encounters a new electric technology, or a new extension of man'.[10] So for McLuhan what was important about the 1960s was the spread of electronic technology that brought along the ubiquity of the TV above all, but also the innovation of the computer, the wider effects of which McLuhan did not live to see but which form the basis for the current RMA, as well as a wider social transformation.

McLuhan characterises this change from print to electronic communication in interesting ways. For him print is not simply a highly efficient way to spread information, but it also models a mindset, and by so universally modelling a way of thinking it does something to bring that way of thinking into existence, with all that follows as a consequence of that way of thinking being, in a sense, the real content of that medium of print. McLuhan characterises print culture as fundamentally analytic, one with a 'place for everything and everything in its place'. But it is also productive of a culture in which the individual is newly privileged, broken 'out of the traditional group' by a new private engagement with the technology of knowledge. Simultaneously print provides a model and tool for 'repeatable precision' that allows the '[adding] of individual to individual in massive agglomerations of power'. Print thereby provides the possibility of the modern state and the corporation. It also produces what McLuhan characterises as the possibility of cool detachment, disinterestedness, the 'power to act without reaction'.[11]

For McLuhan this disinterested cool world contrasts sharply with what was happening when he was writing in 1964. The world of print was then encountering a revolutionary new technology, and he claimed that 'Electric means of moving information are altering our typographic cultures as sharply as print modified medieval manuscript and scholastic culture'. Under these new conditions the fragmentation of the tribe into individuals that literacy produced (and with it the modern world) is reversed: 'Electric light and speed pour upon him, instantly and continuously, the concerns of all other men'. In the new age of post-literate information propagation, 'He becomes tribal once more. The human family becomes one tribe again'.[12]

This is the famous global village for which McLuhan is perhaps best known, and it is not a place of cool detachment. In a mode resonant for our times, in *The Gutenberg Galaxy* he describes it as follows:

> We shall at once move into a phase of panic terrors, exactly befitting a small world of tribal drums, total interdependence, and superimposed co-existence. [...] Terror is the normal state of any oral society, for in it everything affects everything all the time. [...] In our long striving to recover for the western world a unity of sensibility and of thought and feeling we have no more been prepared to accept the tribal consequences of such unity than we were ready for the fragmentation of the human psyche by print culture.[13]

'Print technology', he writes in his later work *The Medium is the Massage*, 'created the public. Electric technology created the mass'.[14] We are (or *were*, in McLuhan's day?) all doing, hearing, thinking the same thing at the same time, addressable as a unitary audience, easily manipulated as a unitary force. Subject, as Foucault might put it, to an effective biopolitics. But clearly the acceleration of technological change has continued since McLuhan. His version of the electric era's effects may already have been superseded by a new era, the era of the silicon chip, of parallel processing, of the huge momentum of change announced by Moore's law: formulated at about the same moment (1965), Moore's law identified a doubling of processing power of integrated circuits every two years, a trend that has continued in the intervening years, leading to the pocketable computers we call smartphones in every pocket and a vast cloud of information and entertainment available, almost instantly, from those devices.

The apparently centrifugal push of these tools towards creating a newly refragmented audience, watching and listening to different things, is surely a change from McLuhan's centripetal, unifying effects. Or is it? If that was the case, why did a billion people watch 'Gangnam Style'? The new technology has unravelled the mass audience of the TV age, to be sure, in that we have a multitude of choices as to what to watch and when, but somewhat counter-intuitively in some sense we all seem to be choosing to do the same things. And given the corporate consolidation in the tech field perhaps it is not surprising. We search through Google, we watch through its subsidiary YouTube, we shop through Amazon, we watch movies and TV through Netflix. And we do we do it on our Apple iPhones, or an Android-operated rival, probably from Samsung. And this is true almost the world over, reflective of a globalised, corporatised, single marketplace.

Everything we do is noted, measured, recorded and used by those corporations to access us more effectively. And then we tell each other all about it on Facebook, tapping in the data on a phone that along with servicing our needs, indeed as a part of that servicing, tells anyone with access almost exactly where we are. As recent revelations have shown, governments, through agencies such as the National Security Agency (NSA) and Government Communications Headquarters (GCHQ), are able to access all those data. Private life has never been more public, and if that loss of the private is part of the McLuhanite effect of the new digital age then, along with the CCTV camera in the mall and on the street corner, the UAVs circling overhead with their unwearying cameras seem to be another component of that change.

McLuhan's pointer towards the prevalence of terror in the new age may seem prophetic, given the public atmosphere regarding the terrorist threat post 9/11, but in the section on weapons in *Understanding Media*[15] McLuhan also offers an insight that seems relevant to the discussion of the drone. He notes that the characteristic of the electric age of information is 'more power with less and less hardware', in which 'all technology can plausibly be regarded as weapons'. Such weapons are not extensions of our limbs like swords, but '[an extension of] our central nervous system'. Weapons in our times are information gatherers and processors in a global system. Again perhaps prophetically, McLuhan sees that this world cannot be satisfied with a balance of power between states in a fragmented world. Victory means what he calls 'the existence and the end of one society to the exclusion of another'. The exponential growth of processing power that has occurred since McLuhan was writing has only magnified the technological revolution he was announcing. In the digitised world of today, everything is somehow revealed as information – the DNA of reality. This is a perception that holds out the promise of manageability: the connections can be made, the system understood. The world, to actors informed by this logic, with the right information-gathering tools at their disposal, can be grasped and, in turn, shaped. The strong predilection of the US, the sole superpower and dominant culture on the planet, for this kind of technology suggests that they think so, or at least that there has been a powerful set of such ideas circulating in US institutions during the last 20 years or so.

UAVs – with their sophisticated information-gathering capacity, along with their small but effective PGMs, their persistent border-ignoring presence, their extension of the nervous system of a pilot perhaps 10,000 miles away to reach out and monitor or kill individuals, sometimes on the basis of a very biopolitical concept of so-called 'patterns of life' surveillance – seem a very apt expression of this new age, a symptom of and a window into the times in general, and their use is proliferating.

In order to assess the potentially revolutionary nature of the UAV, what it is that they change, what behaviour it is that they enable, it is useful to consider what earlier iterations of the new and even revolutionary have produced in military matters, and beyond.

Sea-Based Artillery

Commander James J. Tritten of the US Navy is aware that, as he puts it, 'The basic model of an RMA, with technology in the leading role, is incomplete. RMAs are also stimulated by doctrinal development'. He notes, by way of example, that the Napoleonic RMA was 'probably more a product of political, social and economic conditions than any specific military technology'. Nevertheless he is able to assert that:

> A clear-cut example of a traditional RMA caused by technology was the introduction of naval artillery during the age of sail. Naval artillery changed the fundamental nature of war at sea from ramming, boarding and hand-to-hand fighting to standoff destruction by shipboard artillery. During the Spanish Armada's defeat in 1588, the Spanish combat concept focused on boarding enemy ships in a general melee. The English kept their distance using long-range artillery to wreak havoc on the Armada.[16]

But he also adds, pointing to the more unlooked for effects of this technological shift, that 'The revolution in sea-based artillery required professional navies to master its potential, and privateers soon disappeared. The end of privateering and using commercial ships in fights caused a major naval-warfare paradigm shift'.[17]

This is useful for the purposes of our analysis here, because in McLuhanite terms what we are doing is raising our gaze from the effect of the sea-borne cannon arising from its use in battle to the larger socio-economic effects of the promulgation of this technology. There is much more to it than the splintering of wooden hulls at a range that avoids the risk of, or need for, boarding the enemy vessel. This may be a more effective way for a navy to fight, but beyond that local effect it may be seen that behaviour changes as a result of that possibility. Tritten's observation that the complexity of producing and fighting the new warships meant that only professional navies could deploy the technology effectively, leads, as he puts it, to the end of the privateer. But implicit in that statement is a larger truth: states now control the world's oceans – and a handful of western states at that. What do they do with this control? At the relatively modest cost of sending an essentially invulnerable gunboat, as opposed to marching an army, they enforce their economic will around the globe. Thus it might be said, albeit with a touch of McLuhanite flamboyance, that the message of the medium of sea-based artillery in the age of sail, was empire. Equally, it might be said that without significant changes in a range of fields, from banking to agriculture, European empires would not have happened. It is unlikely that these naval changes alone would have formed a sufficient condition for empire, but it might be that they were a necessary one.

The Railway

Such unpredicted, and possibly unpredictable, effects can work in other ways too, resulting from the impact of an apparently non-military technology as it is moved into the military arena. For example, consider Colonel Pickering's observation:

> Humble barbed wire, designed for cattle control, proved equally capable of herding large numbers of soldiers into killing zones for these weapons. Railroads, designed for commerce, were able to rapidly move huge armies to the front, and reinforce and sustain them – in effect, to feed raw material to the killing machines.[18]

A given technology can have effects in arenas far beyond their intended application. In the case of the railway, some historians (notably A.J.P. Taylor in his 1969 work, *War by Timetable: How the First World War Began*[19]) have even seen it as the *cause* of World War I, such that such total war might be seen as the outcome of the railway's development. It should be acknowledged that other historians (for example David Stevenson[20]) have taken a less narrowly deterministic view, seeing the railways and the mechanistic nature of mobilisations they enabled as a factor, but not a simplistically or independently causal one.

However, the reasoning behind Taylor's assertion is relevant to this discussion. He was interested in the railway's role in producing what he saw as an *inadvertent* conflict: once one side started to mobilise the others must also mobilise due to the time-consuming complexity of the railway transport process. The decision to go to war was never made – only the decision to mobilise, which due to the nature of the technology involved (in this case railways) inadvertently entailed going to war. He saw a parallel with the nuclear weapons of the age in which he was writing. In other words, he saw such weapons as out of the control of their users, believing that their existence had a logic and a momentum of their own, and that their wider effects might prove to be the annihilation of the human race rather than the stalemate politicians hoped for. As it turned out the Cold War ended without the two sides having gone to war directly, although the annihilation that such weapons threatened still remains a possibility – the logic of the weapon poised short of its conclusion.

Blitzkrieg

The idea of the German lightning war as a transformational expression of a new military capacity stems from its extraordinary rapid success in 1940 against the dominant western continental power, France, and the dominant imperial power, Britain. The German Army seemed to understand the new motorised technology better than its enemies, and their rapid push with tanks and aircraft through the Ardennes caught their hidebound opponents on the hop, allowing them a huge victory against the odds. Bolstered by this experience they then went on to attempt the same thing against the Soviet Union. The latest military analysis (for example Robert M. Citino's recent work in this area) seems to indicate that this led them to disaster, earning them huge victory after huge victory at the battlefield level, while sucking them deeper into the maw of a strategically unconquerable Red Army.

Rolf Hobson argues that the support by defence scholars for the blitzkrieg as a key example of a technologically driven RMA stems less from the historical reality and more from a certain predilection among the scholars themselves for this kind of narrative. This arises especially in the US, such that, as Hobson puts it, blitzkrieg is really 'an American ideal projected backwards into history, and then read out of history as the precursor and precedent of the way in which the United States should preferably wage war'. This arose, he argues, out of attitudes produced by the failures of the Vietnam War, the enthusiasm for blitzkrieg deriving from the idea that the fault lay with the politicians, not the military. Thus the perception of German doctrine as one that traditionally gave operational independence to the commander in the field, and delivered rapid success, looked attractive: 'The moral seems to be: give the generals their head and there will be little collateral damage, no long drawn-out attrition, no need to mobilize the economy or respond to fickle public opinion'.[21]

However, Hobson's view, which, as he writes, reflects the wider contemporary scholarship, is that this enthusiasm for blitzkrieg as the transformational application of the new mechanised technology arises from a distorted emphasis on the highly successful French campaign of 1940, Case Yellow. For Hobson, two things are notable about this. Firstly, at the time the Wehrmacht had no clear doctrine for the use of armoured forces, the idea of blitzkrieg only being consolidated after this success. In its apparent initial application in Belgium in 1940 the Wehrmacht merely 'grafted the new technology of tanks, planes and radio communications onto traditional, nineteenth century operational ideals, specifically the Umfassungsschlacht ("Envelopment battle") that had found expression in the Schlieffen Plan'. Furthermore, he suggests that Germany was fortunate in its opponents' generals, who not only would make mistakes but 'would make good mistakes'.

Therefore, the proper target of a study of blitzkrieg should be the eastern front, Operation Barbarossa and the subsequent events in the war with the Soviet Union. Here the success of the technique of rapid pushes encircling the enemy is less clear-cut. For a while it did deliver massive success at the operational level, with more than 5,000,000 Soviet prisoners being taken in the first year, but in the end the freedom that the generals had to precipitate what they hoped would be the decisive battle actually led to Germany's defeat. Hobson argues, however, that that blitzkrieg failed on two levels: 'at the operational level because the infantry and logistics could not keep up with the advance of the Panzer divisions', and it failed too at the strategic level because the arms output of the economy was not coordinated with the needs of the Wehrmacht. 'The OKW [German high Command] concentrated on its operational tasks and did not seek to secure the resources it needed even to fight a limited campaign',[22] as he puts it.

Blitzkrieg is of interest as an RMA for a number of reasons. It raises the question of whether it *was* an RMA, in as much as the new technology merely acted as a disastrous enabler, allowing the German military to go on doing just what they had been doing for centuries. This prompts a certain intellectual care in leaping to identifying the next RMA. It also raises the question of *why* it is so widely thought to be a good example of an RMA – which seems to be because it is at least *portrayable* as a good modern instance of technology changing the face of war, as long as the military is given leave to do things its own way. To do so requires the suppression of some uncomfortable views about blitzkrieg's real efficacy. Technology functions not just through its intended or actual usage, but also through our attitudes to that usage.

The Digital Revolution and the UAV

Discussion of RMAs became particularly fashionable with the obvious and rapid arrival of digital technology into military equipment. With the Soviet Union fragmenting and the Cold War over, the United States was in a position of unprecedented global military dominance. At the same moment the rapid dissemination of information technology into weaponry handed the US military a set of expensive new military tools, in the form of massively improved surveillance and guidance techniques and highly effective PGMs. Events in the Persian Gulf and the Balkans gave the US government the opportunity to test both its newfound freedom to act in the world, and the new weapons in its military arsenal. The two US-led wars in Iraq, the Kosovo war and the war in Afghanistan offered arenas for watching these new factors play out. The endlessly replayed video footage of single bombs flashing through windows, vents or doors to destroy bunkers, hangars and government buildings, seemed to signify a new era: an efficient military victory was dialled in from afar. 'Collateral damage', the hated euphemism of the times, was greatly reduced. US dominance appeared total, and the technology appeared to be largely responsible.

Most scholars writing on this technological RMA seem to accept the term, but with more than a grain of doctrinal salt. Smart bombs may not provide the one target, one kill perfection that the propaganda suggests, but the selective images of PGMs flashing through doors and windows into protected facilities such as hardened aircraft shelters that so captured the public imagination also reflected a truth: it had in fact become a great deal less costly in term of military effort to destroy a given target. Something had changed, and writing in 2000, albeit acknowledging that 'technology by itself cannot provide enhanced cutting edge cost effectiveness', former Indian Air Vice-Marshal Kapil Kak concluded:

> Sweeping away the idea of war being fought at a recognisable front-line, these technologies potentially blend land, sea and air power to create warspaces that stretch backwards and forward in space and time. Warspaces would be dominated by real time information, instant communications, on-line command and control, lethal long range precision strikes and dramatically fast changing situations. In compressed decision cycles, information dominance may perhaps be as crucial an objective as air superiority or favourable air situation has continued to be for decades.[23]

The later wars in Iraq and Afghanistan did nothing to dispel this idea in their early stages; however, the way these successful information-led technological 'shock and awe' tactics rapidly seemed to degenerate into bloody and intractable insurgencies suggested that something was wrong.

The US Army recently updated its doctrine with a 2012 pamphlet entitled *The U.S. Army Capstone Concept*. General Robert Cone's foreword observes that 'Greater speed, quantity, and reach of human interaction and increased access to military capabilities make the operational environment more unpredictable and complex, driving the likelihood and consequence of disorder'.[24] The need for the new approach seems to arise in part from a perception of the failure of a military approach driven by the kinds of technology the RMA is marked by.

According to Brigadier General H.R. McMaster, in charge of implementing the new US Army doctrinal approach, the revolution is already over. The new ideas he espouses are, according to the *National Journal*,

> A direct repudiation of the narrative that dominated the tech bubble 1990s [...] That era spawned concepts of war that were elegant in terms of PowerPoint diagramming, arrogant in their abiding faith in the 'shock-and-awe' predominance of U.S. technology, and fatally flawed in some of their assumptions about the nature of war.[25]

McMaster says that these weaknesses derive from the idea that technology had changed the 'nature' of war, rather than its *character*. He also points out that the technology had inherent consequences for the way the military operated, as they 'tempted commanders to lead from the rear and micromanage subordinates through a computer or video screen'. Perhaps most interestingly: 'the revolution's ideal of "perfect situational awareness" led to over centralization and risk aversion at the top, as commanders waited for the last piece of the information puzzle that would complete the picture'. Particularly relevant to this discussion of drones, he told the *National Journal* that

> The idea that war could be conducted over the horizon and experienced primarily though bomb-camera videos fostered an insensitivity towards the 'collateral' deaths of civilians – carnage that could alienate the population and derail counterinsurgency operations. Perhaps most important, the sanitary and surgical concept of modern war also bred a Pentagon culture that did not adequately prepare officers, or the revolution's civilian advocates, for the true brutality of war.[26]

The point is that the capacity of the new information technology is such that it allows military action at a distance, so that combat is experienced at a remove. This is a convenient way to wage war but has the unlooked for effects, it seems, of reducing sensitivity to casualties, increasing expectation of 'perfect' situational awareness, and (even more significantly) reducing understanding of the real nature of war, to the final detriment of US goals.

The very quality that the new technology brings to the battlefield – that is, an enhanced situational awareness – may, counter-intuitively, actually undermine the capacity for action, as however good the intelligence there always seems to be the possibility of knowing more. Acting in ignorance of your enemies' actions and capacities has always been a part of the general's requirements, and the temptation to believe that finally the Clausewitzian fog can be lifted must be a powerful one, even if the delivery of that clear sight is endlessly deferred. McMaster is an expert on the Vietnam War, and fought in the counter-insurgency in Iraq, and no doubt these views have been fostered by these particular experiences in wars not of national survival, at least not for the US, but in counter-insurgencies: conflicts in which success is visibly not won in the end on the battlefield, but around the table, by politicians.

So if we are looking for pointers towards the larger-scale unintended unlooked for effects of UAVs, this general discussion of the RMA offers some in the form of this unrealistic attitude to war that the broad category of information technology (and the UAV as an instance of such technology) produces in the minds of military commanders. The RMA brought a transformative capacity to deliver certain military effects, to be sure, but it did not change the nature of war. However, it may be that it changed leaders' attitudes to war – the unlooked for outcome of the application of a new technology.

In a further but more specific example of this kind of attitudinal effect, following recent revelations regarding the use by the US of a base in Saudi Arabia for its drone operations in Yemen, the *Guardian* quoted Mustafa Alani of the Gulf Research Centre in Dubai: 'These planes are unmanned so there will not be the same impact as when American planes were flying from the Prince Sultan base. No one will say that the Americans are occupying the country'.[27] People at both ends of the weapon perceive the UAV differently from the manned aircraft, and this allows different behaviour. Part of this behaviour is seen in the targets of these strikes: individuals form those targets, rather than armies, states, or populations, in a kind of nano-warfare. These targeted killings have become an increasingly popular tool both in areas of 'legitimate' military activity, such as Afghanistan, and in areas of more ambiguous jurisdiction, such as Pakistan's tribal lands or Palestine's West Bank. The UAV is the tool of choice, especially in the second case, where alternatives such as kill/capture missions by special forces are seen as more risky, and more of an intrusion. Such UAV attacks have rapidly increased under the Obama administration, and this has happened as the 'small' wars the US has been engaged in have been winding down, and in some sense therefore stand as an alternative, a new phase of state military action.

The lesson of military history is that care should be taken not to overstate the impact of the UAV on military affairs. In its prime characteristic – the way in which it removes the operator from the field of battle, enforcing a certain asymmetry in the nature of military conflict – the UAV is only the latest in a long list of technological attempts to do just that. As part of a wider RMA arising from the massive increase in processing power and shrinkage in the size of computer systems, the reality of a military step change in the energy needed to achieve particular effects certainly prompts the usage of the word 'revolutionary'. But the specific changes attached to UAV use are nevertheless significant too, not least in the way we perceive the UAV: in its very unmannedness it eliminates the risk of casualties (while challenging the warrior ideal) in an era when sensitivity to casualties in the public perception is very high; we also see it as less 'there', which means it is able to go where manned vehicles cannot. Its revolutionary character may in fact be found less as part of the late twentieth-century shock and awe RMA, and more in the way it works as an enabler of a new kind of tightly focused military action that avoids the user getting sucked into the kinds of bloody stalemated insurgencies that marked the wars since 9/11. If the warship in the age of empire allowed the European powers to cheaply exert their will around the globe against the pre-industrial world by sending a near-invulnerable gunboat, then the revolution of the UAV is to restore that capacity to intervene overseas with impunity to today's powers, at least with regard to the global south, through the sending of a drone. If that is the message of this new medium, in McLuhan's terms, then perhaps we need to address the question of whether this is a desirable effect in terms of global security. It would be our contention that it is not.

Notes

Introduction

1. Marshall McLuhan and Quentin Fiore, *The Medium is the Massage: An Inventory of Effects*, New York: Bantam Books, 1967, p. 12.
2. Richard Sclove, *Democracy and Technology*, New York: Guilford Press, 1995, p. 3.
3. Marjorie Cohn, 'Bombing of Afghanistan Is illegal and must be stopped', *Jurist*, 6 November 2001 <http://jurist.law.pitt.edu/forum/forumnew36.htm>.
4. Greg Miller and Bob Woodward, 'Secret memos reveal explicit nature of US, Pakistan agreement on drones', *Washington Post*, 24 October 2013.
5. Marshall McLuhan, *Understanding Media: The Extensions of Man*, New York: Signet, 1964, p. 23.
6. McLuhan, *Understanding Media*, p. 24.
7. McLuhan, *Understanding Media*, p. 156.
8. Karl Marx, 'The second observation', in *The Poverty of Philosophy*, New York: International Publishers, 1992 (1847), p. 119.
9. Neil Postman, 'Five things we need to know about technological change', talk delivered in Denver, Colorado, March 1998, <http://www.cs.ucdavis.edu/~rogaway/classes/188/materials/postman.pdf>.
10. Matthew Power, 'Confessions of a drone warrior', *Gentleman's Quarterly*, 23 October 2013.
11. Nabeel Khoury, 'In Yemen, drones aren't a policy', *Cairo Review of Global Affairs*, 23 October 2013.
12. Christof Heyns, *Report of the Special Rapporteur on Extrajudicial, Summary or Arbitrary Executions*, UN General Assembly, 13 September 2013, para. 16.
13. McLuhan, *Understanding Media*, p. 199.

1.   From Balloons to Big Safari: UAV Development

1. Carl Baner (Major), 'Defining aerospace power', *Air & Space Power Journal*, 11 March 1999.
2. This account based on Curtis Peebles, *The Moby Dick Project: Reconnaissance Balloons over Russia*, Washington, DC: Smithsonian Books, 1991.
3. New Mexico Museum of Space History, 'Archibald M. Low', *The International Space Hall of Fame* 2005–2013 <http://www.nmspacemuseum.org/halloffame/index.php>.

4. Thomas J. Mueller, 'On the birth of micro air vehicles', *International Journal of Micro Air Vehicles*, Vol. 1, Issue 1, 2009, pp. 1–12.

5. Anthony Finn and Steve Scheding, *Developments and Challenges for Autonomous Unmanned Vehicles: A Compendium*, Intelligent Systems Reference Library, Volume 3, Berlin: Springer, 2010, p. 12.

6. Edgar O. Lyons, 'Ghost fleet for war and peace', *Popular Science*, February 1932, p. 24.

7. Robin Braithwaite, 'Queen Bee', *Light Aviation*, June 2012, p. 52.

8. *Hargrave*, 'Reginald Denny and Walter Righter: UAV pioneers', *Hargrave Aviation and Aero-Modelling: Interdependent Evolutions and Histories*, <http://www.ctie.monash.edu.au/hargrave/index.htm>.

9. Delmar S. Fahrney, 'The birth of guided missiles', *US Naval Proceedings*, December 1980, p. 56.

10. Fahrney, 'The birth of guided missiles'.

11. L. Newcome, *Unmanned Aviation: A Brief History of Unmanned Aerial Vehicles*, Reston, VA: American Institute of Aeronautics and Astronautics, 2004, p. 69.

12. Newcome, *Unmanned Aviation*, p. 69.

13. Quoted in Thomas Ehrhard, *Air Force UAVs: The Secret History: A Mitchell Institute Study*, The Air Force Association, 2010, <http://www.afa.org> p. 2.

14. Newcome, *Unmanned Aviation*, p. 70.

15. Ehrhard, *Air Force UAVs*, p. 5.

16. Newcome, *Unmanned Aviation*, p. 72.

17. Newcome, *Unmanned Aviation*, p. 72.

18. Christopher A. Jones, 'Unmanned aerial vehicles (UAVs): An assessment of historical operations and future possibilities', *USAF Research Paper*, presented to the Research Department Air Command and Staff College, March 1997, p. 2.

19. Jones, 'Unmanned aerial vehicles', p. 2.

20. Ehrhard, *Air Force UAVs*, p. 6.

21. Erhhard, *Air Force UAVs*, p. 9.

22. Paul W. Elder, *Project CHECO South East-Asia Report Buffalo Hunter (U) 1970–1972*, USAF, 1973, <http://www.dtic.mil> p. 3.

23. Lawrence Spinetta, 'The rise of unmanned aircraft', *Aviation History*, Vol. 21, Issue 3, January 2011, p. 36.

24. Elder, *Project CHECO*, p. 2.

25. Elder, *Project CHECO*, p. xii.

26. National Museum of the USAF, 'Lavochkin La-17m Target Drone', <http://www.nationalmuseum.af.mil/factsheets/factsheet_print.asp?fsID=13266>.

27. Kimberley Hsu, Craig Murray, Jeremy Cook and Amalia Feld, 'China's military unmanned aerial vehicle industry', *U.S.-China Economic and Security Review*, Commission Staff Research Backgrounder, 13 June 2013, p. 3.

28. Israeli Air Force, 'The first UAV squadron', <http://www.iaf.org>.

29. Reg Austin, *Unmanned Aircraft Systems: UAVs Design, Development and Deployment*, Chichester: Wiley, 2010, p. 310.
30. Ehrhard, *Air Force UAVs*, p. 5.
31. Ehrhard, *Air Force UAVs*, p. 19.
32. Ehrhard, *Air Force UAVs*, p. 30.
33. Ehrhard, *Air Force UAVs*, p. 37.
34. S. Tsach, J. Chemla, D. Penn and D. Budianu, 'History of UAV development in IAI & road ahead', paper presented at the 24th International Congress of the Aeronautical Sciences, Yokohama, Japan, 29 August–3 September 2004, p. 2.
35. Tsach, et al., 'History of UAV development', p. 5.

2.   The Drone Takes Off

1. Quoted in Richard Whittle, 'Predator's Big Safari', *Mitchell Paper* 7, The Mitchell Institute for Air Power Studies, 2011, p.14.
2. Government Accountability Office, 'Nonproliferation: agencies could improve information sharing and end-use monitoring on unmanned aerial vehicle exports', July 2012.
3. Kristin Roberts, 'When the whole world has drones', *The National Journal*, 22 March 2013, <http://www.nationaljournal.com>.
4. Jeremiah Gertler, *U.S. Unmanned Aerial Systems*, Report for the Congressional Research Service, 2012.
5. Gertler, *U.S. Unmanned*, p. 1.
6. Roberts, 'When the whole world has drones'.
7. Gertler, *U.S. Unmanned*, p. 2.
8. *Economist*, 'The Dronefather', 1 December 2012.
9. Thomas Ehrhard, *Air Force UAVs: The Secret History: A Mitchell Institute Study*, The Air Force Association, 2010, <http://www.afa.org>, p. 41.
10. Federation of American Scientists, 'General Atomic GNAT-750 Lofty View', *Intelligence Resource Programme*, 27 November 1999.
11. John Croft, 'Send in the Global Hawk', *Air and Space*, January 2005.
12. Quoted in Whittle, 'Predator's Big Safari', p. 10.
13. David A. Fulghum, 'Star unmanned aircraft faces bureaucratic fight', *Aviation Week & Space Technology*, Vol. 154, Issues 11/12, March 2001, p. 28.
14. Mark Mazzetti, *The Way of the Knife: The CIA, a Secret Army, and the War at the Ends of the Earth*, New York: Penguin, 2013.
15. Quoted in Whittle, 'Predator's Big Safari', p. 17.
16. Whittle, 'Predator's Big Safari', p. 17.
17. Human Rights Watch, *Losing Humanity: The Case Against Killer Robots*, 2012, <http://www.hrw.org/reports/2012/11/19/losing-humanity-0>.

18. George Tenet, 'Written statement for the record of the Director of Central Intelligence before the National Commission on terrorist attacks upon the United States', 24 March 2004, p. 15.

19. Whittle, 'Predator's Big Safari', p. 25.

20. *Bureau of Investigative Journalism*, 'Covert drone war', <http://www.thebureauinvestigates.com/category/projects/drones/>.

21. UAS Vision, 'Shadow is US military's favourite unmanned asset in Afghanistan', 15 August 2013 <http://www.uasvision.com/2013/08/15/shadow-is-us-militarys-favourite-unmanned-asset-in-afghanistan/>.

22. Jason Dangel, 'UAVs role key ingredient to success in Iraq', 15 August 2008, <http://www.army.mil/article/11684/>.

23. Dangel, 'UAVs role key'.

24. Dangel, 'UAVs role key'.

25. Derek Gregory, 'The biopolitics of Baghdad: counterinsurgency and the counter-city', *Human Geography*, Vol. 1, Issue 1, 2008, pp. 6–27.

26. *Defense Industry Daily*, 'ER/MP Gray Eagle: enhanced MQ-1C Predators for the army', 2 July 2013, <https://www.defenseindustrydaily.com/warrior-ermp-an-enhanced-predator-for-the-army-03056/>.

27. Sandra I. Erwin, 'UAV programs illustrate DoD's broken procurement system', *National Defense*, May 2009.

28. Thales UK, 'Thales's Hermes 450 service exceeds 50,000 flight hours in Afghanistan', press release, 6 September 2011, <http://www.thalesgroup.com/Press_Releases/>.

29. Nick Hopkins, 'Nearly 450 British military drones lost in Iraq and Afghanistan', *Guardian*, 12 February 2013.

30. Craig Hoyle, 'Watchkeeper UAV nears service use', *Flight Global*, 11 October 2013.

31. *Defense Update*, 'German Herons log 15,000 combat-operation hours in Afghanistan', 22 July 2013, < http://defense-update.com/20130722_german_heron_afghanistan.html>.

32. *Defense Aerospace*, 'French Air Force details UAV operations', 2 September 2012, <http://www.defense-aerospace.com/article-view/feature/117835/french-uav-operations-in-afghanistan.html>.

33. W.J. Hannigan, 'Army lets air out of battlefield spyship project', *Los Angeles Times*, 23 October 2013.

34. *Israel Defense Forces Blog*, 'Army of the future: the IDF's unmanned vehicles', 28 February 2012, <http://www.idfblog.com/2012/02/28/army-future-idfs-unmanned-vehicles/>.

35. Michele K. Esposito, 'The Israeli arsenal deployed against Gaza during Operation Cast Lead', *Journal of Palestine Studies*, Vol. 38, Issue 3, Spring 2009, pp. 175–91.

36. Human Rights Watch, 'Gaza airstrikes violated laws of war', 12 February 2013, <http://www.hrw.org/news/2013/02/12/israel-gaza-airstrikes-violated-laws-war>.

37. *Defense Industry Daily*, 'Ravens, mini-UAVs winning gold in Afghanistan's "commando olympics"', 22 April 2012, <http://www.defenseindustrydaily.com/raven-uavs-winning-gold-in-afghanistans-commando-olympics-01432/>.

38. Joshua Edwards, '2CR troops use Raven to patrol skies', 26 June 2013, <http://www.army.mil/article/98798/2CR_Troops_use_Raven_to_patrol_skies/>.

39. *BBC*, 'Black Hornet spycam is a "lifesaver" for British troops', 13 February 2013, <http://www.bbc.co.uk/news/uk-21450456>.

40. Hopkins, 'Nearly 450 British military'.

41. Yasmin Tadjdeh, 'Small UAV demand by U.S. Army ebbs as overseas market surging', *National Defense*, September 2013.

42. Richard B. Gasparre, 'Size matters – small is sexy in the UAV microcosm', 23 April 2008, <http://www.army-technology.com/features/feature1789/>.

43. Greg Zacharis and Mark Maybury, *Report on Operating Next-Generation Remotely Piloted Aircraft for Irregular Warfare*. United States Air Force Scientific Advisory Board. April 2011.

44. General Atomics, 'Aircraft platforms: Predator C Avenger', <http://www.ga-asi.com/products/aircraft/predator_c.php>.

45. Craig Whitlock and Barton Gellman, 'U.S. documents detail al-Qaeda's efforts to fight back against drones', *Washington Post*, 3 September 2013.

46. Whitlock and Gellman, 'US Documents'.

47. Department of Defense, *Unmanned Systems Integrated Roadmap FY2011-2036*, October 2011, p. 43.

48. David Donald, 'Taranis and Mantis UAVs move forward towards active service', *AINonline*, 8 July 2012, <http://www.ainonline.com/aviation-news/2012-07-08/taranis-and-mantis-uavs-move-forward-towards-active-service>.

49. Douglas Barrie, 'China's "sharp sword"', *12th IISS Asia Security Summit*, 29 May 2013, <http://www.iiss.org/en/shangri-la%20voices/blogsections/2013-6cc5/barrie-china-sharp-sword-28bb>.

50. Anton Denisov 'MiG signs attack drone R&D contract', *RIANovosti*, 1 May 2013, www.en.rian.ru/military.

3.   *The UAV and Military Doctrine*

1. Jeffrey Sluka, 'Death from above: UAVs and losing hearts and minds', *Military Review*, 2011, Vol. 91, Issue 3, pp. 70–6, p. 74.

2. John D. Jogerst, 'Air power trends 2010: the future is closer than you think', *Air & Space Power Journal*, Vol. 23, Issue 2, 2009, p. 109.

3. MOD, *Joint Doctrine Note 2/1: The UK Approach To Unmanned Aircraft Systems*. 2011.

4. MOD, *Joint Doctrine Note*, p. 1.1.

5. MOD, *Joint Doctrine Note*, p. 1.4.

6. MOD, *Joint Doctrine Note*, p. 1.2.

7. MOD, *Joint Doctrine Note*, p. 1.4.

8. MOD, *Joint Doctrine Note*, p. 3.4.

9. MOD, *Joint Doctrine Note*, p. 3.5.

10. MOD, *Joint Doctrine Note*, p. 3.5.

11. *Reuters*, 'US Marines extend K-MAX unmanned helicopter's use in Afghanistan', 18 March 2013, <http://www.reuters.com/article/2013/03/17/lockheed-unmanned-helicopter-idUSL1N0C603420130317>.

12. MOD, *Joint Doctrine Note*, p. 3.6.

13. Norton Schwartz, 'Air force strategic choices and budget priorities', *Brief at the Pentagon*, US Department of Defense, 27 January 2012.

14. *Research and Markets*, 'United States defence and security report Q1 2012', 2012, p. 64.

15. MOD, *Joint Doctrine Note*, p. 1.3.

16. USAF, 'Unmanned aircraft systems flight plan 2009–2047', Headquarters, United States Air Force, Washington, DC, 18 May 2009.

17. MOD, *Joint Doctrine Note*, p. 3.1.

18. MOD, *Joint Doctrine Note*, p. 3.1.

19. Government Accountability Office, 'Unmanned aerial vehicles: improved strategic and acquisition planning can help address emerging challenges', *GAO Report*, 9 March 2005.

20. MOD, *Joint Doctrine Note*, p. 6.3.

21. MOD Defence Science and Technology, 'Technologies for unmanned air systems, call for research proposals', 4 November 2011.

22. MOD, 'Miniature surveillance helicopters help protect front line troops', *News Story*, 4 February 2013.

23. Craig Hoyle, 'Unmanned Taranis has flown', *Flight Global*, 25 October 2013.

24. MOD, *Joint Doctrine Note*, p. 5.9.

25. MOD, *Joint Doctrine Note*, p. 3.8.

26. MOD Official, Personal Communication, 3 September 2012.

27. USAF, 'Unmanned aircraft systems'.

28. MOD, *Joint Doctrine Note*, p. 3.10.

29. Nick Turse, 'America's secret empire of drone bases', 16 October 2011, <http://www.tomdispatch.com/blog/175454/>.

30. BAE Systems, 'BAe systems completes first flight test of persistent surveillance system to protect U.S. Army soldiers', *Press Release*, 8 February 2010.

31. Travis A. Burdine, 'The Army's "organic" unmanned aircraft systems', *Air and Space Power Journal*, 2009, Vol. 23, Issue 2, p. 95.

32. Burdine, 'The Army's Unmanned', p. 97.

33. Burdine, 'The Army's Unmanned', p. 99.

34. David Kilcullen, 'Counter-insurgency redux', *Survival: Global Politics and Strategy*, Vol. 48, Issue 4, 2006, p. 112.

35. US Army/Marine Corps, *Counter-Insurgency Field Manual*, Chicago: University of Chicago Press 2006. Quoted in Ben Anderson, 'Facing the future enemy: US counterinsurgency doctrine and the pre-insurgent', *Theory Culture and Society*, Vol. 28, 2011, pp. 216–40.

36. Kilcullen, 'Counter-insurgency redux', p. 122.

37. Raids by special forces aimed at capturing or killing individuals have been carried out in countries with which the US is not otherwise engaged in war, most famously of course in the case of the SEAL raid that finally killed Osama Bin Laden in Pakistan, and more recently (October 2013) raids in Libya and Somalia.

38. Sluka, 'Death from above', p. 75.

39. Scott Shane, 'Election spurred a move to codify U.S. drone policy', *New York Times*, 24 November 2012.

40. Anderson, 'Facing the future enemy'.

41. Department of Defense, *Report of the Defense Science Board Task Force on Defense Intelligence Counterinsurgency (COIN) Intelligence, Surveillance, and Reconnaissance (ISR) Operations*, February 2011, p. vii.

42. *BBC Newsworld*, 'UN launches inquiry into drone killings', 24 January 2013.

4. *The Consequences of Killing Without Consequences*

1. Graham Greene, *The Third Man*, London: Faber and Faber, 1968, p. 97.

2. Alison Williams, 'Enabling persistent presence? Performing the embodied geopolitics of the unmanned aerial vehicle assemblage', *Political Geography*, Vol. 30, 2011, pp. 381–90, p. 387.

3. Jennie Germann Molz, '"Watch us wander": mobile surveillance and the surveillance of mobility', *Environment and Planning A*, Vol. 38, 2006, pp. 377–93, p. 377.

4. Matt J. Martin, with Charles W. Sasser, *Predator – The Remote-Control Air War over Iraq and Afghanistan: A Pilot's Story*, Minneapolis: Zenith Press, 2010, p. 286.

5. Derek Gregory, 'Deadly embrace: war, distance and intimacy', keynote to British Academy, London, 14 March 2012, audio file available at <http://www.britac.ac.uk/events/2012/Gregory-balec.cfm>.

6. Quoted in P. Adey, M. Whitehead and A.J. Williams, 'Introduction – air-target: distance, reach and the politics of verticality', *Theory, Culture and Society*, Vol. 28, 2011, pp. 173–187, p. 179.

7. An infamous example of what mediated war looks like – US soldiers in helicopters in Iraq gunning down a so-called insurgent group that included *Reuters* journalists and children – was Wikileaks, 'Collateral Murder',

3 April 2010, Sunshine Press, <http://www.youtube.com/watch?gl=CA&v= 5rXPrfnU3G0>.

8. Henry Crumpton, *The Art of Intelligence: Lessons from a Life in the CIA's Clandestine Service*, New York: Penguin, 2012, p. 223.

9. Col Pete Gerston, commander of the 432nd Air Expeditionary Wing at Creech, quoted in Megan McCloskey, 'The war room: daily transition between battle, home takes a toll on drone operators', *Stars and Stripes*, 27 October 2009.

10. Williams, 'Enabling persistent presence?', p. 388.

11. Mary A. Favret is quoted in Gregory, 'Deadly embrace'.

12. See: Jefferson Morely, 'Boredom, terror, deadly mistakes: secrets of the new drone war', *Salon*, 3 April 2012; and Martin, *Predator*, pp. 30–1.

13. *Global Edition*, 'Drone pilot ejects from office chair', 5 December 2012.

14. See, for example, Jason S. McCarley and Christopher D. Wickens, *Human Factors Implications of UAVs in the National Airspace*, Institute of Aviation, Aviation Human Factors Division University of Illinois at Urbana-Champaign, 2007, p. 13.

15. Missy Cummings, 'Impact of workload on operator performance in human supervisory control systems', 20 August 2009, The University of Texas at Austin, <http://www.youtube.com/watch?v=VeII-AxiZ30>.

16. Martin, *Predator*, p. 31.

17. Amir Mizroch, 'Israel's rocket-intercepting ace who started out on Warcraft', *Wired*, UK edition, 19 November 2012.

18. USAF Scientific Advisory Board, *Report on Operating Next-Generation Remotely Piloted Aircraft for Irregular Warfare* (SAB-TR-10–03), April 2011, <http:// publicintelligence.net/usaf-drones-in-irregular-warfare/ >, p. 1.

19. Martin, *Predator*, p. 141.

20. McCloskey, 'The war room'.

21. Morely, 'Boredom'.

22. Martin, *Predator*, p. 121.

23. J. Ouma, W. Chappelle and A. Salinas, *Facets of Occupational Burnout Among US Air Force Active Duty and National Guard/Reserve MQ-1 Predator and MQ-9 Reaper Operators* (Report No AFRL-SA-WP-TR-2011–0003), Wright-Patterson AFB OH: Air Force Research Laboratory, June 2011, executive summary.

24. USAF Scientific Advisory Board, *Report*.

25. Martin, *Predator*, p. 20.

26. ISAF/NATO, 'U.S. releases Uruzgan investigation findings', press release, 28 May 2010.

27. Martin, *Predator*, p. 140.

28. Martin, *Predator*, p. 51.

29. Martin, *Predator*, p. 55.

30. Martin, *Predator*, p. 77.

31. Michael Walzer, *Just and Unjust Wars: A Moral Argument with Historical Illustrations*, Harmondsworth: Pelican Books, 1980, p. 141.

32. Peter Asaro, 'How just could a robot war be?', in P. Brey, A. Briggle and K. Waelbers (eds), *Current Issues in Computing And Philosophy*, Amsterdam: IOS Press, 2008, pp. 50–64, p. 13.

33. Adi Robertson, 'US military announces new medal for cyberwarfare and drone operation', *Verge*, 13 February 2013.

34. Mike Hoffman, 'Congress questions low UAV pilot promotion rates', *Defensetech*, 2 January 2013.

35. David Blair, 'Ten thousand feet and ten thousand miles: reconciling our air force culture to remotely piloted aircraft and the new nature of aerial combat', *Air and Space Power*, May/June 2012, pp. 61–9.

36. Blair, 'Ten Thousand', p. 65.

37. Adey et al., 'Introduction', p. 178.

38. Caren Kaplan, 'Mobility and war: the cosmic view of US "air power"', *Environment and Planning A*, Vol. 38, Issue 2, 2006, pp. 395–407, p. 402.

39. The phrase is Habermas's. See E. Mendieta, 'America and the world: a conversation with Jurgen Habermas', *Logos*, Summer 2004.

40. Martin, *Predator*, p. 121.

41. Martin, *Predator*, p. 55.

42. Keen is quoted by Kaplan, 'Mobility and war', p. 403.

43. Michael Hastings, 'The rise of the killer drones: how America goes to war in secret', *Rolling Stone*, 26 April 2012.

44. Martin, *Predator*, p. 49.

45. Martin, *Predator*, p. 52.

46. Adey et al., 'Introduction', p. 175.

47. Martin, *Predator*, p. 140.

5.   Targets: The View From Below

1. Quoted in Pir Zubair Shah, 'My drone war', *Foreign Policy*, March/April 2012, pp. 56–62, p. 56.

2. Tami Davis Biddle, 'Learning in real time: the development and implementation of air power in the First World War', in *Air Power History: Turning Points from Kitty Hawk to Kosovo*, S. Cox and P. Gray (eds), London: Frank Cass, 2002, p. 8. See especially pp. 8–14.

3. Nick Turse, *Kill Anything that Moves: The Real American War in Vietnam*, New York: Metropolitan Books, 2013, p. 80.

4. Ben Anderson, 'Facing the future enemy: US counterinsurgency doctrine and the pre-insurgent', *Theory Culture and Society*, Vol. 28, 2011, pp. 216–40, p. 219.

5. Shah, 'My drone war', p. 58.

6. Anderson, 'Facing the future enemy', p. 223.

7. T. Wall and T. Monahan, 'Surveillance and violence from afar: the politics of drones and liminal security-scapes', *Theoretical Criminology*, Vol. 15, Issue 3, 2011, pp. 239–54, p. 240.

8. Alison Williams, 'Enabling persistent presence? Performing the embodied geopolitics of the Unmanned Aerial Vehicle assemblage', *Political Geography*, Issue 30, 2011, pp. 381–90.

9. Wall and Monahan, 'Surveillance', p. 240.

10. Tom Curry, 'Poll finds overwhelming support for drone strikes', *NBC News*, 5 June 2013. The poll was jointly conducted by NBC and the *Wall Street Journal*.

11. The account of this strike is from International Human Rights and Global Conflict Resolution Clinic at Stanford Law School and Global Justice Clinic at NYU School of Law, *Living Under Drones: Death, Injury, and Trauma to Civilians from US Drone Practices in Pakistan*, September 2012, pp. 57–62, p. 60.

12. *Living Under Drones*, pp. 58–59.

13. See for example the account offered by the *Bureau of Investigative Journalism*, 'Obama 2011 Pakistan strikes', 17 March 2011, <http://www.thebureauinvestigates.com/2011/08/10/obama-2011-strikes/>.

14. *Reprieve*, 'Pakistan court orders government to stop "war crime" drone strikes', 9 May 2013.

15. Faisal bin Ali Jaber, 'Letter to Obama and Hadi on Yemeni drones', *Middle Eastern Monitor*, 2 August 2013.

16. *Bureau of Investigative Journalism*, 'Somalia: reported US covert actions 2001–2013', 22 February 2012, <http://www.thebureauinvestigates.com/2012/02/22/get-the-data-somalias-hidden-war/>.

17. E. Mendieta, 'America and the world: a conversation with Jurgen Habermas', *Logos*, Summer 2004.

18. Quoted in International Crisis Group, 'Drones: myths and reality in Pakistan', *Asia Report*, No. 247, 21 May 2013, p. 9.

19. See Mark Mazzetti, *The Way of the Knife: The CIA, a Secret Army, and the War at the Ends of the Earth*, New York: Penguin, 2013, for an excellent account of the complexities of this web of relationships.

20. International Crisis Group, 'Drones', p. 6.

21. Pew Research, 'On eve of elections, a dismal public mood in Pakistan', *Global Attitudes Project*, 7 May 2013.

22. The quote is from *Hampton Roads International Security Quarterly*, 22 March 2009, and is reproduced in Michael Quinion's article on the etymology of the term AfPak, 18 April 2009, <http://www.worldwidewords.org/turnsofphrase/tp-afp1.htm>.

23. Mark Duffield, 'Governing the borderlands: decoding the power of aid', *Disasters*, Vol. 25, No. 4, 2001, pp. 308–20, p. 309.

24. Kevin Heller, '"One hell of a killing machine": signature strikes and international law', *Research Paper No.* 634, University of Melbourne Legal Studies, 30 October 2012, p. 3.

25. John O. Brennan, 'The ethics and efficacy of the President's counterterrorism strategy', speech delivered at the Woodrow Wilson International Center for Scholars, 30 April 2012, my emphasis.

26. David Luban, 'What would Augustine do?', *Boston Review*, 6 June 2012, p. 9.

27. UNAMA, *Afghanistan Mid-Year Report 2013: Protection of Civilians in Armed Conflict*, Kabul, July 2013, pp. 40–2.

28. Daniel Brunstetter and Megan Braun, 'The implications of drones on the just war tradition', *Ethics and International Affairs*, 22 September 2011, pp. 337–58, p. 338.

29. Spencer Ackerman, 'Under McChrystal, drone strikes in Afghanistan quietly rise as civilian casualties *drop*', *Washington Independent*, 14 January 2010.

30. UNAMA, *Afghanistan*, p. 24.

31. UNAMA, *Afghanistan*, p. iii.

32. UNAMA, *Afghanistan*, p. 18.

33. *Living Under Drones*, p. 55.

34. *Living Under Drones*, p. 96.

35. *Living Under Drones*, p. 163.

36. Ofilio Mayorga, 'Double tap drone strikes and the denial of quarter in IHL', Program on Humanitarian Police and Conflict Research, Harvard University, 8 May 2013, <http://hpcrresearch.org/blog/ofilio-mayorga/2013–05–08/double-tap-drone-strikes-and-denial-quarter-ihl>.

37. Chris Wood and Mushtaq Yusufzai, 'Get the data: the return of double-tap drone strikes', *Bureau of Investigative Journalism*, 1 August 2013.

38. See ICRC, 'Practice relating to rule 46: orders or threats that no quarter will be given', Customary IHL, <http://www.icrc.org/customary-ihl/eng/docs/v2_rul_rule46>.

39. Chris Wood, 'Bureau investigation finds fresh evidence of CIA drone strikes on rescuers', *Bureau of Investigative Journalism*, 1 August 2013.

40. Ken Dilanian, 'Congress zooms in on drone killings', *Los Angeles Times*, 25 June 2012.

41. *Living Under Drones*, p. 76.

42. Fawad Ali, 'Security situation: four times as many people killed in FATA in 2012', *The Express Tribune*, 1 February 2013.

6.   Unlegal: Justifying a Drone War

1. Barack Obama, 'The future of our fight against terrorism', speech given at National Defense University, Fort McNair, 23 May 2013.

2. Faisal bin Ali Jaber, 'Letter to Obama and Hadi on Yemeni drones', *Middle Eastern Monitor*, 2 August 2013.

3. The UN special rapporteur on human rights, Ben Emmerson, the UN special rapporteur on extrajudicial killings, Christof Heyns, Amnesty International

and Human Rights Watch are among those who have flagged numerous concerns about US policy. See Jeffrey Bachman, 'The Obama administration may be guilty of war crimes', *Guardian*, 5 November 2013.

4. E. Mendieta, 'America and the world: a conversation with Jurgen Habermas', *Logos*, Summer 2004.

5. David Michael Jackson, 'Jus ad bellum', in *Encyclopedia of Global Justice*, Deen K. Chatterjee (ed.), Dordrecht: Springer, 2011, p. 581.

6. Michael Walzer, 'Responsibility and proportionality in state and nonstate wars', *Parameters*, Spring 2009, pp. 40–52, p. 41.

7. Peter Asaro, 'How just could a robot war be?', in P. Brey, A. Briggle and K. Waelbers (eds), *Current Issues in Computing And Philosophy*, Amsterdam: IOS Press, 2008, pp. 50–64, p. 56.

8. Mark Rigstad, 'Jus ad bellum after 9/11: a state of the art report', *IPT Beacon*, Issue 3, June 2007, p. 2.

9. David Luban, 'What would Augustine do?', *Boston Review*, 6 June 2012, p. 8.

10. Daniel Brunstetter and Megan Braun, 'The implications of drones on the just war tradition', *Ethics and International Affairs*, 22 September 2011, pp. 337–58, p. 343.

11. John O. Brennan, 'Remarks of John O. Brennan, assistant to the President for homeland security and counterterrorism, on ensuring al-Qa'ida's Demise – as prepared for delivery', White House press release, 29 June 2011.

12. Michael Byers, *War Law*, Vancouver: Douglas and McIntyre, 2005.

13. This is a revisionist interpretation founded on the 1986 Shultz Doctrine that maintains, 'if states have just cause for armed self-defense against sub-state terrorist organizations, then they also have just cause to use such arms against states that support, train, and harbor terrorists'. See Rigstad, 'Jus ad bellum', p. 14.

14. Jonathan Masters, 'Targeted killings', Council on Foreign Relations, 23 May 2013.

15. Rigstad, 'Jus ad bellum', p. 14.

16. Robert P. Abele, 'Just war theory and the invasion of Iraq', in *Encyclopedia of Global Justice*, Deen K. Chatterjee (ed.), Dordrecht: Springer, 2011, p. 588.

17. These figures are based on the *Bureau of Investigative Journalism*'s casualty estimates, accessed 30 Sept 2013.

18. Ingrid Detter, *The Law of War*, 2nd edition, Cambridge: Cambridge University Press, 2000, p. 22.

19. American Civil Liberties Union, 'National security: targeted killings', < https:// www.aclu.org/national-security/targeted-killings >.

20. Mark Mazzetti, *The Way of the Knife: The CIA, a Secret Army, and the War at the Ends of the Earth*, New York: Penguin, 2013, p. 121.

21. Mazzetti, *The Way of the Knife*, p. 125.

22. Peter Bergen, 'Drone is Obama's weapon of choice', *CNN Opinion*, 19 September 2012.

23. Jackson, '*Jus ad bellum*', p. 584.

24. David Chandler, 'War without end(s): grounding the discourse of "global war"', *Security Dialogue*, Vol. 40, Issue 3, 2009, pp. 243–62, p. 260.

25. Luban, 'Augustine', p. 9.

26. See Kevin Jon Heller, '"One hell of a killing machine": signature strikes and international law', *Research Paper*, No. 634, University of Melbourne Legal Studies, 30 October 2012.

27. Owen Bowcott, 'Drone strikes threaten 50 years of international law, says UN rapporteur', *Guardian*, 21 June 2012.

28. This according the UK-based justice organisation Reprieve.

29. J. Boone, 'Bin Laden killing: official report criticises Pakistan and US', *Guardian*, 9 July 2013.

30. This discussion is based on Heller, 'Killing machine'. The quote is from J. Sifton, 'A brief history of drones', *The Nation*, 7 February 2012.

31. Heller, 'Killing machine', p. 2.

32. According to the *New York Times*, 'Counterterrorism officials insist this approach is one of simple logic: people in an area of known terrorist activity, or found with a top Qaeda operative, are probably up to no good'. Jo Becker and Scott Shane, 'Secret "kill list" proves a test of Obama's principles and will', *New York Times*, 29 May 2012.

33. Walzer, 'Responsibility', p. 51.

34. Johnsen is quoted in Spencer Ackerman, 'Barrage of drone strikes in Yemen show flaws of US counter-terrorism strategy', *Guardian*, 12 August 2013.

35. Brunstetter and Braun, 'The implications of drones', p. 7.

36. International Crisis Group, 'Drones: myths and reality in Pakistan', *Asia Report*, No. 247, 21 May 2013, p. 11.

37. Jeremy Scahill, *Dirty Wars: The World is a Battlefield*, New York: Nation Books, 2013, chapter 10. See also: Jack Serle, 'US and others have "licence to ignore international law" in Somalia', *Bureau of Investigative Journalism*, 24 September 2012.

38. Stephen David, 'Israel's policy of targeted killing', *Ethics and International Affairs*, Vol. 1, Issue 7, April 2003, p. 5.

39. David, 'Israel's policy', p. 5.

40. Yotam Feldman and Uri Blau, 'Consent and advise', *Haaretz*, 29 January 2009.

41. Project on Extrajudicial Executions, 'Possible involvement of civilian contractors in covert targeting operations in Pakistan', 28 July 2010, <http://www.extrajudicialexecutions.org>.

42. Lisa Hajjar, 'Lawfare and armed conflict: comparing Israeli and US targeted killing policies and challenges against them', *Research Report*, Issam Fares Institute for Public Policy and International Affairs, January 2013, p. 4.

43. Feldman and Blau, 'Consent and advise'.

44. E. Flanagan, 'Notorious drug lord executed by China over "Golden Triangle" smuggling, hijackings', *NBC News*, 1 March 2013.

45. Michael Walzer, *Just and Unjust Wars: A Moral Argument with Historical Illustrations*, Harmondsworth: Pelican Books, 1980, p. 143.
46. T. Simpson, 'Robots, trust and war', *Philosophy and Technology*, Vol. 24, May 2011, pp. 325–35, p. 330.
47. Quoted in Glenn Greenwald, 'Times Square bomber: cause and effect in the War on Terror', *Salon*, 6 October 2010.

7. Killer Robots

1. R. Latiff and P. McCloskey, 'With drone warfare, America approaches the robo-rubicon', *Wall Street Journal*, 14 March 2013.
2. T. Simpson, 'Robots, trust and war', *Philosophy and Technology*, Vol. 24, May 2011, pp. 325–35, p. 326.
3. Human Rights Watch, *Losing Humanity: The Case Against Killer Robots*, 2012, <http://www.hrw.org/reports/2012/11/19/losing-humanity-0>, p. 1.
4. UN Office of the High Commissioner for Human Rights, 'UN human rights expert calls for a moratorium on lethal autonomous robots', press release, 30 May 2013, <http://www.ohchr.org/EN/NewsEvents/Pages/DisplayNews.aspx?NewsID=13380&LangID=E>.
5. Quoted in Zack Beauchamp, 'France calls for talks over banning Cylons, the Terminator, and other killer robots', *Thinkprogress.org*, 9 October 2013, <http://thinkprogress.org/security/2013/10/09/2756751/france-calls-for-talks-over-banning-the-terminator/>.
6. *Science Daily*, 'New survey shows widespread opposition to "killer robots," support for new ban campaign', 19 June 2013.
7. R. Arkin, 'Building trust in combat robots', interview in *Military History*, October 2007, pp. 14–15, p. 14.
8. *NBC News/Wall Street Journal* poll quoted by J. Proctor and B. Wanger, 'The truth about the "drones" that have so many so bothered', *Forbes*, 28 June 2013.
9. RUSI/YouGov poll quoted by T. Royle, 'Drones and the UK', *Herald Scotland*, 21 July 2013.
10. Human Rights Watch, *Losing Humanity*, p. 4.
11. Nick Hopkins, 'Welsh airfield at the centre of Britain's drone revolution', *Guardian*, 6 May 2013.
12. Human Rights Watch, *Losing Humanity*, p. 2.
13. Human Rights Watch, *Losing Humanity*, p. 4, fn. 2.
14. This discussion, including quotes, draws on Peter Asaro, 'How just could a robot war be?', in P. Brey, A. Briggle and K. Waelbers (eds), *Current Issues in Computing And Philosophy*, Amsterdam: IOS Press, 2008, pp. 50–64.
15. Asaro, 'How just could a robot war be?'.
16. G. Lubold and J. Reed, 'This drone just made history: but now where does it go?', *Foreign Policy: Killer Apps*, 10 July 2013, <http://complex.foreignpolicy.

com/posts/2013/07/10/this_drone_just_made_history_but_now_where_does_it_go>.

17. Government Accountability Office, 'Non-proliferation: agencies could improve information sharing and end use monitoring on unmanned aerial vehicle exports', GAO-12–536, July 2012, p. 9.

18. Human Rights Council, *Report of the Special Rapporteur on Extrajudicial, Summary or Arbitrary Executions, Christof Heyns*, May 2013, p. 6.

19. USAF, 'Unmanned aircraft systems flight plan 2009–2047', Headquarters, United States Air Force, Washington, DC, 18 May 2009, p. 16.

20. USAF, 'Unmanned aircraft systems', p. 41.

21. Proctor and Wanger, 'The Truth'.

22. Arkin, 'Building trust', p. 15.

23. Georgia Tech College of Computing, 'Robot ethics proposal funded by DoD', Press Release, 13 July 2006, <http://www.cc.gatech.edu/news/robot-ethics-proposal-funded-dod>.

24. Ronald Arkin, 'The case for ethical autonomy in unmanned systems', *Journal of Military Ethics*, Vol. 9, Issue 4, 2010, pp. 332–41, p. 334.

25. Arkin, 'The case', p. 339.

26. Human Rights Watch, *Losing Humanity*, p. 27.

27. See the excellent discussion of the many problems with Arkin's work in Andreas Matthias, 'Is the concept of an ethical governor philosophically sound?', paper presented at the TILTing Perspectives 2011 conference held at Tilburg University, Netherlands, 11–12 April 2011, <http://www.academia.edu/473656/Is_the_Concept_of_an_Ethical_Governor_Philosophically_Sound>.

28. New America Foundation, 'A new technology takes flight', in *The Drone Next Door Conference Proceedings*, Washington, DC, 7 May 2013.

29. In Afghanistan the figures for those killed in action are: Army, 1,419; Marine Corps, 417; USN, 92; USAF, 75. Source: *New York Times*, '2,003 deaths in Afghanistan', 21 August 2012. For Iraq the rank order is the same: Army, 3,583; Marine Corps, 1,138; USN, 109; USAF, 55. Source: *PBS Newshour*, 'US casualties in Iraq searchable database' (statistics cover 3 March 2003–21 October 2011).

30. S. Preston and E. Buzzell, 'Mortality of American troops in Iraq', *PSC Working Paper Series*, Population Studies Center, University of Pennsylvania, 2006, p. 3.

31. Philip Alston, 'The CIA and targeted killings beyond borders', *Public Law and Legal Theory Research Paper Series*, Working Paper, No. 11–64, New York University, September 2011, pp. 35, 37.

32. Karin Brulliard, 'Drone operators blamed in airstrike that killed Afghan civilians in February', *Washington Post*, 30 May 2010.

33. Ryan Tonken, 'Should autonomous robots be pacifists?', *Ethics and Information Technology*, 16 May 2012, pp. 1–15, p. 10.

34. Human Rights Watch, *Losing Humanity*, p. 4.

35. Matthias, 'Ethical governor', p. 15.

36. New America Foundation, 'A new technology'.

37. Langdon Winner, 'Do artifacts have politics?', *Daedalus*, Vol. 109, Issue 1, Winter 1980, pp. 121–36, p. 121.

38. Winner, 'Artifacts', p. 126.

39. Winner, 'Artifacts', p. 121.

40. Winner, 'Artifacts', p. 129.

41. Winner, 'Artifacts', p. 130, his emphasis.

42. See C.J. Chivers, *The Gun*, New York: Simon and Schuster, 2010.

43. Joanna Bourke, *An Intimate History of Killing: Face to Face Killing in the Twentieth Century*, London: Granta, 1999, p. 74. See her book generally for the immense difficulties involved in training people to kill in battle.

44. Arie Egozi, 'Israeli F-16 downs another Hezbollah UAV', *Flight*, 25 April 2013.

45. Larry Lessig, quoted in Matthias, 'Ethical governor', p. 5.

46. Alison Williams, 'Enabling persistent presence? Performing the embodied geopolitics of the Unmanned Aerial Vehicle assemblage', *Political Geography*, Vol. 30, Issue 7, 2011, pp. 381–90, p. 384.

47. Lyon is quoted in J. Molz, '"Watch us wander": mobile surveillance and the surveillance of mobility', *Environment and Planning A*, Vol. 38, Issue 2, 2006, pp. 377–93, p. 380.

48. Williams, 'Enabling', p. 387.

49. Williams, 'Enabling', p. 385.

50. Michel Foucault, *Discipline and Punish: The Birth of the Prison*, New York: Vintage Books, 1995, p. 188. Emphasis in original: the quote is attributed to Kropotkin.

51. Quoted in J. Ralph, 'War as an institution of international hierarchy: Carl Schmitt's theory of the partisan and contemporary US practice', *Millennium*, Vol. 39, Issue 2, 2010, pp. 279–98, p. 290.

52. The phrase is actually from John M. Culkin, 'A schoolman's guide to Marshall McLuhan', *Saturday Review*, 18 March 1967, p. 70.

53. Neil Postman, 'Five things we need to know about technological change', talk delivered in Denver, Colorado, March 1998, <http://www.cs.ucdavis.edu/~rogaway/classes/188/materials/postman.pdf>, p. 3.

54. The International Committee of the Red Cross (ICRC) is quoted in Human Rights Watch, *Losing Humanity*, p. 21.

8.   *From Man O' War to Nano-War: Revolutions in Military Affairs*

1. Joseph Conrad, *Heart of Darkness*, 2nd edition, Peterborough, ON: Broadview Press, 1999, pp. 80–1

2. Philip Alston, *Report of the Special Rapporteur on Extrajudicial, Summary or Arbitrary Executions. Addendum: Study on Targeted Killings*, UN Human Rights Council, 2010.

3. John F. Guilmartin, Jr, 'The military revolution in warfare at sea during the early modern era: technological origins, operational outcomes and strategic consequences', *Journal for Maritime Research*, Vol. 13, Issue 2, November 2011, pp. 129–37.

4. W.L. Pickering, 'Revolutions in military affairs: fact or fiction', *Canadian Army Journal*, Vol. 2, Issue 2, May 1999, pp. 36–49, p. 64.

5. Barry D. Watts, *The Maturing Revolution in Military Affairs*, A Centre for Budgetary and Strategic Assessments Study, 2011.

6. Watts, *Maturing Revolution*, p. 1.

7. Andrew F. Krepinovich, *The Military-Technical Revolution: A Preliminary Assessment*, Washington, DC: Centre for Strategic and Budgetary Assessments, 2002, p. 6.

8. Krepinovich, *The Military-Technical Revolution*, p. 6.

9. Marshall McLuhan, *Understanding Media: The Extensions of Man*, New York: Signet. 1964, p. 24.

10. McLuhan, *Understanding Media*, p. 156.

11. McLuhan, *Understanding Media*, pp. 156–62.

12. McLuhan, *Understanding Media*, p. 156.

13. Marshall McLuhan, *The Gutenberg Galaxy: The Making of Typographic Man*, Toronto: University of Toronto Press, 1962, p. 32.

14. Marshall McLuhan and Quentin Fiore, *The Medium is the Massage: An Inventory of Effects*, New York: Bantam. 1967.

15. McLuhan, *Understanding Media*, pp. 298–300.

16. James J. Tritten, 'Revolutions in military affairs: from the sea', *Military Review*, Vol. 80, Issue 2, 2000, p. 79.

17. Tritten, 'Revolutions in military affairs', p. 79.

18. Pickering, *Revolutions in Military Affairs*, p. 35.

19. A.J.P. Taylor, *War by Timetable: How the First World War Began*, Barnsley: Pen and Sword Books, 2005.

20. David Stevenson, 'War by timetable? The railway race before 1914', *Past & Present*, Vol. 162, Issue 1, 1999, pp. 163–94.

21. Rolf Hobson, 'Blitzkrieg, the revolution in military affairs, and defense intellectuals', *Journal of Strategic Studies*, Vol. 33, Issue 4, 2010, pp. 625–43.

22. Hobson, 'Blitzkrieg', p. 632.

23. Kapil Kak, 'Revolution in military affairs: an appraisal', *Strategic Analysis*, Vol. 24, Issue 1, 2000, p. 15.

24. TRADOC (Training and Doctrine Command), *The U.S. Army Capstone Project*, 19 December 2012, p. iii.

25. Sydney J. Freedberg, 'The army looks beyond Afghanistan', *National Journal*, 11 December 2009.
26. Freedberg, 'The army'.
27. Ian Black, 'CIA using Saudi base for drone assassinations in Yemen', *Guardian*, 6 February 2013.

Bibliography

Abele, Robert P., 'Just war theory and the invasion of Iraq', in *Encyclopedia of Global Justice*, Deen K. Chatterjee (ed.), Dordrecht: Springer, 2011.

Ackerman, Spencer, 'Under McChrystal, drone strikes in Afghanistan quietly rise as civilian casualties *drop*', *Washington Independent*, 14 January 2010.

Ackerman, Spencer, 'Barrage of drone strikes in Yemen show flaws of US counter-terrorism strategy', *Guardian*, 12 August 2013.

Adey, P., M. Whitehead and A.J. Williams, 'Introduction – air-target: distance, reach and the politics of verticality', *Theory, Culture and Society*, Vol. 28, 2011, pp. 173–87.

Ali, Fawad, 'Security situation: four times as many people killed in FATA in 2012', *The Express Tribune*, 1 February 2013.

Alston, Philip, *Report of the Special Rapporteur on Extrajudicial, Summary or Arbitrary Executions, Addendum: Study on Targeted Killings*, UN Human Rights Council, 2010.

Alston, Philip, 'The CIA and targeted killings beyond borders', *Public Law and Legal Theory Research Paper Series*, Working Paper, No. 11–64, New York University, September 2011.

American Civil Liberties Union, 'National security: targeted killings', <https://www.aclu.org/national-security/targeted-killings>.

Anderson, Ben, 'Facing the future enemy: US counterinsurgency doctrine and the pre-insurgent', *Theory Culture and Society*, Vol. 28, 2011, pp. 216–40.

Asaro, Peter, 'How just could a robot war be?', in P. Brey, A. Briggle and K. Waelbers (eds), *Current Issues in Computing And Philosophy*, Amsterdam: IOS Press, 2008, pp. 50–64.

Arkin, Ronald, 'Building trust in combat robots', interview in *Military History*, October 2007, pp. 14–15.

Arkin, Ronald, 'The case for ethical autonomy in unmanned systems', *Journal of Military Ethics*, Vol. 9, Issue 4, 2010, pp. 332–41.

Austin, Reg, *Unmanned Aircraft Systems: UAVs Design, Development and Deployment*, Chichester: Wiley, 2010, p. 310.

Bachman, Jeffrey, 'The Obama administration may be guilty of war crimes', *Guardian*, 5 November 2013.

BAE Systems, 'BAe systems completes first flight test of persistent surveillance system to protect U.S. Army soldiers', *Press Release*, 8 February 2010.

Baner, Carl (Major), 'Defining aerospace power', *Air & Space Power Journal*, 11 March 1999.

Barrie, Douglas, 'China's "sharp sword"', *12th IISS Asia Security Summit*, 29 May 2013, < http://www.iiss.org/en/shangri-la%20voices/blogsections/2013-6cc5/barrie-china-sharp-sword-28bb >.

BBC, 'Black Hornet spycam is a "lifesaver" for British troops', 13 February 2013, < http://www.bbc.co.uk/news/uk-21450456 >.

BBC Newsworld, 'UN launches inquiry into drone killings', 24 January 2013.

Beauchamp, Zack, 'France calls for talks over banning Cylons, the Terminator, and other killer robots', *Thinkprogress.org*, 9 October 2013, < http://thinkprogress.org/security/2013/10/09/2756751/france-calls-for-talks-over-banning-the-terminator/ >.

Becker, Jo and Scott Shane, 'Secret "kill list" proves a test of Obama's principles and will', *New York Times*, 29 May 2012.

Bergen, Peter, 'Drone is Obama's weapon of choice', *CNN Opinion*, 19 September 2012.

Biddle, Tami Davis, 'Learning in real time: the development and implementation of air power in the First World War', in *Air Power History: Turning Points from Kitty Hawk to Kosovo*, S. Cox and P. Gray (eds), London: Frank Cass, 2002.

Black, Ian, 'CIA using Saudi base for drone assassinations in Yemen', *Guardian*, 6 February 2013.

Blair, David, 'Ten thousand feet and ten thousand miles: reconciling our air force culture to remotely piloted aircraft and the new nature of aerial combat', *Air and Space Power*, May/June 2012, pp. 61–9.

Boone, J., 'Bin Laden killing: official report criticises Pakistan and US', *Guardian*, 9 July 2013.

Bourke, Joanna, *An Intimate History of Killing: Face to Face Killing in the Twentieth Century*, London: Granta, 1999.

Bowcott, Owen, 'Drone strikes threaten 50 years of international law, says UN rapporteur', *Guardian*, 21 June 2012.

Braithwaite, Robin, 'Queen Bee', *Light Aviation*, June 2012, p. 52.

Brennan, John O., 'Remarks of John O. Brennan, assistant to the President for homeland security and counterterrorism, on ensuring al-Qa'ida's Demise – as prepared for delivery', White House press release, 29 June 2011.

Brennan, John O., 'The ethics and efficacy of the President's counterterrorism strategy', speech delivered at the Woodrow Wilson International Center for Scholars, 30 April 2012.

Brulliard, Karin, 'Drone operators blamed in airstrike that killed Afghan civilians in February', *Washington Post*, 30 May 2010.

Brunstetter, Daniel and Megan Braun, 'The implications of drones on the just war tradition', *Ethics and International Affairs*, 22 September 2011, pp. 337–58.

Burdine, Travis A., 'The Army's "organic" unmanned aircraft systems', *Air and Space Power Journal*, 2009, Vol. 23, Issue 2, pp. 88–100.

Bureau of Investigative Journalism, 'Covert drone war', < http://www.thebureau investigates.com/category/projects/drones/ >.

Bureau of Investigative Journalism, 'Obama 2011 Pakistan strikes', 17 March 2011, <http://www.thebureauinvestigates.com/2011/08/10/obama-2011-strikes/>.

Bureau of Investigative Journalism, 'Somalia: reported US covert actions 2001–2013', 22 February 2012, <http://www.thebureauinvestigates.com/2012/02/22/get-the-data-somalias-hidden-war/>.

Byers, Michael, *War Law*, Vancouver: Douglas and McIntyre, 2005.

Chandler, David, 'War without end(s): grounding the discourse of "global war"', *Security Dialogue*, Vol. 40, Issue 3, 2009, pp. 243–62.

Conrad, Joseph, *Heart of Darkness*, 2nd edition, Peterborough, ON: Broadview Press, 1999.

Culkin, John M., 'A schoolman's guide to Marshall McLuhan', *Saturday Review*, 18 March 1967.

Cummings, Missy, 'Impact of workload on operator performance in human supervisory control systems', 20 August 2009, The University of Texas at Austin, <http://www.youtube.com/watch?v=VeII-AxiZ30>.

Chivers, C.J., *The Gun*, New York: Simon and Schuster, 2010.

Cohn, Marjorie, 'Bombing of Afghanistan is illegal and must be stopped', *Jurist*, 6 November 2001 <http://jurist.law.pitt.edu/forum/forumnew36.htm>.

Croft, John, 'Send in the Global Hawk', *Air and Space*, January 2005.

Crumpton, Henry, *The Art of Intelligence: Lessons from a Life in the CIA's Clandestine Service*, New York: Penguin, 2012.

Curry, Tom, 'Poll finds overwhelming support for drone strikes', *NBC News*, 5 June 2013.

Dangel, Jason, 'UAVs role key ingredient to success in Iraq', 15 August 2008, <http://www.army.mil/article/11684/>.

David, Stephen, 'Israel's policy of targeted killing', *Ethics and International Affairs*, Vol. 1, Issue 7, April 2003.

Defense Aerospace, 'French Air Force details UAV operations', 2 September 2012, <http://www.defense-aerospace.com/article-view/feature/117835/french-uav-operations-in-afghanistan.html>.

Defense Industry Daily, 'Ravens, mini-UAVs winning gold in Afghanistan's "commando olympics"', 22 April 2012, <http://www.defenseindustrydaily.com/raven-uavs-winning-gold-in-afghanistans-commando-olympics-01432/>.

Defense Industry Daily, 'ER/MP Gray Eagle: enhanced MQ-1C Predators for the army', 2 July 2013, <https://www.defenseindustrydaily.com/warrior-ermp-an-enhanced-predator-for-the-army-03056/>.

Defense Update, 'German Herons log 15,000 combat-operation hours in Afghanistan', 22 July 2013, < http://defense-update.com/20130722_german_heron_afghanistan.html>.

Denisov, Anton, 'MiG signs attack drone R&D contract', *RIANovosti*, 1 May 2013, <http://www.en.rian.ru/military>.

Department of Defense, *Report of the Defense Science Board Task Force on Defense Intelligence Counterinsurgency (COIN) Intelligence, Surveillance, and Reconnaissance (ISR) Operations*, February 2011.

Department of Defense, *Unmanned Systems Integrated Roadmap FY2011-2036*, October 2011.

Detter, Ingrid, *The Law of War*, 2nd edition, Cambridge: Cambridge University Press, 2000.

Dilanian, Ken, 'Congress zooms in on drone killings', *Los Angeles Times*, 25 June 2012.

Donald, David, 'Taranis and Mantis UAVs move forward towards active service', *AINonline*, 8 July 2012, < http://www.ainonline.com/aviation-news/2012-07-08/taranis-and-mantis-uavs-move-forward-towards-active-service >.

Duffield, Mark, 'Governing the borderlands: decoding the power of aid', *Disasters*, Vol. 25, Issue 4, 2001, pp. 308–20.

Economist, 'The Dronefather', 1 December 2012.

Edwards, Joshua, '2CR troops use Raven to patrol skies', 26 June 2013, < http://www.army.mil/article/98798/2CR_Troops_use_Raven_to_patrol_skies/ >.

Egozi, Arie, 'Israeli F-16 downs another Hezbollah UAV', *Flight*, 25 April 2013.

Ehrhard, Thomas, *Air Force UAVs: The Secret History: A Mitchell Institute Study*, The Air Force Association, 2010, < http://www.afa.org >.

Elder, Paul W. *Project CHECO South East-Asia Report Buffalo Hunter (U) 1970–1972*, USAF, 1973, < http://www.dtic.mil >.

Erwin, Sandra I., 'UAV programs illustrate DoD's broken procurement system', *National Defense*, May 2009.

Esposito, Michele K., 'The Israeli arsenal deployed against Gaza during Operation Cast Lead', *Journal of Palestine Studies*, Vol. 38, Issue 3, Spring 2009, pp. 175–91.

Fahrney, Delmar S., 'The birth of guided missiles', *US Naval Proceedings*, December 1980, p. 56.

Federation of American Scientists, 'General Atomic GNAT-750 Lofty View', *Intelligence Resource Programme*, 27 November 1999.

Feldman, Yotam and Uri Blau, 'Consent and advise', *Haaretz*, 29 January 2009.

Finn, Anthony and Steve Scheding, *Developments and Challenges for Autonomous Unmanned Vehicles: A Compendium*, Intelligent Systems Reference Library, Volume 3, Berlin: Springer, 2010, p. 12.

Flanagan, E., 'Notorious drug lord executed by China over "Golden Triangle" smuggling, hijackings', *NBC News*, 1 March 2013.

Foucault, Michel, *Discipline and Punish: The Birth of the Prison*, New York: Vintage Books, 1995.

Freedberg, Sydney J., 'The army looks beyond Afghanistan', *National Journal*, 11 December 2009.

Fulghum, David A., 'Star unmanned aircraft faces bureaucratic fight', *Aviation Week & Space Technology*, Vol. 154, Issues 11/12, March 2001, p. 28.

Gasparre, Richard B., 'Size matters – small is sexy in the UAV microcosm', 23 April 2008, <http://www.army-technology.com/features/feature1789/>.

General Atomics, 'Aircraft platforms: Predator C Avenger', <http://www.ga-asi.com/products/aircraft/predator_c.php>.

Georgia Tech College of Computing, 'Robot ethics proposal funded by DoD', press release, 13 July 2006, <http://www.cc.gatech.edu/news/robot-ethics-proposal-funded-dod>.

Gertler, Jeremiah, *U.S. Unmanned Aerial Systems*, Report for the Congressional Research Service, 2012.

Global Edition, 'Drone pilot ejects from office chair', 5 December 2012.

Government Accountability Office, 'Non-proliferation: agencies could improve information sharing and end use monitoring on unmanned aerial vehicle exports', GAO-12–536, July 2012.

Government Accountability Office, 'Unmanned aerial vehicles: improved strategic and acquisition planning can help address emerging challenges', *GAO Report*, 9 March 9 2005.

Greene, Graham, *The Third Man*, London: Faber and Faber, 1968.

Greenwald, Glenn, 'Times Square bomber: cause and effect in the War on Terror', *Salon*, 6 October 2010.

Gregory, Derek, 'The biopolitics of Baghdad: counterinsurgency and the counter-city', *Human Geography*, Vol. 1, Issue 1, 2008, pp. 6–27.

Gregory, Derek, 'Deadly embrace: war, distance and intimacy', keynote to British Academy, London, 14 March 2012, audio file available at <http://www.britac.ac.uk/events/2012/Gregory-balec.cfm>.

Guilmartin, Jr, John F., 'The military revolution in warfare at sea during the early modern era: technological origins, operational outcomes and strategic consequences', *Journal for Maritime Research*, Vol. 13, Issue 2, November 2011, pp. 129–37.

Hajjar, Lisa, 'Lawfare and armed conflict: comparing Israeli and US targeted killing policies and challenges against them', *Research Report*, Issam Fares Institute for Public Policy and International Affairs, January 2013.

Hannigan, W.J., 'Army lets air out of battlefield spyship project', *Los Angeles Times*, 23 October 2013.

Hargrave, 'Reginald Denny and Walter Righter: UAV pioneers', *Hargrave Aviation and Aero-Modelling: Interdependent Evolutions and Histories*, <http://www.ctie.monash.edu.au/hargrave/index.htm>.

Hastings, Michael, 'The rise of the killer drones: how America goes to war in secret', *Rolling Stone*, 26 April 2012.

Heller, Kevin Jon, '"One hell of a killing machine": signature strikes and international law', *Research Paper*, No. 634, University of Melbourne Legal Studies, 30 October 2012.

Heyns, Christof, *Report of the Special Rapporteur on Extrajudicial, Summary or Arbitrary Executions*, UN General Assembly, 13 September 2013.

Hobson, Rolf, 'Blitzkrieg, the revolution in military affairs, and defense intellectuals', *Journal of Strategic Studies*, Vol. 33, Issue 4, 2010, pp. 625–43.

Hoffman, Mike, 'Congress questions low UAV pilot promotion rates', *Defensetech*, 2 January 2013.

Hopkins, Nick, 'Nearly 450 British military drones lost in Iraq and Afghanistan', *Guardian*, 12 February 2013.

Hopkins, Nick, 'Welsh airfield at the centre of Britain's drone revolution', *Guardian*, 6 May 2013.

Hoyle, Craig, 'Watchkeeper UAV nears service use', *Flight Global*, 11 October 2013.

Hoyle, Craig, 'Unmanned Taranis has flown', *Flight Global*, 25 October 2013.

Hsu, Kimberly, Craig Murray, Jeremy Cook and Amalia Feld, 'China's military unmanned aerial vehicle industry', *U.S.-China Economic and Security Review*, Commission Staff Research Backgrounder, 13 June 2013.

Human Rights Council, *Report of the Special Rapporteur on Extrajudicial, Summary or Arbitrary Executions, Christof Heyns*, May 2013.

Human Rights Watch, *Losing Humanity: The Case Against Killer Robots*, 2012, <http://www.hrw.org/reports/2012/11/19/losing-humanity-0>.

Human Rights Watch, 'Gaza airstrikes violated laws of war', 12 February 2013, <http://www.hrw.org/news/2013/02/12/israel-gaza-airstrikes-violated-laws-war>.

ICRC, 'Practice relating to rule 46: orders or threats that no quarter will be given', Customary IHL, <http://www.icrc.org/customary-ihl/eng/docs/v2_rul_rule46>.

International Crisis Group, 'Drones: myths and reality in Pakistan', *Asia Report*, No. 247, 21 May 2013.

International Human Rights and Global Conflict Resolution Clinic at Stanford Law School and Global Justice Clinic at NYU School of Law, *Living Under Drones: Death, Injury, and Trauma to Civilians from US Drone Practices in Pakistan*, September 2012, pp. 57–62.

ISAF/NATO, 'U.S. releases Uruzgan investigation findings', press release, 28 May 2010.

Israel Defense Forces Blog, 'Army of the future: the IDF's unmanned vehicles', 28 February 2012, <http://www.idfblog.com/2012/02/28/army-future-idfs-unmanned-vehicles/>.

Israeli Air Force, 'The first UAV squadron', <http://www.iaf.org>.

Jackson, David Michael, 'Jus ad bellum', in *Encyclopedia of Global Justice*, Deen K. Chatterjee (ed.), Dordrecht: Springer, 2011.

Jaber, Faisal bin Ali, 'Letter to Obama and Hadi on Yemeni drones', *Middle Eastern Monitor*, 2 August 2013.

Jogerst, John D., 'Air power trends 2010: the future is closer than you think', *Air & Space Power Journal*, Vol. 23, Issue 2, 2009, pp. 101–26.

Jones, Christopher A., 'Unmanned aerial vehicles (UAVs): An assessment of historical operations and future possibilities', *USAF Research Paper*, presented to the Research Department Air Command and Staff College, March 1997.

Kak, Kapil, 'Revolution in military affairs: an appraisal', *Strategic Analysis*, Vol. 24, Issue 1, 2000, p. 15.

Kaplan, Caren, 'Mobility and war: the cosmic view of US "air power"', *Environment and Planning A*, Vol. 38, Issue 2, 2006, pp. 395–407.

Khoury, Nabeel, 'In Yemen, drones aren't a policy', *Cairo Review of Global Affairs*, 23 October 2013.

Kilcullen, David, 'Counter-insurgency redux', *Survival: Global Politics and Strategy*, Vol. 48, Issue 4, 2006, pp. 111–30.

Krepinovich, Andrew F., *The Military-Technical Revolution: A Preliminary Assessment*, Washington, DC: Centre for Strategic and Budgetary Assessments, 2002.

Latiff R. and P. McCloskey, 'With drone warfare, America approaches the robo-rubicon', *Wall Street Journal*, 14 March 2013.

Luban, David, 'What would Augustine do?', *Boston Review*, 6 June 2012.

Lubold, G. and J. Reed, 'This drone just made history: but now where does it go?', *Foreign Policy: Killer Apps*, 10 July 2013, <http://complex.forcignpolicy.com/posts/2013/07/10/this_drone_just_made_history_but_now_where_does_it_go>.

Lyons, Edgar O., 'Ghost fleet for war and peace', *Popular Science*, February 1932.

Martin, Matt J. with Charles W. Sasser, *Predator – The Remote-Control Air War over Iraq and Afghanistan: A Pilot's Story*, Minneapolis: Zenith Press, 2010.

Marx, Karl, *The Poverty of Philosophy*, New York: International Publishers, 1992 (1847).

Masters, Jonathan, 'Targeted killings', Council on Foreign Relations, 23 May 2013.

Matthias, Andreas, 'Is the concept of an ethical governor philosophically sound?', paper presented at the TILTing Perspectives 2011 conference held at Tilburg University, Netherlands, 11–12 April 2011, <http://www.academia.edu/473656/Is_the_Concept_of_an_Ethical_Governor_Philosophically_Sound>.

Mayorga, Ofilio, 'Double tap drone strikes and the denial of quarter in IHL', Program on Humanitarian Police and Conflict Research, Harvard University, 8 May 2013, <http://hpcrresearch.org/blog/ofilio-mayorga/2013–05–08/double-tap-drone-strikes-and-denial-quarter-ihl>.

Mazzetti, Mark, *The Way of the Knife: The CIA, a Secret Army, and the War at the Ends of the Earth*, New York: Penguin, 2013.

McCarley, Jason S. and Christopher D. Wickens, *Human Factors Implications of UAVs in the National Airspace*, Institute of Aviation, Aviation Human Factors Division University of Illinois at Urbana-Champaign, 2007.

McCloskey, Megan 'The war room: daily transition between battle, home takes a toll on drone operators', *Stars and Stripes*, 27 October 2009.

McLuhan, Marshall, *The Gutenberg Galaxy: The Making of Typographic Man*, Toronto: University of Toronto Press, 1962.

McLuhan, Marshall, *Understanding Media: The Extensions of Man*, New York: Signet. 1964.

McLuhan, Marshall and Quentin Fiore, *The Medium is the Massage: An Inventory of Effects*, New York: Bantam. 1967.

Mendieta, E., 'America and the world: a conversation with Jurgen Habermas', *Logos*, Summer 2004.

Miller, G. and B. Woodward, 'Secret memos reveal explicit nature of US, Pakistan agreement on drones', *Washington Post*, 24 October 2013.

Mizroch, Amir, 'Israel's rocket-intercepting ace who started out on Warcraft', *Wired*, UK edition, 19 November 2012.

MOD, *Joint Doctrine Note 2/1: The UK Approach To Unmanned Aircraft Systems*. 2011.

MOD, 'Miniature surveillance helicopters help protect front line troops', *News Story*, 4 February 2013.

MOD Defence Science and Technology, 'Technologies for unmanned air systems, call for research proposals', 4 November 2011.

Molz, Jennie Germann, '"Watch us wander": mobile surveillance and the surveillance of mobility', *Environment and Planning A*, Vol. 38, Issue 2, 2006, pp. 377–93.

Morely, Jefferson, 'Boredom, terror, deadly mistakes: secrets of the new drone war', *Salon*, 3 April 2012.

Mueller, Thomas J., 'On the birth of micro air vehicles', *International Journal of Micro Air Vehicles*, Vol. 1, Issue 1, 2009, pp. 1–12.

National Museum of the USAF, 'Lavochkin La-17m Target Drone', <http://www.nationalmuseum.af.mil/factsheets/factsheet_print.asp?fsID=13266>.

New America Foundation, 'A new technology takes flight', in *The Drone Next Door Conference Proceedings*, Washington, DC, 7 May 2013.

New York Times, '2,003 deaths in Afghanistan', 21 August 2012.

Newcome, L., *Unmanned Aviation: A Brief History of Unmanned Aerial Vehicles*, Reston, VA: American Institute of Aeronautics and Astronautics, 2004.

New Mexico Museum of Space History, 'Archibald M. Low', *The International Space Hall of Fame* 2005–2013 <http:// www.nmspacemuseum.org/halloffame/index.php>.

Obama, Barack, 'The future of our fight against terrorism', speech given at National Defense University, Fort McNair, 23 May 2013.

Ouma, J., W. Chappelle and A. Salinas, *Facets of Occupational Burnout Among US Air Force Active Duty and National Guard/Reserve MQ-1 Predator and MQ-9 Reaper Operators* (Report No AFRL-SA-WP-TR-2011–0003), Wright-Patterson AFB OH: Air Force Research Laboratory, June 2011, executive summary.

PBS Newshour, 'US casualties in Iraq searchable database' (statistics cover 3 March 2003–21 October 2011).

Peebles, Curtis, *The Moby Dick Project: Reconnaissance Balloons over Russia*, Washington, DC: Smithsonian Books, 1991.

Pew Research, 'On eve of elections, a dismal public mood in Pakistan', *Global Attitudes Project*, 7 May 2013.

Pickering, W.L., 'Revolutions in military affairs: fact or fiction', *Canadian Army Journal*, Vol. 2, Issue 2, May 1999, pp. 36–49.

Postman, Neil, 'Five things we need to know about technological change', talk delivered in Denver, Colorado, March 1998, <http://www.cs.ucdavis.edu/~rogaway/classes/188/materials/postman.pdf>.

Power, Matthew, 'Confessions of a drone warrior', *Gentleman's Quarterly*, 23 October 2013.

Preston, S. and E. Buzzell, 'Mortality of American troops in Iraq', *PSC Working Paper Series*, Population Studies Center, University of Pennsylvania, 2006.

Proctor J. and B. Wanger, 'The truth about the "drones" that have so many so bothered', *Forbes*, 28 June 2013.

Project on Extrajudicial Executions, 'Possible involvement of civilian contractors in covert targeting operations in Pakistan', 28 July 2010, <http://www.extrajudicialexecutions.org>.

Quinion, Michael, 'Afpak', 18 April 2009, <http://www.worldwidewords.org/turnsofphrase/tp-afp1.htm>.

Ralph, J., 'War as an institution of international hierarchy: Carl Schmitt's theory of the partisan and contemporary US practice', *Millennium*, Vol. 39, Issue 2, 2010, pp. 279–98.

Reprieve, 'Pakistan court orders government to stop "war crime" drone strikes', 9 May 2013.

Research and Markets, 'United States defence and security report Q1 2012', 2012.

Reuters, 'US Marines extend K-MAX unmanned helicopter's use in Afghanistan', 18 March 2013, <http://www.reuters.com/article/2013/03/17/lockheed-unmanned-helicopter-idUSL1N0C603420130317>.

Rigstad, Mark, '*Jus ad bellum* after 9/11: a state of the art report', *IPT Beacon*, Issue 3, June 2007.

Robertson, Adi, 'US military announces new medal for cyberwarfare and drone operation', *Verge*, 13 February 2013.

Royle, T., 'Drones and the UK', *Herald Scotland*, 21 July 2013.

Roberts, Kristin, 'When the whole world has drones', *The National Journal*, 22 March 2013, <http://www.nationaljournal.com>.

Scahill, Jeremy, *Dirty Wars: The World is a Battlefield*, New York: Nation Books, 2013.

Science Daily, 'New survey shows widespread opposition to "killer robots," support for new ban campaign', 19 June 2013.

Sclove, Richard E., *Democracy and Technology*, New York: Guilford Press, 1995.

Schwartz, Norton, 'Air force strategic choices and budget priorities', *Brief at the Pentagon*, US Department of Defense, 27 January 2012.

Serle, Jack, 'US and others have "licence to ignore international law" in Somalia', *Bureau of Investigative Journalism*, 24 September 2012.

Shah, Pir Zubair, 'My drone war', *Foreign Policy*, March/April 2012, pp. 56–62.

Shane, Scott, 'Election spurred a move to codify U.S. drone policy', *New York Times*, 24 November 2012.

Sifton, J., 'A brief history of drones', *The Nation*, 7 February 2012.

Simpson, T., 'Robots, trust and war', *Philosophy and Technology*, Vol. 24, May 2011, pp. 325–35.

Singer, P.W., *Wired for War: The Robotics Revolution and Conflict in the 21st Century*, New York: Penguin, 2009.

Sluka, Jeffrey. 'Death from above: UAVs and losing hearts and minds', *Military Review*, 2011, Vol. 91, Issue 3, pp. 70–6.

Spinetta, Lawrence, 'The rise of unmanned aircraft', *Aviation History*, Vol. 21, Issue 3, January 2011.

Stevenson, David, 'War by timetable? The railway race before 1914', *Past & Present*, Vol. 162, Issue 1, 1999, pp. 163–94.

Tadjdeh, Yasmin, 'Small UAV demand by U.S. Army ebbs as overseas market surging', *National Defense*, September 2013.

Tenet, George, 'Written statement for the record of the Director of Central Intelligence before the National Commission on terrorist attacks upon the United States', 24 March 2004.

Thales UK, 'Thales's Hermes 450 service exceeds 50,000 flight hours in Afghanistan', press release, 6 September 2011, < http://www.thalesgroup.com/Press_Releases/ >.

Tonken, Ryan, 'Should autonomous robots be pacifists?', *Ethics and Information Technology*, 16 May 2012, pp. 1–15.

Tritten, James J., 'Revolutions in military affairs: from the sea', *Military Review*, Vol. 80, Issue 2, 2000, p. 79.

Tsach, S., J. Chemla, D. Penn and D. Budianu, 'History of UAV development in IAI & road ahead', paper presented at the 24th International Congress of the Aeronautical Sciences, Yokohama, Japan, 29 August–3 September 2004.

TRADOC (Training and Doctrine Command), *The U.S. Army Capstone Project*, 19 December 2012.

Turse, Nick, 'America's secret empire of drone bases', 16 October 2011, < http://www.tomdispatch.com/blog/175454/ >.

Turse, Nick, *Kill Anything that Moves: The Real American War in Vietnam*, New York: Metropolitan Books, 2013.

UNAMA (United Nations Assistance Mission in Afghanistan), *Afghanistan Mid-Year Report 2013: Protection of Civilians in Armed Conflict*, Kabul, July 2013.

UN Office of the High Commissioner for Human Rights, 'UN human rights expert calls for a moratorium on lethal autonomous robots', press release, 30 May 2013, < http://www.ohchr.org/EN/NewsEvents/Pages/DisplayNews.aspx?NewsID=13380&LangID=E >.

USAF, 'Unmanned aircraft systems flight plan 2009–2047', Headquarters, United States Air Force, Washington, DC, 18 May 2009.

USAF Scientific Advisory Board, *Report on Operating Next-Generation Remotely Piloted Aircraft for Irregular Warfare* (SAB-TR-10–03), April 2011, <http://publicintelligence.net/usaf-drones-in-irregular-warfare/>.

UAS Vision, 'Shadow is US military's favourite unmanned asset in Afghanistan', 15 August 2013 <http://www.uasvision.com/2013/08/15/shadow-is-us-militarys-favourite-unmanned-asset-in-afghanistan/>.

Wall, T. and T. Monahan, 'Surveillance and violence from afar: the politics of drones and liminal security-scapes', *Theoretical Criminology*, Vol. 15, Issue 3, 2011, pp. 239–54.

Walzer, Michael, *Just and Unjust Wars: A Moral Argument with Historical Illustrations*, Harmondsworth: Pelican Books, 1980.

Walzer, Michael, 'Responsibility and proportionality in state and nonstate wars', *Parameters*, Spring 2009, pp. 40–52.

Watts, Barry D., *The Maturing Revolution in Military Affairs*, A Centre for Budgetary and Strategic Assessments Study, 2011.

Whitlock, Craig and Barton Gellman, 'U.S. documents detail al-Qaeda's efforts to fight back against drones', *Washington Post*, 3 September 2013.

Whittle, Richard, 'Predator's Big Safari', *Mitchell Paper* 7, The Mitchell Institute for Air Power Studies, 2011.

Williams, Alison, 'Enabling persistent presence? Performing the embodied geopolitics of the unmanned aerial vehicle assemblage', *Political Geography*, Vol. 30, Issue 7, 2011, pp. 381–90.

Winner, Langdon, 'Do artifacts have politics?', *Daedalus*, Vol. 109, Issue 1, Winter 1980, pp. 121–36.

Wood, Chris and Mushtaq Yusufzai, 'Get the data: the return of double-tap drone strikes', *Bureau of Investigative Journalism*, 1 August 2013.

Wood, Chris, 'Bureau investigation finds fresh evidence of CIA drone strikes on rescuers', *Bureau of Investigative Journalism*, 1 August 2013.

Zacharis, Greg, and Mark Maybury. *Report on Operating Next-Generation Remotely Piloted Aircraft for Irregular Warfare*. United States Air Force Scientific Advisory Board. April 2011.

Index